"Across the globe, it is widely assumed that management is natural and universal, serving everyone's interests equally. So it is refreshing to read a new book which challenges these assumptions in the context of public services, and which recognises the interests being served by the managerialist systems which now dominate many country's public sectors. Its international set of authors all hold senior positions and are trying to get things done, in spite of the ideological dominance of today's quasi-competition and league tables. Their work is complex, and any successes are often paradoxical, but their personal narratives in the book are all the more compelling for the challenges involved. Their stories represent vital reading for anyone who wants to make a similar difference when faced with the neoliberal modes of governance that have become so widely used in today's society."

Mark Learmonth, *Professor Emeritus, Nottingham Trent University*

"A refreshing perspective on managerialism and a highly recommended read. The book offers a unique window into senior practitioners' lived experiences of their management role within the public sector within the UK and internationally. A very useful resource for managers, consultants and academics faced with complexity and the dilemma of making sense of their role and the context they find themselves in."

Dr Julia Gale, *Associate Dean (Special Projects), Faculty of Health, Social Care and Education, a joint enterprise of Kingston University and St. George's, University of London*

"Resonates absolutely with the reality and tumult of public sector leadership. The authors clearly describe the realities of improvement in the public sector, and help our understanding of the mismatch between overly simplistic rhetoric and the complex reality leaders and their teams experience."

Danny Mortimer, *Chief Executive of NHS Employers, Deputy CEO of the NHS Confederation*

COMPLEXITY AND THE PUBLIC SECTOR

Since the early 1990s, public sector organisations have been overwhelmed with what has come to be termed New Public Management (NPM) methods. NPM idealises performance, metrics, transparency and marketisation. This book explores some of the tensions which arise in institutions where NPM methods prevail, introduces different ways of thinking about the task of managing for public good and offers a radical challenge to the dominant assumptions regarding why and how professional communities of practice may (or may not) come to change their working practices.

In this third book in the *Complexity and Management* series, the expert authors bring together their experiences to provide vibrant accounts of how to manage in everyday public sector organisational situations using practical judgement. The book includes a brief introduction to complexity and public sector management, real-world narratives illustrating concrete dilemmas in the workplace and a concluding chapter that draws together the practical and theoretical implications of a complexity perspective.

With both theoretical grounding and practical insights from senior managers and consultants, the book provides an ideal resource for students on management or executive leadership programmes for the public sector, as well as managers in and consultants to the sector.

Chris Mowles is Professor of Complexity and Management at the University of Hertfordshire Business School and Director of the Doctor of Management programme there. He is the author of *Complexity: A Key Idea for Business and Society* (2021) also published by Routledge.

Karen Norman is Visiting Professor at the University of Hertfordshire Business School, UK, and Visiting Professor at the School of Nursing, Kingston University and St George's, University of London, UK. She also works as a Non-Executive Director at Queen Victoria Hospital NHS Foundation Trust.

Complexity and Management

SERIES EDITOR: CHRIS MOWLES, UNIVERSITY OF HERTFORDSHIRE, UK

The Complexity of Consultancy
Exploring Breakdowns within Consultancy Practice
Edited by Nicholas Sarra, Karina Solsø and Chris Mowles

Complexity and Leadership
Edited by Kiran Chauhan, Emma Crewe and Chris Mowles

Complexity and the Public Sector
Edited by Chris Mowles and Karen Norman

For more information about this series, please visit: www.routledge.com/Complexity-and-Management/book-series/CM

COMPLEXITY AND THE PUBLIC SECTOR

Edited by
Chris Mowles and Karen Norman

LONDON AND NEW YORK

Cover image: Getty Images / sssimone

First published 2023
by Routledge
4 Park Square, Milton Park, Abingdon, Oxon OX14 4RN

and by Routledge
605 Third Avenue, New York, NY 10158

Routledge is an imprint of the Taylor & Francis Group, an informa business

© 2023 selection and editorial matter, Chris Mowles and Karen Norman; individual chapters, the contributors

The right of Chris Mowles and Karen Norman to be identified as the authors of the editorial material, and of the authors for their individual chapters, has been asserted in accordance with sections 77 and 78 of the Copyright, Designs and Patents Act 1988.

All rights reserved. No part of this book may be reprinted or reproduced or utilised in any form or by any electronic, mechanical, or other means, now known or hereafter invented, including photocopying and recording, or in any information storage or retrieval system, without permission in writing from the publishers.

Trademark notice: Product or corporate names may be trademarks or registered trademarks, and are used only for identification and explanation without intent to infringe.

British Library Cataloguing-in-Publication Data
A catalogue record for this book is available from the British Library

Library of Congress Cataloging-in-Publication Data
Names: Mowles, Chris, editor. | Norman, Karen, editor.
Title: Complexity and the public sector / Edited by Chris Mowle and Karen Norman.
Description: Abingdon, Oxon ; New York : Routledge, 2023. | Series: Complexity and management | Includes bibliographical references and index.
Subjects: LCSH: Public administration. | Administrative agencies—Management.
Classification: LCC JF1351 .C589 2023 (print) | LCC JF1351 (ebook) | DDC 351—dc23/eng/20220628
LC record available at https://lccn.loc.gov/2022015490
LC ebook record available at https://lccn.loc.gov/2022015491

ISBN: 978-0-367-54473-7 (hbk)
ISBN: 978-0-367-56920-4 (pbk)
ISBN: 978-1-003-09992-5 (ebk)

DOI: 10.4324/9781003099925

Typeset in Joanna
by codeMantra

To Ralph Stacey, in loving memory.

CONTENTS

	Notes on Contributors	xi
	Preface to the Complexity and Management series CHRIS MOWLES	xiii
	Acknowledgements	xxv
1	**The Complexity of Managing in the Public Sector: Introduction** CHRIS MOWLES AND KAREN NORMAN	1
2	**Calls to Interprofessionalism and 'Best' Practice in Healthcare Distract Attention from Everyday Experience: Practical Implication for Leaders and Practice Consultants** MARION BRIGGS	19
3	**The Double Bind of Metrics** EMMA ELKINGTON	50
4	**Working with Difference: The Emergence of Prejudice When Integrating Care in the National Health Service (NHS)** FIONA YUNG	72
5	**Trust, Metrics and Complexity in Meaning-Making** SARA FILBEE	95

6 Corporate Social Responsibility (CSR) in the UK University:
   From Idealism to Pragmatism   117
   JANA FILOSOF

7 Reflections on How Differing Values and Power
   Relationships Impact on the Local Implementation of
   Central Policy Directives in the UK National Health Service   143
   SHEILA MARRIOTT

8 Reworking Meaning through Process Consultancy
   Interventions   168
   ÅSA LUNDQUIST COEY

9 Complexity and the Public Sector: Key Themes   191
   CHRIS MOWLES AND KAREN NORMAN

   Index   201

CONTRIBUTORS

Marion Briggs graduated from the DMan programme, University of Hertfordshire, in 2012. She has held senior leadership roles in the Canadian health service, including as a Practice Consultant, ensuring practitioners worked together well to bring about optimal patient outcomes. Latterly, she worked in medical education.

Emma Elkington is a Middle Manager within a senior leadership team of a large and diverse business school in a UK university, having previously trained and practiced as a Chartered Accountant. Emma has recently graduated from the Doctor of Management programme from the Business School at the University of Hertfordshire in the UK, where she explored the role of middle managers and managing using metrics in Higher Education and the processes of subjugation and subterfuge that emerge.

Sara Filbee has had a varied career, including as a Corporate Law Partner at a leading law firm in Nova Scotia, as banking executive for the Canadian Imperial Bank of Commerce and as Assistant Deputy Minister Public Service of Canada. She has served most recently as Public Servant in Residence with the Dalhousie University School of Public

Administration, Halifax, Nova Scotia, and Research Fellow with the Institute of Governance, Ottawa, Ontario.

Jana Filosof is a Principal Lecturer and a Director of the Executive Programmes Suite at the Hertfordshire Business School. Her research interests are Corporate Social Responsibility, Complexity Sciences and Leadership.

Åsa Lundquist Coey is an experienced management consultant, author and key note presenter. She holds a Doctor of Management and Complexity from Hertfordshire Business School and is a Member of the faculty of SSE, Stockholm School of Economics Executive Education, where she regularly lectures within Advanced Management.

Sheila Marriott is a nurse who has held executive management roles in the UK NHS. She is currently a Regional Director at the Royal College of Nursing, a professional organisation and trade union. She has also held various trustee posts within the UK health sector.

Chris Mowles is Professor of Complexity and Management and Director of the Doctor of Management (DMan) programme at Hertfordshire Business School. His most recent book *Complexity: A Key Idea for Business and Society* is also published by Routledge.

Karen Norman is Visiting Professor at the University of Hertfordshire Business School, UK, and Visiting Professor at the School of Nursing, Kingston University and St George's, University of London, UK. She also works as a Non-Executive Director at Queen Victoria Hospital NHS Foundation Trust.

Fiona Yung is a Senior Operational Manager for a large NHS acute teaching hospital in London with many years' experience of working across health and social care. She holds a Doctorate in Management and Complexity from Hertfordshire University and is also a Registered Dietitian.

PREFACE TO THE COMPLEXITY AND MANAGEMENT SERIES

The Key Ideas of Complex Responsive Processes of Relating and Their Recent Development

Chris Mowles

Our experience at work tells us that we make plans but they rarely turn out as we intended. We communicate as clearly as we can, but we are still often misunderstood. Even when acting with the best of intentions we can cause harm. Sometimes, leaders and managers become brutally aware that they may be in charge, but they are not always in control because work life has the quality of being predictably unpredictable. Management training and education have become much more widespread since the 1990s yet still largely rely on assumptions of predictability and control. Often dealing with abstractions and idealisations, the majority of management discourse rests on assumptions of an orderly world where leaders and managers propose and dispose using tools and techniques of technical rationality (Stacey, 2012).

The minority disciplines within the natural sciences, the sciences of complexity, have been an alternative source domain for thinking differently about the stable instability of organisational life for more than 30 years. Even so, management as a tradition finds it hard to shake off old habits. Just as it is now widely accepted that organisations are sites of complex activity, so there are tendencies within organisational scholarship that assume that even complexity can be managed, putting the manager back in control. For example, it may be assumed that the manager can decide whether a situation is simple, complicated or complex, thus determining whether a 'complexity approach' is needed or not. Alternatively, it may be suggested that a manager can 'unleash/embrace/encourage' complexity, as though complexity is always good and is at the manager's command, thus reinstating managerial control.

Uniquely, then, the books, articles and teaching which have emerged from the faculty group at the University of Hertfordshire (UH), and graduates of the Doctor of Management (DMan) programme there, have taken up insights from the complexity sciences, but have tried at the same time to cleave to their radical implications. It has been a decades-long experiment working with the idea that ultimately the social world is uncontrollable, but that we need to find ways to go on together anyway. This is not the same as saying that there is nothing to be done. Rather, the perspective developed at UH, termed 'complex responsive processes of relating', takes management seriously as a contingent group activity that requires highly reflective and reflexive individuals to negotiate and improvise, particularly in situations of high uncertainty. It assumes that some ways of managing are more helpful than others, and that with practice, it is possible to become more skilful.

Between 2000 and 2008, Routledge produced a series of volumes, both single author and curated books of chapters written by faculty and graduates from the DMan programme, which set out this perspective. The foundational volume was the jointly authored book by Ralph Stacey, Doug Griffin and Patricia Shaw entitled *Complexity and Management: Fad or Radical Challenge to Systems Thinking*. In it the authors interpreted the complexity sciences by analogy and drew on the social sciences to locate it as a resource for social science thinking and research. It marked a radical departure for organisational theory, and was a pioneering attempt to mobilise complexity theory to understand organisational life. The subsequent series of edited volumes was entitled *Complexity and the Experience of Organizing* and comprised titles on research, managing and leading in the public sector, emergence, improvisation, values and leadership (Stacey 2005; Stacey and Griffin 2005a, 2005b, 2008; Shaw and Stacey 2006; Stacey et al. 2000). These volumes evolved out of the research work undertaken by students on the DMan, which had become an experiential doctorate run along psychodynamic lines. The volumes had wide appeal and demonstrated the importance of taking everyday complex experience seriously, inquiring into it as a participant rather than from an assumed independent position.

This current series reimagines the experience of 15 years ago with the programme under the directorship of Chris Mowles and faculty colleagues, Nick Sarra, Karen Norman, Emma Crewe, Karina Solsø and Kiran Chauhan. To date, more than 70 DMan students have successfully completed their doctorates. Over recent years, the graduates in the programme have drawn on an ever-widening variety of scholars and ideas to illuminate their work, including anthropology, social psychology, political economy, feminism, intersectionality and critical organisational theory.

The faculty also continues to develop the perspective of complex responsive processes (Mowles, 2021). In these co-edited volumes (Leadership, Consultancy and Management in the public sector), the first in a new series, a group of vibrant, engaged researchers inquire into complex phenomena at work and write about the insights they have gained as a way of provoking resonance, recognition and insight in the reader. This is very different from the more orthodox entity-based research which is more typical in business schools, or research which is undertaken to increase the effectiveness or efficiency of organisations or to test some tool or technique of management. Rather, the research in this volume is driven by doubt and curiosity to draw out the plurality of everyday interactions in organisations. Aimed at producing complex knowledge, it is governed simply by paying attention to what is going on and what sense people are making of it, including the researcher. The generalisability of the findings, their usefulness if you like, is to be found in the extent to which the reader finds this resonant, provoking, insightful and wise. There are no tools and techniques of stepwise methods to be found here.

Readers of the original Routledge series may be interested in comparing and contrasting methods and references from the previous publications to judge how thinking has changed. But first, it is worth going back over some of the original scholarship which shaped the thinking of the founding of the DMan and the perspective it embodied, which I do briefly now as a way of providing some context for the chapters which follow. This review does not do justice to the wide variety of sources which students and graduates now draw on for their research, but it may help frame the key tenets of thinking which pervade the chapters in this volume.

Theoretical and Practical Origins

At the beginning of the millennium, three colleagues at the UH, Ralph Stacey, Doug Griffin and Patricia Shaw, decided to start a new professional doctorate. The trio's aim was to combine all that was productive, if sometimes uncomfortable, from their shared experience of group-based pedagogy with an interdisciplinary research perspective combining the natural and social sciences. This perspective was forged in a very close friendship between the three colleagues, a fact consonant with the perspective they were developing, and which highlights the centrality of relationships to understanding social life.

Starting the DMan also marked a theoretical break from Stacey's previous oeuvre and fascination with the complexity sciences. Staceyhad been working with researchers in groups for some time, but in his previous publications he had argued that organisations were complex adaptive systems (CAS), or that they were like them, using the complexity sciences as metaphor. CAS are computer-based models comprising multiple interacting agents. He even argued that complexity thinking applied in certain situations and not others, the subject of the still ubiquitous Stacey diagram.[1] After many heated hours of discussion, Stacey, Griffin and Shaw moved from simple metaphor to interpret the CAS by analogy, identifying properties of interest in the models and refracting them to the social domain. In doing so, they tried to hang on to the generative tension of keeping an in-depth understanding of CAS to set alongside a granular interpretation of relevant social theory and argued that complexity applies in all situations and at all degrees of scale.

I explore what the two domains share in common, and what the conceptual implications are later. But the combined perspective these colleagues developed, complex responsive processes of relating, is an example of what the French philosopher Edgar Morin (2005) later expressed as a necessary development in dealing with insights from the complexity sciences. Morin argued that there needed to be a transition from a restricted understanding of complexity to a general understanding. He set out to encourage new ways of thinking that brought the natural and social sciences together. For him, there was further to go than simply collapsing some of the radical implications of taking the complexity sciences seriously into orthodox natural science thinking based on disaggregation, prediction and control:

> The principle of disjunction, of separation (between objects, between disciplines, between notions, between subject and object of knowledge), should be substituted by a principle that maintains the distinction, but that tries to establish the relation.
>
> (Morin 2005: 7)

The perspective of complex responsive processes of relating is an attempt at describing such a new paradigm of thinking, researching and acting which privileges relationships, process and collaboration, uniting the knower and the known in paradoxical tension.

The body of ideas originally wove together four principal traditions of thought: the complexity sciences, in particular evolutionary CAS; pragmatic philosophy; process sociology, especially Norbert Elias; and group analytic thinking and practice. I briefly explore these four influences sequentially. The purpose of the following paragraphs is to point to some of the key assumptions which inform the work of authors contributing to this volume, so that the reader might better locate their arguments.

Complexity – Radically Different Assumptions about Stability and Change

More orthodox theories of management often contain assumptions about social life drawing on systems theory, which depend upon spatial metaphors, notions of equilibrium, and consider organisations as entities. Organisations are described as operating at different 'levels', are disaggregated into parts and whole and go through distinct and managed processes of change. There is an assumption that managers are somehow outside the organisation understood as a system and can therefore operate upon it. As an example, in everyday ways of talking about organisations, managers are thought to be able to 'move it in the right direction', to 'create the right culture' and to 'drive change'. These assumptions hide in plain sight: they are taken for granted and are therefore often not alluded to or justified because they are dominant assumptions. This is the way that ideology works. When I present complexity ideas to groups of managers, they often rightly ask me to work hard to justify them, often without acknowledging that their own ideas about stability and change in organisations are informed by a set of assumptions which are equally questionable.

The perspective of complex responsive processes of relating interprets CAS in particular as having profound implications for thinking about stability and change in social life. For example, first CAS models are never at rest, but iterate, then reiterate. The implication by analogy is that this is equally true for social life. Assuming this problematises more orthodox theories of management which propose that organisations have to undergo periods of change from an undesired stable state to an ideal stable state; stability is contrasted with change. Instead, to corrupt Churchill's observation about history, from a complexity perspective, we might think that organising is simply one damned thing after another. Even states of stability are dynamically maintained.

Second, in CAS, population-wide patterns of stable-instability arise as a result of what all agents are doing together in their local interactions, and may change as a result of the amplification of small differences. Cause and effect are in a non-linear relationship. Interpreting this characteristic by analogy challenges thinking about wholesale, often top-down, change predicated on linear cause and effect. To transpose this insight to organisations, is to assume that whatever happens does so as a combination of managerial framing and employee interpretation in local interactions, which in turn feeds managerial framing. As an example, and to give a complexity perspective on why wholesale organisational change programmes often fail, what everyone is doing together in their local interactions may be precisely to resist the proposed change.

Third, in CAS, agents negotiate conflicting constraints in their local interactions. By analogy, this directs us to think about how people in organisations negotiate their mutual constraints, their power relationships at work. Power and politics are often avoided in contemporary organisations and orthodox organisational scholarship, and when they are, we avoid the ethical implications of the negotiation of how to go on together. Fourth, in CAS, there is no controlling agent or group of agents which direct activity. Interpreting this characteristic by analogy deflates the common assumption that individual leadership is everything. Thinking about general patterns of influence is not the same as denying the importance of leaders, but rather broadens our thinking to consider the exercise of authority as an improvisational group activity.

And lastly, CAS have a paradoxical movement: local interaction creates the global pattern, while at the same time the global pattern shapes local activity. In organisational life, we can only take up idealisations of global patterns, call them strategies, in local activity. At the same time, our local improvisations produce what we might think of as strategy in practice. In everyday management thinking, contradictions are resolved by splitting them out with the manager able to choose one pole over the other, leaders or followers, transformation or transaction, strategy or implementation. Interpreting insights from the complexity sciences from a complex responsive process perspective implies that there is no splitting and no choosing, and so no escaping the paradox.

Evolutionary CAS interpreted by analogy do offer a different source domain for thinking about what's going on when we're at work trying to get things done with other people. But they only take us so far, and are, after all, models which run on computers. In order to develop a more subtle, durable suite of ideas, in a move from a restricted to a general understanding of complexity, complex responsive processes draws on three additional strands of thinking from the social sciences/humanities. In doing so, it sketches out a more comprehensive theory of mind, of action, of identity, of communication, of ethics and of the paradox of stability and change.

Pragmatic Philosophy

Complex responsive processes of relating are infused with pragmatic thinking. Pragmatic philosophy, particularly the works of G.H. Mead (1932, 1934) and John Dewey (1929, 1946; Dewey and Bentley, 1949) directs us to consider the importance of everyday experience. We mobilise our human capacity for doubt, the ability to reflect on what we are doing. If, as the CAS suggest, global patterns arise simply and only from what we are all doing together acting locally, then the pragmatists' preoccupation with experience, which turns on the exploration of what we are doing together, and what sense we make of it, is a useful perspective. Rather than proceeding from abstract ideas, from the idea of systems, pragmatism is concerned with what people are saying and doing in the co-construction of their social worlds. Both Mead and Dewey assume a thoroughly social self, that the body is in the social world and the social world is in the body. We are formed by the social world, just as we form it, the same dynamic of forming and being formed that I drew attention to in CAS.

The perspective of complex responsive processes of relating draws on Mead's complex theory of communication, that in order to understand each other, we communicate in shared significant symbols. Equally, the perspective borrows his idea about the predictable unpredictability of conversation, that meaning arises in our gestures towards one another taken together with the responses these provoke, both in ourselves and in others. We may start out by knowing what it is we want to say, but change our minds as we hear ourselves speaking and as we notice and respond to our interlocutors. Consonant with Morin's suggestion that we consider the subject and object of knowledge in relation, so pragmatism works to overcome dualisms, self and other, I, me and we, and reframes them as paradoxes. Both Dewey and Mead were concerned with an emergent theory of ethics which addresses the competing goods in any dynamic situation.

Process Sociology

The main sociological informant of the original statement of complex responsive processes of relating is Norbert Elias (1978, 2000, 2001) who also considers the 'I' and 'we' element of our personality structures to be two sides of the same coin. For Elias, the relatively contemporary idea that we are discrete, autonomous individuals cut off from one another is an illusion which doesn't serve us well. Instead, we are highly interdependent, social selves with no 'inside' and no 'outside', just as there is no outside of social life from which we gain a privileged view. Elias frames the structure/agency discussion at the heart of sociology as a paradox: society is made up of highly social individuals who together create the habitus, the dynamic recognisable patterns of behaviour which we shape and which shape us. Our place in the social network we are born into, and the groups we belong to produces our sense of self: paradoxically it individualises us. I argue that this is a shared assumption between Mead, Dewey and Elias, and is consonant with the interpretation I made from CAS previously.

Though Elias developed his oeuvre long before there were computers, he develops similar insights about society that I drew by interpretation from CAS. Elias is preoccupied by the fact that language and thinking represent entities at rest much better than they do relationships in motion. Instead, he uses the analogy of the game both to understand the constant change in social life and to frame the role of power and reflective detachment in gaining social advantage. We are interdependent and have need of one another: the greater the need, the greater the power disadvantage. But so too greater power accrues to those who are able to notice their own participation in the game of social life. This too is resonant with the value that Dewey in particular attributes to our human capacity for reflection and thought in the deepening of experience.

Group Analytic Theory

S.H. Foulkes, the founder of group analytic theory and practice (1964; Foulkes and Anthony, 1957) had a troubled friendship with his fellow German Jewish refugee, Nobert Elias. Both were concerned with inherent sociality of human beings, and shared the insight that we could act more wisely if we gained insight into group dynamics and our own participation in them. For Foulkes, the best way to find out about a group was to participate in a group, so he developed a method of running agendaless, free-flowing inquiry in groups, where the principal task is to talk about what is going on. This brings to mind the focus of the pragmatists and their interest in what it is we are doing together and how we come to think and talk about it. In the course of inquiry, a variety of perspectives emerge: there is no need for consensus, and no need to take action, except the action of noticing and reflecting. The point is to be together with no particular end in view and to pay attention to relationships. Foulkes called this the development of 'group mindedness', which we might understand as a form of decentring of the self, or reflexivity.

Experiential groups run in the tradition of Foulkesian thinking are at the heart of the method adopted by the DMan, and every graduate of the programme will have experienced a minimum of 36 group meetings lasting 90 minutes run without anyone in charge and without a task, except to talk about what the participants have on their minds.

Summary – Key Ideas which Inform the Chapters in this Volume

All four strands of intellectual tradition which inform the perspective of complex responsive processes of relating privilege history, sociality, and paradox. The social theory which underpins the insights from the complexity sciences weave together the traditions of Aristotle, Hegel and Darwin to focus on the processual and evolutionary qualities of social life.

All the chapters in this volume borrow from and develop the founding ideas of complex responsive processes and borrow from the intellectual traditions outlined earlier. They also supplement and deepen them with their own reading. In doing so, they take what is considered a micro-social approach to researching organisations and depend upon narrative and interpretation. The focus on everyday interaction arises from the key insight informing the perspective of complex responsive processes that whatever happens does so as a result of what everyone is doing together. As a set of intellectual assumptions, complex responsive processes are concerned with the structured flux of relationships, power, practical judgement and ethics. The focus is on complexifying our thinking about the social world, but nonetheless to draw distinctions, to generalise, to call out resonance and to provoke.

To be clear that there are no easy answers in working out how to go on together is not the same as giving up and claiming that there is nothing to be done. Rather, the emphasis in the chapters in this volume is to make sense of what the researchers have been doing in the hope of acting more wisely in future, and on producing complex and plural ways of thinking more helpful in navigating uncertain times.

References

Dewey, J. (1929/2008) *The Quest for Certainty: The Later Works 1925–1953*, Vol. 4. Carbondale: Southern Illinois University Press.

Dewey, J. (1946) *The Public and Its Problems*. New York, NY: Gateway Books.

Dewey, J. and Bentley, A. (1949) *Knowing and the Known*. Boston, MA: Beacon Press.

Elias, N. (1978) *What Is Sociology?* London: Hutchinson and Co.

Elias, N. (2000) *The Civilising Process: Sociogenetic and Psychogenetic Investigations*. Oxford: Blackwell.

Elias, N. (2001) *The Society of Individuals*. London: Continuum Books.

Foulkes, S.H. (1964/2002) *Therapeutic Group Analysis*. London: Karnac Book.

Foulkes, S.H. and Anthony, E.J. (1984 [1957]) *Group Psychotherapy: The Psychoanalytic Approach*. London: Karnac Books.

Mead, G.H. (1932/2002) *The Philosophy of the Present*. New York, NY: Prometheus Books.

Mead, G.H. (1934) *Mind, Self and Society from the Standpoint of a Social Behaviourist*. Chicago, IL: University of Chicago Press.

Morin, E. (2005) Restricted complexity, general complexity. Presented at the Colloquium "Intelligence de la complexite: "epistemologie et pragmatique", Cerisy- La- Salle, France, June 26th, 2005". Translated from French by Carlos Gershenson.

Mowles, C. (2021) *Complexity: A Key Idea for Business and Society*. London: Routledge.

Shaw, P. and Stacey, R. (2006) *The Experience of Risk, Spontaneity and Improvization in Organizational Change: Working Live*. London: Routledge.

Stacey, R. (ed.) (2005) *Experiencing Emergence in Organizations: Local Interaction and the Emergence of Global Pattern*. London: Routledge.

Stacey, R. (2012) *The Tools and Techniques of Leadership and Management: Meeting the Challenge of Complexity*. London: Routledge.

Stacey, R. and Griffin, D. (eds.) (2005a) *A Complexity Perspective on Researching Organizations: Taking Experience Seriously*. London: Routledge.

Stacey, R. and Griffin, D. (eds.) (2005b) *Complexity and the Experience of Managing in the Public Sector*. London: Routledge.

Stacey, R. and Griffin, D. (eds.) (2008) *Complexity and the Experience of Values, Conflict and Compromise in Organizations*. London: Routledge.

Stacey, R., Griffin, D. and Shaw, P. (2000) *Complexity and Management: Fad or Radical Challenge to Systems Thinking*. London: Routledge.

ACKNOWLEDGEMENTS

We are indebted to the founder members of the Doctorate of Management programme at the University of Hertfordshire, Ralph Stacey, Doug Griffin and Patricia Shaw, for starting the community of practice which has enriched our professional and personal lives in so many ways (not all of them comfortable.)

Heartfelt thanks go to our fellow faculty members, Nick Sarra, Emma Crewe, Karina Solsø and Kiran Chauhan, for their encouragement, support and friendship, which enabled us all to complete a books series in the midst of a pandemic whilst moving a residential programme online.

We are deeply grateful to our authors, Marion Briggs, Emma Elkington, Sara Filbee, Jan Filosof, Fiona Yung, Sheila Marriott and Åsa Lundquist Coey, without whom this volume would not have been possible. Our thanks go to our Doctorate of Management alumni and the wider complex responsive processes community, whose contributions to our annual conference provide an ongoing provocation to our thoughts and ideas and development of our respective intellectual traditions. Likewise, to our examiners, whose thoughtful and constructive assessment of our students enriches their contribution to knowledge and practice. We have appreciated the support and diligence of Lauren Whelan and the team at Routledge for their help with the production of our manuscript. Finally, we express our love and gratitude to our respective partners Nikki Van Der Gaag and Chris Wilson, for their patience and support, often at the expense of our holidays and weekends.

NOTE

1 Stacey abandoned the diagram when he accepted that complexity wasn't a special condition that applied in certain circumstances, but is a quality of all human relating. Additionally, he was concerned that such diagrams, which are ubiquitous in business schools, give false reassurance that managers are still in control.

1

THE COMPLEXITY OF MANAGING IN THE PUBLIC SECTOR

Introduction

Chris Mowles and Karen Norman

The authors in this volume write about the experience of managing in the public sector where a particular understanding of how to manage is dominant. A phenomenon which is more or less consistent across public sectors in the global North, and through the aid mechanism, in the global South, is the pervasiveness of what is termed managerialism (Pollitt, 1993, 2002, 2016; Barberis, 2012, Klikauer, 2013). What we take managerialism to mean is an ideology which has arisen over the last 40 years and which makes a claim for management as a quasi-scientific discipline universal in its applicability, irrespective of context and economic sector, and even beyond the organisation to society more widely. As an example of the kind of thinking which underpins managerialism, one of the prime movers, the eminent management scholar Peter Drucker claimed the following:

> [I]t is managers and management that make institutions perform. Performing, responsible management is the alternative to tyranny and our only protection against it... For management is the organ, the life-giving, acting, dynamic organ of the institution it manages.
>
> (Drucker, 1974: x)

DOI: 10.4324/9781003099925-1

There is nothing wrong with wanting to ensure that organisations are well managed per se, and as with any profession seeking status and recognition, it is inevitable that the discipline of management should also undergo phases of development. What makes the claim ideological, Klikauer (2013) posits, and visible in the Drucker quote are the scale of the claims and the move to render them both natural and value neutral. It encourages a taken-for-granted view that management methods based on assumptions of continuous change, predictability and control aiming for maximum effectiveness and efficiency, and based on commercial practices, are in everyone's interests and are applicable everywhere. To accept this assumption has big implications for the way that the public sector is managed and led, and towards which ends.

To consider the success of the managerialist project, we need only pause a minute to reflect on the way that business terms have pervaded our everyday thinking and acting: we are encouraged to manage our anger and our feelings, to manage our relationships, to treat ourselves as a brand, to 'make a business case' for putting an idea forward in an organisation or to treat students in universities as 'customers' (Mowles, 2021: 170), just to give a few examples. Managerialism's rise has been aided by the burgeoning of business schools across the globe with an output of tens of thousands of graduates with business degrees, including MBAs. Having a management qualification has become a prerequisite for climbing the greasy career pole in whichever sector one finds oneself working. Managerialism has also been amplified by the creation of new identities and roles for managers, consultants and big management consultancy firms offering 'management best practice'.

So, managerialist assumptions have arisen in all sectors of the economy and as a general background discourse for the way we should think about our lives in general. In the scholarly literature, managerialism in the public sector is discussed as New Public Management (NPM), a subcategory of managerialism and a term coined by political scientist Christopher Hood (1991). Dawson and Dargies (2002) argue that politicians and policymakers coalesced as a movement in promoting the ideology that private and public institutions could be organised similarly in many countries where there were strong, centrally driven public services, like New Zealand, Australia, the UK and Sweden, and even in countries where services were more decentralised, such as the US. Although it is always a fiction to find one origin story for an ideology, NPM is often said to have become particularly prominent with the publication of Osborne and Gaebler's *Reinventing Government: how the entrepreneurial spirit is transforming the public sector* (1993). This book became very popular during the Clinton presidency, and latterly with the Blair administration in the UK, and encapsulated the spirit of commercialism and entrepreneurialism based on constant change, referred to as transformation, that managerialism advocates. There are broad characteristics of NPM, which are given different emphases depending on the country context, but these are the creation of quasi-markets in the public services in order to encourage competition, cost control and choice; the preference for contracts and standards of service to encourage commercial relationships and a focus on quality for the citizen as the 'consumer' of services, and thus a reliance on performance metrics and league tables as indicators of quality; an assumption that public services are too dominated by the professions which work in them, which has brought about a challenge to the power of trade unions and professional associations through legislation and threats of privatisation. Pollitt (2022) argues that the heartlands of managerialism have been North America, the UK and Australasia, with other countries in Europe like the Netherlands and the Scandinavian countries borrowing ideas selectively but never in wholesale fashion. While no one would stand in favour of inefficient services, and most of us would be concerned to get the best value for money from collectively funded services, the way we might achieve this is contestable and involves negotiation of what we choose to value.

We mentioned earlier that managerialism and greater marketisation of society are not necessarily the same thing, but that they have become entwined together over the last 40 years or so; managerialism has been interwoven with the set of economic policies usually referred to as neoliberalism.[1] The most comprehensive neoliberal policies have been adopted by Anglo governments, although they appear in more diluted form globally (and have been imposed on developing countries seeking aid through structural reform known as the 'Washington consensus'). To clarify the distinction between the two, Klikauer (2013) argues that where neoliberalism is a philosophy grounded in economics, privileging individual liberty through deregulating markets, deregulating labour and industrial relations, reducing welfare and privatising the state, managerialism is a discourse and an ideology: knowledge in the service of interests. So, although managerialism and neoliberalism are distinct, formally trained managers with management degrees act as facilitators of the programme that neoliberal governments have wanted to bring about. In the public sector, this has meant making organisations more 'business-like' and creating a permanent revolution of change dressed as 'reform', with some of these reforms leading to greater privatisation. To make managing in the public sector harder, many countries across the Global North responded to the banking collapse of 2007–2008 with what were termed austerity measures, shrinking the size of the state and its commitment to welfare benefits in particular. Pollitt (2016) thinks of austerity as being a pre-NPM intervention based on an economic view of the world that has little regard for managerial efficiency and effectiveness. But cuts in the public budget broadly fit within a managerialist discipline of getting more for less.

To manage in the public sector, then, means adopting practices which are assumed to be technical and rational, universally applicable and in everyone's interest at a time when much greater emphasis has been placed on marketisation and privatisation. Grand claims have been made for the efficacy of the discipline of management which we have termed ideological, and as ideology, they tend to cover over contestation and different valuations of the good. In this volume, the authors explore some of the tensions that managerialist expectations lead to in public organisations, which are often hidden from view.

Some Broad Characteristics of Managerialist Practices

Here are some of the principal characteristics of a managerialist practice in managing public sector organisations, which form the background for the chapters in this volume. Given how diverse countries are and how broad and different public services can be even within one country, we do not claim that managerialism is the only ideology in play, nor that it works out everywhere the same.

Managerialist organisations in the public realm are in constant states of manager-inspired change, often described as 'transformation', which is deemed both necessary and inevitable. Transformational change in the public sector is often presented as progressive, reforming and modernising, and aims to make public sector organisations more like businesses. It is also understood as linear progression away from a deficient present towards an idealised future, which can be 'driven' by committed managers. In situations where public sector organisations face cuts to their budgets, there is a much greater emphasis on innovation and entrepreneurialism as compensation for shrinking resources to get more from less. Change programmes are often understood in terms of systems, where whole organisation change is the principle aim (Stacey and Mowles, 2016). Consistent with an epistemological claim that management is a universal discipline, in change processes managers look to borrow 'best practice' from other organisations which have attempted similar undertakings. The authors in this volume document the way that they are encouraged to overcome difficulties in their own organisation by first looking for examples from elsewhere, or for national guidance or blueprints.

It is important to mention the special place of metrics and targets in the NPM firmament, both in defining change and shaping the response to it, and which have a particular role in surveilling and disciplining public sector employees. In public sector organisations which are moved closer to market relations with citizens, metrics are supposed to act as proxy measures for price and quality so that 'consumers' can make better choices. Managerial organisations then create progress checkers, auditors and change champions in what Power has described as an audit society (1999, 2004). Audit has a particular function in the public sector both in the creation of quasi-markets but also for the purposes of surveillance and public accountability. Public sector organisations may be ranked and graded using metrics which are proxy measures, as a public display of performance.

Though ostensibly rationalist in its claims to predict and control, the degree to which managerialism depends on affect, positivity and the appeal to the religious imagination is often hidden. As examples of the affectual and the imaginative appeal of the discourse, however, employees may be invited to 'believe' in the vision or mission of the organisation, or encouraged to be committed to organisational values, assuming an organisation can 'have values', to the exclusion of their own. In wholescale change programmes, managers may aspire to transforming or optimising the organisational culture, which are based on idealised versions of co-operation and team working which deny the more complete spectrum of emotions and feelings involved in being human, such as envy, anger, anxiety, competitiveness and prejudice. A number of chapters, particularly 2, 4 and 8 in this volume, turn on the experience of idealisations taken up as a managerial intervention.

Nor is the public sector immune from the inflated and charismatic discourse on leadership in the corporate sector (Learmonth and Morrell, 2019) where leaders are assumed to have superhuman powers of insight and influence, and thus justify their grand salaries that their special powers are deemed to deserve. If public and private sector are no different, then the skills you need to lead in one are exactly the same as you need to lead in the other, thus resulting in corporate-scale salaries of some leaders in the public sector along with the tendentious justifications for awarding them. Equally, if the difference between private gain and public service is problematised, there is no difficulty in employing managers with no public sector experience in senior positions, and nor is there a problem of the 'revolving door' where senior civil servants or public managers end up working for corporations which have an interest in privatising public services. Public sector values of equity and impartial service do still prevail in many public sector organisations, but they compete with consequentialist ethics (if it 'works', then the outcome justifies the means) and the manager's right to manage.

In sum, to manage in the public sector usually means engaging with a body of taken-for-granted NPM ideas about the most professional way to manage services. This assumes that managing in a public sector organisation is the same as managing a commercial one and the same discipline applies. In the process, public sector organisations have become more like private sector organisations, more financialised and commercialised, and with proxy measures for producing market-like mechanisms to approximate the price mechanism. The tools and techniques of management presuppose that managers can predict outcomes and control whole organisations towards pre-reflected ends using methods drawn from a relatively stable body of knowledge, often claimed to be 'evidence-based'. The appeal to evidence carries with it the potential to evade contestation or alternative valuations of the good. Public sector organisations may lend themselves to these kinds of assumptions, particularly if they are organised centrally and have large numbers of employees. Methods which purport to allow politicians to 'see like a state' (Scott, 1998) may have particular valency, especially if they can be framed as based in science.

None of the above is to claim that managerialism holds sway as a unified doctrine or is unopposed. Pollitt argues that public management consists of 'a complex and unstable process of layering, displacement, drift and the general hybrid co-existence of different doctrines and styles', which he describes as a marbling of disciplines (2016: 433). And even in the most managerial of organisations, employees often adopt strategies of subversion and evasion which sometimes capture and ameliorate the worst aspects of managerial control (Lozeau et al., 2002). But alongside changes in the political economy towards greater marketisation and privatisation, the grand claims of management do require particular scrutiny in terms of what they lead to in practice, what they allow and disallow and how helpful they are in bringing about the changes they aspire to, which is the focus of this volume.

Some Added Complexities of Managing Public Services

One way of thinking about the public sector is that the way it is funded and managed is a reflection of the organised attitudes of citizens to the state, to the market and towards each other; the degree to which they consider themselves interdependent. In different countries, the public sector is organised differently and may evoke different meanings for those who use them and manage in them. As with all organisations, the public sector is dynamic and changes over time to reflect the way that the political economy changes and is caught in the currents of political contestation. There are a number of other factors which make public organisations more complex to manage than those in the private sector.

Public services not only figure in our daily lives in practical ways but also play a role in our imagination. They inform our sense of identity about what it means to be a citizen of a particular country, our 'we identity' as Elias puts it (Elias, 2001). Swedes, for example, have traditionally been proud of their social democratic model based on principles of egalitarianism, and have developed public services to reflect this.[2] Meanwhile one eminent UK politician argued that the National Health Service (NHS) is the closest thing British people have to a national religion with doctors and nurses as the priesthood.[3] As testimony, we point to the way that the NHS was dramatically imagined in the 2012 opening ceremony to the Olympic Games based in London. The recent pandemic will only have enhanced this idealisation of respective health services in most countries, even if funding does not match the degree of idealisation. In contrast, for conservative political traditions in the United States, there is strong resistance to the idea of a large public sector, which denotes for them dependency, even moral and political failing, famously captured by President Reagan's observation that 'The nine most terrifying words in the English language are "I'm from the government and I'm here to help"'.

Unlike the latter which we may opt to use or not, as citizens, we have no choice but to use police, drive on roads, borrow books from libraries and thrive or not as a consequence of the environment being properly monitored and regulated. In different countries, health and education services may have a more or less public provision. Our experience of the recent pandemic will have taught us a lot about the degree to which we depend on our government's disaster preparedness, for example, for our survival. It is for these sorts of existential concerns that Hoggett (2006) points out that the public sector can also be a container for citizens' anxieties, whether they are conscious or unconscious. How far will the public sector protect, educate and look after me, my family and my community if we are sick? Public sector managers are also citizens, so these currents of anxiety and what they mean are inherent in the job they do, and will show up in their day-to-day activities.

Questions of political ideology, decided either locally or nationally through elections, then affect funding and policy, which then turn into matters of life and death, good care or poor care, access to resources or deprivation. Anyone with a child in school or a relative in hospital will have felt the effects of the contestation over public sector resourcing and management and in turn will work out their satisfactions, their anxieties and their feelings of recognition directly with public servants. Most societies are highly diverse and represent a whole jumble of claims and needs, all of which have to be mediated through state services. But not all communities are treated equally and have the confidence and know-how to access the services they need. When the encounter is extremely negative or frustrating, the experience can feel like being on the losing side of a power relationship, which, according to some scholars, can sometimes manifest as structural violence (Graeber, 2012). It has long been observed that in situations of crisis or enhanced uncertainty, it is the already marginalised and vulnerable who are most likely to suffer the greatest (Douglas, 1986/2012; Marris, 1996). Managers in the public sector may then find themselves, in turn, coping with highly ambivalent feelings about being responsible for services which they believe to be underfunded or to be allocating resources or not allocating them in ways which they find ethically compromising.

Additionally, public sector organisations are obliged to be more open to scrutiny than the private sector. Over the last three decades in particular, public sector organisations have been subjected to a much greater degree of surveillance as a result of changes to the political economy and the spread and development of technology. There are a variety of examples of public sector organisations misleading the public or covering over bad practice, but in general they are unable to hide so effectively behind the defence of commercial confidentiality. Accountability to the public and the constant surveillance that this involves add an extra dimension of anxiety to managing in the public sector. However, as the Cambridge moral philosopher Onora O'Neill has pointed out (2002), a huge increase in publicly available information has not necessarily led to greater trust in UK services, which is often predicated instead on people's direct experience of the services they try to access and the employees they meet. Rather, it may lead to greater confusion and disappointment, particularly if the ambition to provide greater information is linked to the ephemeral notion of 'choice' in service, a concept borrowed from the private sector which assumes that citizens should exercise choice between competing public institutions.

The congruence of managerialism and neoliberalism presents a challenge to the public sector in the way it aspires to shape perceptions of the public good in commercial terms, leading to ethical and epistemic difficulties. Scholars have noted the way that neoliberalism 'disenchants politics with economics' (Davies, 2014) and systematically reduces the scope for political contestation more generally (Brown, 2015), an echo of Hannah Arendt's concerns (1958) that modern governments transform politics into administration. Crouch (2016) points to the way that the neoliberalism privileges the knowledge of the market over the knowledge of the professions, which can lead to the disparagement of experts and a suspicion of the practical judgement of professionals. The chapters in this volume explore the ways in which the everyday judgement and experience of professionals can be trumped by the instrumental or commercial demands of managerialism, leading to what the hermeneutic philosopher HG Gadamer referred to as social irrationalities (1993), or what we might recognise as unhelpful practice when we are forced to 'feed the beast' rather than make the decision the situation more readily demands.

The public sector, then, is a domain where we experience directly the practical outcomes of broader patterns of political contestation and struggle and where our hopes, expectations and anxieties as citizens are invested. Our attitude towards and our encounter with public services shapes us as members of the public of a particular culture, whether it is a positive or a negative experience, and gives us a sense of our 'we-ness'. To manage in this setting is to dwell in all of these tensions and to have the performance as managers open to scrutiny of the public and politicians. Leaders and managers are held responsible, but are rarely fully in control of either resources or policy. In order to manage such diverse expectations, some manifestation of Weberian bureaucracy predicated on hierarchy, professionalisation, written rules and technical qualification is, of course, necessary to achieve what he termed the rationality and impartiality of bureaucracy. The particular characteristic of management rationality that has emerged over the last period, however, is worth investigating further in the kind of granular detail that the authors in this volume do.

The Chapters in This Volume in More Detail

In this volume, chapter contributors from the UK, Canada and Sweden, who are graduates of the Doctor of Management or PhD programmes at the University of Hertfordshire, discuss the complexity of organising within the public sector using anonymised accounts of their work. Each of them has held, or holds, a senior role in management or is very experienced in offering consultancy to the sector. They draw on their doctoral theses for their inspiration, where they were encouraged to take their everyday experience at work as the subject and object of exploration. As we describe in the preface to this volume, their perspective has been informed by the body of ideas referred to as complex responsive processes of relating, which combines insights from the complexity sciences, pragmatic philosophy and process sociology. The book is aimed at managers in and consultants to the public sector, and those who consider themselves scholar-practitioners, combining as it does granular narratives about the experience of trying to get things done with other people, while drawing in relevant scholarly material to better understand what might be going on.

In writing directly from their experience, the authors describe the day-to-day dilemmas and disruptions of making sense of managing in the context of often diminishing resources yet enhanced expectations. They also try to make sense of the dominant managerialist assumptions about what is required of them as managers and consultants. However, rather than dwelling in abstractions and reflections on 'best-practice' each of the authors describe in detail the complex dynamics of group politics conducted in a particular place at a particular time. In doing so, they bring alive the necessary politics, conflict and comprise, the ethical choices and value considerations which are often hidden from view in more orthodox accounts of managing in the public sector. They also describe situations in which strong feelings are evoked, which are often occluded in orthodox accounts of what it means to manager skilfully in the public sector.

In Chapter 2, Marion Briggs, a qualified health professional, senior manager and latterly academic, tackles the concept of interprofessional collaborative practice (ICP) in health care. In a health context where many medical disciplines come together to provide care on a minute-by-minute basis, the advantages of multidisciplinary teams working as seamlessly as possible together are obvious, but difficult to achieve. Briggs argues that in a health context, particular value is placed on the evidence base for interventions, where evidence is understood from a natural science perspective. The highest form of evidence in a medical setting is derived from randomised control trials (RCTs) which is a method predicated on eliminating researcher bias to produce universal, abstract and generalisable knowledge. Briggs questions the relevance of this kind of knowledge in social contexts, which are always unique, and in where any patterns we do discern never repeat in exactly the same way. Briggs claims that practice has its own particular logic, is always contextual and involves specific people trying to achieve particular things at a particular time. She argues that in the idealisation of ICP, notions of 'best practice' can get in the way of paying attention to the here and now. This requires a different understanding of knowledge and ethics, not as fully pregiven, but as emerging in the complex encounter between patient and health professionals. As Briggs points out: 'Practice can never be fully described or prescribed in advance of its enactment in real time' and is a paradox of the particular and the general. She recommends health teams become more skilled in paying attention to the here and now and to what emerges between interprofessional teams trying to get things done together.

In Chapter 3, Elkington draws on dualisms too, but as a senior middle manager in a UK business school she finds herself caught up in a double bind rather than a paradox. On the one hand, she is obliged to use the metrics that govern her role as a team leader of academics, and on the other hand, she finds herself in turn inescapably dominated by others above her in the hierarchy as they hold her to account for her (departmental) metrics: she is literally stuck in the middle. In her argument, she points to the way in which metrics can sometimes bring about the exact opposite of what they are intended to achieve. Where the justification for using metrics is made that they put an end to contestation by revealing 'facts' about the work, conveying confidence, accuracy and neutrality, Elkington shows how they are often proxy measures for qualities, such as skilful teaching, which cannot be reduced to a set of numbers. Ironically, metrics are justified in terms of creating a rational basis for making managerial judgements about the work, but they may also have the effect of provoking strong feelings in those obliged to use them, leading to anxiety, rivalry and subversion, effects quite other than what was intended. Elkington observes that in contemporary managerial organisations, it is unlikely that managers can operate without metrics, but the same time they provoke as many problems as they solve. She explores how managers in metric-dominated organisations may feel they are hemmed in with a reduced ability to act. As a remedy, she recommends paying attention to how the taking up of metrics plays out in a group allows for a greater degree of agency and criticality.

Fiona Yung also explores strong feelings in organisational life (Chapter 4), provoked in her case during a merger between two health facilities in the NHS. As a senior manager responsible for leading the planned merger, she is conscious that in similar situations she would be expected to follow a stepwise procedure to 'align values' and develop a sense of unity and harmony. The assumption in the literature is that she can do this from a position somehow outside what is going on with an appeal to national health values to which everyone present subscribes. What ensued instead in her particular example, however, was a rancorous and rivalrous exchange between the two groups which revealed a depth of unexplored prejudice about the culture and functioning of the other group. Yung felt that she failed to deal with the conflict and was unable to respond skilfully to the strong feelings in the room, including her own. So, in this chapter she takes the idea of prejudice seriously and questions the idea that we can ever be entirely free of prejudice, given that we always have prejudgements about the world, some of which are helpful shortcuts to getting things done. Given that we are members of different groups with their own particular traditions, we inevitably see the world in different ways. So rather than passing over our differences and aspire for an unrealistic sense of idealised unity, Yung recommends instead dwelling for longer in the uncertainty of exploration of our prejudgements, where the inevitable conflict of doing so may lead to changes in identity. Unity is a temporary state which is achieved through negotiation, rather than an abstract good.

As a senior manager in the civil service in Canada, Sara Filbee (Chapter 5) was responsible for policy development and monitoring, which inevitably involved the discussion of metrics to make judgements about the work. What interests Filbee, however, is the extent to which the function of metrics encourages or inhibits trust between colleagues. Measurements and calculations are assumed to give us greater certainty in an uncertain world, particularly in Filbee's working environment where she is encouraged to bring 'no surprises' (an injunction which also informs the work of public sector colleagues in Lundquist Coey's account in Chapter 8). In society more generally we are encouraged to have trust in numbers as a claim to objectivity (Porter, 1995), a trend which various authors in this book draw attention to (Elkington, Chapter 3, Filosof, Chapter 6). However, in taking trust seriously, she explores the extent to which it is an unalloyed good in the functioning of teams, as is usually supposed in more orthodox management literature. In some situations, she argues, particularly when trust is uncritical, it can lead to underperformance and group think. Like Elkington, Filbee notes the ways in which the use and abuse of metrics can stir up strong feelings in groups of employees committed to 'doing the right thing' and following the evidence, where the invitation to trust the numbers may be mobilised in a way which closes down inquiry. Trust between colleagues is made and unmade in many, many interactions that take place daily, and is an emergent quality of relationships, both constraining and enabling the work.

In Chapter 6, Jan Filosof, who was appointed to head a new initiative to develop corporate social responsibility (CSR) in her school in the university, explores the extent to which we can keep complex questions of importance open in the face of a management regime which wants to reduce phenomena to numbers. In the UK, universities are in the forefront of the struggle over the extent to which market thinking is applicable in a sector where education used to be considered a good in and of itself. In an institution taken over by NPM, is it possible not to play the managerial game? Filosof argues that the approach to CSR in businesses has often been instrumental, and CSR initiatives are expected to make a contribution to the 'bottom line'. She questions the degree to which the idea of CSR is relevant and appropriate to an educational institution, particularly when 'the bottom line' is inchoate and involves questions of the public good. How might one measure the longer-term development of relationships between a university and its local community, for example? Filosof brings the question of ethics and values reflexively back to herself to pay attention to her own struggles to keep matters of value which are important to her open, and the extent to which she was caught up in game-playing. This is necessary to keep alive vital questions of critique, given that it is all too easy to find oneself in the critical position and claiming the moral high ground. Metrics, even ones which try to measure the unmeasurable, may be necessary to provoke a conversation and to manage at a distance, even if they are insufficient.

Sheila Marriott was a senior nurse manager in the NHS, a senior manager in a nursing union and professional body and now acts as a consultant. In Chapter 7, she inquires into the concept of innovation, an idea which has gained currency in public services which have tight budget restraints. In the NHS, a huge and disparate organisation, local health organisations are still obliged to follow national guidance on service improvement and innovation, much of which rests on systemic assumptions and the development of plans and 'blueprints'. Where there may be heavy sanctions for not following guidance strictly, so teams may game the regime they are obliged to follow, or compete with each other so that criticism does not fall on them. Marriott finds herself mediating between colleagues in the health service whose relationship is poor, partly because they symbolise two competing narratives about NHS values: on the one hand, efficient and effective services, cutting waiting lists, for example, and on the other, the best possible care for the patients, which may involve practices which appear 'inefficient' in financial terms. Rather than looking to abstract schemata for achieving innovation in the health service, Marriott draws on the complexity sciences by analogy to argue that novelty emerges in the exploration of difference in the interactions between colleagues competing and co-operating to try and get things done together. In doing so, we negotiate power differentials, which are often difficult to talk about in organisational life.

In Chapter 8, experienced organisational consultant Åsa Lundquist Coey writes about the stresses in the public sector in Sweden for both employees and consultants in an environment of NPM which imposes unrealistic targets for the work, resulting in high levels of anxiety and shame. Following a period of increased marketisation of public services in Sweden, Coey finds herself facilitating a meeting just after a new government directive had instituted a procedure to monitor the activity of employees accessing files on a central computer system. This felt to many like even more disciplining surveillance for employees already subjected to targets and metrics. For Coey, this created something of a dilemma of how to go on. On the one hand, her contractor was keen to avoid the opening up of tensions and conflict, and on the other hand, there was no way of proceeding while this matter was weighing so heavily on participants' minds. In general, the role of the consultant is to pour oil on troubled water and to bring about harmony, what is often referred to as 'alignment', so to work in the way that she did, encouraging colleagues to explore their differences, was countercultural in the public sector and to a particular understanding of what it means to be a consultant. Consultancy can sometimes turn on finding ritualised ways of avoiding conflict.

Summing Up the Focus of This Book

The sociologist Norbert Elias (1997) observed that highly diverse mass societies depend upon symbols, like flags, to crystallise and organise what we might understand as 'national character'. Some of these symbols, like the NHS in the UK, can have a cult-like value in the national imagination and therefore become hard to question. In our public services, we see ourselves and our values reflected back: love of the symbol is a kind of self-love, Elias argues, so there is a lot at stake for us. This might lead to a quasi-heroic sense of feeling we are caring and compassionate in talking about our health and public services, or more ambivalent feelings in our attitude towards, for example, the benefits system (and for benefit claimants themselves, how the services are organised will enhance or mitigate their sense of marginalisation and vulnerability). In general, public services are informed by an ethic of impartiality and equity, which call out huge expectations and can provoke strong feelings in people, particularly if they don't directly experience this in their dealings with services. Public sector managers are no less caught up in these complex dynamics, given that they are citizens too and are placed in the position of negotiating competing goods with limited resources.

In this book, authors who have long experience as managers in or consultants to the public sector explore how the broader trends of mass expectation and identity and contestation over the role of the public sector in our lives as citizens manifest in their minute particulars. Each chapter holds on to the paradox of the general and the particular, general schemata for improving or transforming the work taken up in particular contexts. So, too, public services lend themselves to abstractions and idealisations, which are the currency of the current phase of managerialism, which shows up in its public sector form as NPM. And to manage at scale does imply whole organisation interventions and national guidance and policies to some degree. Public sector managers need to be fluent with blueprints, tools and techniques and 'best-practice' models for change, particularly if there are sanctions for not doing so. The authors in this volume make no case for ignoring national guidance; but in most cases, they regard it as necessary but insufficient, and point to the inevitable struggle of contextualisation and negotiation over the specific context in which they are working. Rendering the general particular often provokes strong feelings, conflict and negotiation over different valuations of the good. Being a public sector manager or consultant is about managing in the hurly-burly of complex needs and complex responses.

Notes

1. We use 'neoliberalism' here in the broadest sense, recognising what economic historian Venugopal observes (2015) that the term becomes too vague and contradictory when taken up outside an economic context.
2. Even in Sweden though, politicians are experimenting with greater marketisation, as the chapter by Lundquist Coey shows, and the country went through its own period of structural austerity in the 1990s, a decade earlier than other countries in Europe.
3. Former Conservative Chancellor Nigel Lawson made this observation in 1992, but didn't mean it in a positive sense. Rather, he rued the idea that the British people seemed to be impervious to the idea of privatising it (https://www.kingsfund.org.uk/blog/2018/02/30-years-public-views-nhs-public-spending).

References

Arendt, H. (1958) *The Human Condition*, Chicago, IL: University of Chicago Press.

Barberis, P. (2012) The managerial imperative: Fifty years' change in UK public administration, *Public Policy and Administration*, 28(4): 327–345.

Brown, W. (2015) *Undoing the Demos: Neoliberalism's Stealth Revolution*, New York: Zone Books.

Crouch, C. (2016) *The Knowledge Corrupters: Hidden Consequences of the Financial Takeover of Public Life*, Cambridge: Polity Press.

Davies, W. (2014) *The Limits of Neoliberalism: Authority, Sovereignty and the Logic of Competition*, London: Sage.

Dawson, S. and Dargies, C. (2002) New public management: A discussion with particular reference to UK health, in McLaughlin, K., Osborne, S. and Ferlie, E. (eds) *New Public Management: Current Trends and Future Prospects*, London: Routledge, pp. 34–56.

Douglas, M. (1986/2012) *How Institutions Think*, London: Routledge Revivals.

Drucker, P. (1974) *Management: Tasks, Responsibilities, Practices*, London: Heinemann.

Elias, N. (1997) *The Germans: Power Struggles and the Development of Habitus in the Nineteenth and Twentieth Centuries*, Cambridge: Polity Press.

Elias, N. (2001) *The Society of Individuals*, London: Continuum Books.

Gadamer, H.-G. (1993) *Reason in the Age of Science*, Cambridge, MA: MIT Press.

Giddens, A. (1998). *The Third Way*, London: Polity Press.

Graeber, D. (2012) Dead zones of the imagination: On violence, bureaucracy, and interpretive labor, The Malinowski Memorial Lecture, 2006, *HAU: Journal of Ethnographic Theory*, 2(2): 105–128.

Hoggett, P. (2006) Conflict, ambivalence, and the contested purpose of public organizations, *Human Relations*, 59(2): 175–194.

Hood, C. (1991) A public management for all seasons, *Public Administration*, 69: 3–19.

Klikauer, T. (2013) What is managerialism? *Critical Sociology*, 0(0): 1–17.

Learmonth, M. and Morrell, K. (2019) *Critical Perspectives on Leadership: The Language of Corporate Power*, London: Routledge.

Lozeau, D., Langley, A. and Denis, J-L. (2002) The corruption of managerial techniques by organizations, *Human Relations*, 55(5): 537–564.

Marris, P. (1996) *The Politics of Uncertainty: Attachment in Private and Public Life*, London: Routledge.

Mowles, C. (2021) *Complexity: A Key Idea for Business and Society*, London: Routledge.

O'Neill, O. (2002) *A Question of Trust: Reith Lectures 2002*, Cambridge: Cambridge University Press.

Osborne, D. and Gaebler, T. (1993) *Reinventing Government: How the Entrepreneurial Spirit Is Transforming the Public Sector*, New York: Prentice Hall.

Pollitt, C. (1993) *Managerialism and Public Services*, Oxford: Blackwell.

Pollitt, C. (2002) The new public management in international perspective: An analysis of impacts and effects, in McLaughlin, K., Osborne, S. and Ferlie, E. (eds) *New Public Management: Current Trends and Future Prospects*, London: Routledge.

Pollitt, C. (2016) Managerialism redux, *Financial Accountability & Management*, 32(4): 429–447.

Porter, T.M. (1995) *Trust in Numbers: The Pursuit of Objectivity in Science and Public Life*, Princeton, NJ: Princeton University Press.

Power, M. (1999) *The Audit Society: Rituals of Verification*, Oxford: Oxford University Press.

Power, M. (2004) Counting, control and calculation: Reflections on measuring and management, *Human Relations*, 57(6): 765–783.

Scott, J.C. (1998) *Seeing Like a State: How Certain Schemes for to Improve the Human Condition Have Failed*, New Haven, CT: Princeton University Press.

Stacey, R.D. and Mowles, C. (2016) *Strategic Management and Organisational Dynamics: The Challenge of Complexity to Ways of Thinking about Organizations*, London: Pearson Education, 7th Edition.

Venugopal, R. (2015) Neoliberalism as concept, *Economy and Society*, 44(2): 165–187.

2

CALLS TO INTERPROFESSIONALISM AND 'BEST' PRACTICE IN HEALTHCARE DISTRACT ATTENTION FROM EVERYDAY EXPERIENCE

Practical Implication for Leaders and Practice Consultants

Marion Briggs

Introduction

In this chapter, I propose an understanding of healthcare practices that takes up and develops insights from the perspectives of complex responsive processes of relating (see Preface to this volume) and practice theory (Bourdieu 1980/1990; Gabbay and le May 2004, 2011; Gherardi 2009; MacIntyre 1984; Nicolini 2013; Sandberg and Tsoukas 2011, 2014; Schatzki 2010; Tsoukas 2005, 2011, 2017, 2019). Practice theorists view practice as social phenomena that emerge in embodied real-time interpersonal interactions. Scholars in both groups agree on the significant contribution of

American pragmatism (Dewey 1958; James 2004; Mead 1934; Peirce 1997) to their field – notably, that knowing the world is inseparable from our participation within it. Finally, because practices involve human interactions, ethics and values are important. Thus, this chapter also draws insights from philosophers and ethicists, such as Heidegger (1927/1996), MacIntyre (1984), Scott (1998), Niebuhr (1963), and Barad (2007).

Readers in practice contexts outside healthcare may also find this way of thinking helpful as it is broadly situated in the practice theory domain rather than healthcare per se. I will start with a brief discussion of the call to interprofessional collaborative practice (ICP) and the demand for 'best' or 'evidence-based practice' (EBP) and explore how the emphasis on these concepts can be a problem in the public sector.

The Call to Interprofessional Collaborative Practice

The ubiquitous call for interprofessional collaboration in healthcare is not new (Linker 2005), but it remains loud and insistent. Without ICP, healthcare pundits worry that compassionate, patient-centered care would be impossible, co-ordinated and efficient practices improbable, and adherence to best EBP unlikely. An abundant literature explores the ideals of teamwork. One framework developed in 2010 by the Canadian Interprofessional Health Collaborative (CIHC 2010) (Figure 2.1) has been widely used in Canada and elsewhere to support interprofessional education and practice. The framework defines interprofessional collaboration as 'a partnership between a team of health providers and a client in a participatory, collaborative, and coordinated approach to shared decision-making around health and social issues' (CIHC 2010, p. 11). Elements of this collaboration deemed essential for its effective enactment include a shared understanding of the role and scope of practice of each team member, effective methods for conflict resolution, common understanding of and commitment to team functioning, collaborative leadership (including reduced professional hierarchy), successful interprofessional communication practices, and an unrelenting focus on patient-/community-centered care (CHIC 2010) (Figure 2.1).

Why Could This Emphasis on ICP Be a Problem for the Public Sector?

I do not contest that collaboration is helpful. I do argue that when practitioners idealise a model of ICP that has particular characteristics when it is done

CALLS TO INTERPROFESSIONALISM 21

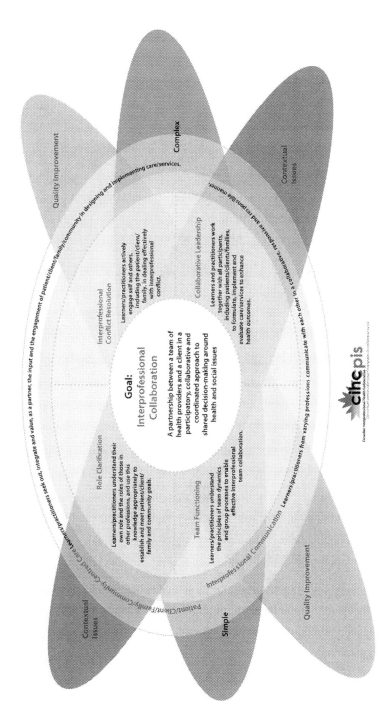

Figure 2.1 National Interprofessional Competency Framework

'right', efforts to deal with everyday issues focus on how they are failing to enact the model correctly. If practitioners follow the CIHR model, for example, they may focus on actions that clarify roles and scope of practice or improve systems of communication (e.g. tweaking when team rounds are held, who attends, or how the decisions to come out of team rounds are communicated). I suggest that it is impossible not to collaborate, but understand that the processes and outcomes of working together are almost always a combination of what people hope and expect them to be and at the same time unexpected or unwelcome. Thus, ICP as an idealised model is often felt as an aspirational goal that remains frustratingly out of reach. Instead of asking, 'Why aren't we doing this right'?, it would be more fruitful to ask, 'What are we experiencing together'? ICP has become idealised (one right way) and reified (an object that exists separate from everyday experience), and that prevents a more granular look at what practitioners are actually doing and to what extent their actions and habits are helpful or not to moving toward shared goals.

Like ICP, 'best practices' (or EBPs) have been a hot topic in healthcare since the mid-1980s. Practitioners are called on to 'translate' the best evidence science has to offer into their daily practice. While best practice is generally articulated in the context of the physical and biomedical sciences, I include regulatory and policy directives as they too define ideal standards and even systems of practice that are meant to be directly translated into everyday practice.

The Call to 'Best' Practice

The explosion of scientific knowledge over the last 100 or so years has been nothing short of miraculous. From the mid-1980s, based on work initially published out of McMaster University in Canada (Sackett *et al.* 1997), scholars began to examine the clinically relevant scientific literature and produce synoptic reviews that offer clinicians condensed summaries that represent 'the best evidence' currently available. In the form of clinical algorithms, these synopses become the expected standard of practice. In many jurisdictions, funding formulas are specifically developed to enforce these 'best' practices and funding can be reduced or redirected if the expected practice standards and anticipated results are not achieved. Efforts to incorporate scientific discoveries into practice have been supported by implementation sciences, where the emphasis is on how to support this direct-to-practice translation of summarised science (Stacey 2007).

In healthcare, deviation from documented 'best practice' is viewed harshly; practitioners learn early in their training that being right (e.g. as opposed to being wise or creative) is crucial to their success (see Box 2.1). The physician in Box 1 was in genuine distress as he left the meeting. He wanted to participate and be helpful, but he was so anxious over being asked to create something without benefit of a scientifically validated map to inform the conversation that he could not even stay in the room. Like ICP, best practice has a reality of its own that is so powerful, it is as though it 'speaks for itself' (see Box 2.2).

Like ICP models and best practice algorithms, professional regulations and the policies of entities that fund and manage healthcare intend to direct practices. They certainly influence practice, but practice theorists point to the greater influence (and unpredictability) of human agency in the moments of decision and action (Gabbay and le May 2004, 2011, Schatzki 2002, 2010).

BOX 2.1   'I'M TRAINED TO BE RIGHT'

Early in the conversation among medical and surgical department heads about reimagining the bed map, one physician leader left the meeting, shouting as he went: 'There is not enough here for me to criticize'. Pointing to blank sheets still posted on the conference wall, he offered this explanation for his comment the next day: 'I am trained to be right – not creative. I can't just create something. Surely there is a right way'.

BOX 2.2   'THE EVIDENCE SPEAKS FOR ITSELF'

I asked a chiropractor how he experienced current relations between members of his discipline and physicians – a historically troubled one. He said, 'Well, there are two kinds of chiropractors – philosophical and evidence-based. I am evidence-based, and since the evidence speaks for itself, there is nothing to disagree about anymore'.

How Can an Emphasis on 'Best' Practice Be a Problem in Healthcare?

Uncritical acceptance of idealised interprofessional collaboration and a hegemonic focus on what is considered 'best practice' obscures and draws practitioners' attention away from what is happening in the emergent, interdependent, and agentic world of everyday practice. Practitioners' determination of what is 'best' is informed by many things, but importantly that determination happens in the living, embodied, interactional moments of clinical practice that remain largely unexamined.

The value of science, clinical practice guidelines, professional regulation, and institutional policies is unquestionable. However, these two-dimensional representations of practice are not sufficient to fully express, explain, or explore the practice story and cannot account for local practice variations or how practices change over time. A more robust understanding of how practices are negotiated and iteratively co-expressed through relations of power, values, and identity is needed. Local and population-wide patterns arise in complex, responsive socio-material processes of human relating (see General Preface to the Complexity and Management Series in this volume) and have important ethical features that are undervalued in the dominant discourse.

Thus, with *practice* (not a particular model of practice such as ICP) situated as the phenomenon of interest, I will briefly explore some key elements of practice theory.

Practice as the Phenomenon of Interest

Scholars who think about practices are not unified in their thinking, but agree in general terms that practices are (a) *performative*, in that they have an intention to accomplish something, often referred as teleo-affective intentions – that is, practitioners who work together agree in general terms about what they want to accomplish (e.g. to offer an outstanding stroke treatment program) and how they want to feel as they work together (e.g. valued and respected); (b) *local* (i.e. two internal medicine units even in the same hospital will have a different feel and unique aspects of both how staff work together and what they actually do); (c) *occur in time and place* (i.e. they are concrete and immediate, not abstract); (d) *embodied and socio-material* (i.e. practitioners literally use their bodies in their practices and interact with each other and with equipment and technology in particulars spaces); and (e) *contingent* (i.e. they emerge in response to many things, including but well beyond what is considered 'best' or directed by policies). Representational approaches adopt a *knowledge-based worldview* in which truth is knowable and fixed (at least for now); practice theories emphasise a *knowing worldview*, believing that practices continuously arise in and are transmitted through practitioners' immediate actions and interactions (Chia 1996; Heidegger 1927/1996; Mead 1934; Sandberg and Tsoukas 2011; Schatzki et al. 2001).

What is emphasised is the generative function of the micro interactions between people, material objects, and technology in all aspects of social life. These approaches hold identity, power, conflict, and politics as central concerns (Fenwick *et al.* 2012; Nicolini 2013; Schatzki 2002, 2005; Stacey 2005).

I will explore and build on three facets of practice described by Tsoukas (2011, 2019), Shotter and Tsoukas (2014), Sandberg and Tsoukas (2011), and Sandberg, Langly, and Tsoukas, (2017) as iterative, co-expressed facets of the practices of a community. These facets are representation (or best practices), signification (or sense-making), and improvisation (see Figure 2.2). To understand each, it is necessary to describe them individually, but it is important to keep in mind that they operate neither in sequence nor in isolation of each other. They function in paradoxical tension (all at the same time) and expose multiple perspectives (parallax) that each reveals unique influence, perceptions, interpretations, and learnings (Sameshima 2007, pp. 293–294).

For each facet of practice, I will explore how knowledge and identity is considered, some representative processes and artifacts, and how decisions are made and actions taken in the context of shared values (ethics). These are not separate phenomena. Barad (2007, p. 185) noted:

> What we need is an appreciation of the intertwining of ethics, knowing and being...each intra-action matters, since the possibilities for what the world may become ...precedes each breath before a moment comes into being and the world is remade again.

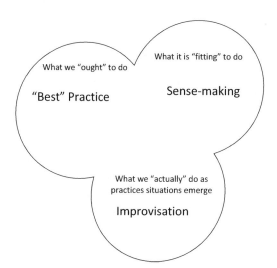

Figure 2.2 Co-Expressed Facets of Practice

I will also explore the key limitations and vital contributions of each, before exploring the practical implications.

Representation/'Best Practice" – What We Ought to Do

How Knowing, Being, and Practice Are Understood

Representationalism is a theory of knowledge that assumes a reality exists and questions human ability to see what is real as opposed to images that people's minds conjure up. This split between what is real and what is imagined necessitates finding and revealing the 'truth' so that it can be represented and then applied (Sandberg and Tsoukas 2011). Having come as close as possible (for now) to the truth, synoptic versions of the evidence are re-presented by other experts as 'best practice' guidelines (rules) and practitioners are expected to translate these directly into their practices. Knowledge is understood as something that is discoverable (largely through the scientific method). Individuals know it through accepting what science – or 'the experts' tell them. The collective (or team) comprises individuals who independently choose their course of action, albeit in consideration of and with others. Practice, in this view, is represented as a largely technical undertaking.

Representative Artifacts and Processes of 'Best' Practice

Synoptic algorithms and practice guidelines, policies, professional regulations, strategic plans, models of practice, even position descriptions are all examples of documents (entities) that represent an ideal. Implementation sciences aim to guide their effective implementation into routine practices. Even though the human side of practice is acknowledged, it takes a back seat to science (including implementation science), and the measures used to assess and improve the degree to which the actual practice – or at least its outcomes – match practice guidelines and policies (quality improvement paradigms).

How Ethics Is Represented

In this facet of practice, ethical constructs tend to follow normative ethics; that is, an ethics framework that assumes it is usually possible to identify a solution to ethical dilemmas by applying ethical 'rules' that indicate what is right under any circumstances (deontology) or an identifiable 'end' that explicates the good that is desired (teleology). Within these broad rules, decision-making is then guided by reference to four ethical principles: non-maleficence (do no harm), beneficence (do good), autonomy (right to self-determination) and distributive justice (balancing individual and common interests) (Beauchamp and Childress 1989; MacIntyre 1984; Niebuhr 1963). Virtue is sometimes added as a fifth principle to acknowledge that ethical conduct is better discerned and more effectively applied when actors are wise and kind. Leaving aside the principle of virtue suggests that if the rules and principles are properly followed, the character of those involved is less important, and then even ethics is understood as a technical application of rules and principles.

Vital Contribution

Representations of best practice are crucial in healthcare. In the coronavirus pandemic, we have seen the devastating impact when leaders and ordinary citizens fail to take science seriously. Representations help to summarise what healthcare practitioners know so far and offer vital information that informs practices, particularly for novice practitioners. Regulations offer form and context to professional identity and help to create a sense of belonging through common language among specific communities of practitioners (MacIntyre 1984). Representations offset the anxiety created by the indeterminacy of practice by their inference that a right answer exists and can be applied. This is more than just a starting point – guidelines, policies, and regulations provide the (back)ground through which practices arise and to which the knowledges of practice return for further study. As recursive, mutually constitutive facets, theory could no more exist without practice than practice could exist without theory, for practice, as the word itself suggests, is experience that continually deepens its own understanding, challenges what people think they know, and offers guidance to the further development of science through the questions that arise in its enactment.

Key Limitations

This way of thinking emphasises the individual – the researcher, the clinician, the manager, or consultant. It is the individual who becomes familiar with the evidence and makes 'right' decisions based on it. Practitioners generally highly value their professional autonomy (arguably, the antithesis of the stated ideals of interprofessionalism and an impediment to idealised collaboration). The paradoxical tensions of professional autonomy and interprofessional collaboration can be difficult to navigate, and practitioners may find it less stressful to work together in linear, sequential ways than through the collaborative ideal expressed in ICP models.

Synoptic knowledge produced by experts intends to function as rules for action (Tsoukas 2011, p. x), but what practitioners believe or are told is 'best', is neither directly nor exclusively causal to what happens in day-to-day practices. Practitioners rarely actually read 'the evidence' and follow it only to the extent that it matches their own experience, whether trusted colleagues have recommended following the practice and whether the practitioner knows and trusts those who produced the evidence (Gabbay and le May 2004, 2016). A recent paper addressing the so-called practice/theory gap suggested that all practitioners should be involved in the production of the evidence to ensure the evidence was put into practice – a daunting and unrealistic task (Horsley et al. 2020).

Reliance on principle-based ethics has been problematic in clinical settings where most ethical dilemmas are complex and can rarely be solved by the simple, acontextual application of rules and principles (Benner et al. 2010; Bergum and Dossetor 2005). In ethics, as in all practices, it is necessary to act even though there is not a clear course of action and the practitioner cannot foresee or control what is likely to happen next. Thus, efforts to simplify and codify practitioners' actions are not always helpful (Tsoukas 2017).

Perhaps the most important limitation of thinking that practice is simply the technical application of science is that it disconnects knowledge from its social construction (Sandberg et al. 2017; Sandberg and Tsoukas 2011, 2020). It is in practice that knowledge encounters 'the wall that only practice can pierce' (Deleuze cited in Foucault 1977/1980, p. 205). The logic of science relies on rational cognition (Shotter 2007, p. 3) and loses the multiple ways in which meaning arises when practices pierce and further inform theory. The very essence of practice as a living, embodied, social phenomenon is denied. Thus, we turn two other facets of practice – sense-making and improvisation.

Sense-Making: What It Is 'Fitting' to Do; Improvisation: What We 'Actually' Do

Introduction

In turning now to two other facets of practice (sense-making and improvisation), I intend a shift in focus from scientific ways of knowing and being to the intertwining of ethics, knowing, and being that emerge together in practitioners' ongoing inter/intra-actions in particular environments (Barad 2007). Sandberg and Tsoukas (2011) refer to the logics of practice, enacted through what University of Hertfordshire scholars (e.g. Mowles 2015; Stacey 2010; Stacey and Griffin 2005) call complex responsive processes of relating (see General Preface to the Complexity and Management Series). These largely preconscious patterns can be noticed most easily when 'first-order breakdowns' occur (Heidegger 1927/1996) in the everyday (habitual) micro-interactions between actors (e.g. see Box 2.3).

BOX 2.3 'THE RUSH TO CLOSE CONVERSATION'

A nurse followed through on an aggressive threat to 'stuff a sock in [the] mouth' of a patient with agitated delirium if he did not stop shouting. A care aide witnessed the incident and ensured the patient was safe but did not report the assault. The nurse bragged about what she did to two other nursing colleagues, neither of whom reported the incident; one of them did tell two other colleagues the next day, and one of them reported the incident. Swift action ensued. The first nurse was terminated and reported to her College and the police; the care aide was suspended without pay for two weeks; the three nurses who knew about but failed to report the incident were suspended without pay for three months and reported to their College; the nurse who reported the incident was praised. The patient's family was advised immediately and, since no harm was evident, legal action was not pursued. The situation was considered resolved and closed. A practice consultant urged a continued focus on this incident, since antecedent factors likely created the conditions of possibility for this to happen and postcedent influences would continue to emerge that may need further attention. What was the context in which this kind of incident could occur? Were there other unreported incidents? Did the incident and its resolution make staff more or less likely to report other incidents in the future? What signs were missed that pointed to the possibility of this occurrence? Were further actions needed to understand this incident and prevent future incidents of unethical care or failure to report? How did this incident change practice, both front line and management, going forward? Would these changes be helpful or harmful? The desire to bring the incident to an end was strong and further discussion was resisted.

Consistently well-functioning interprofessional teams delivering stellar patient-focused care would be an achieved goal, not an aspirational one, if practice were a simple translation of what science and scientific managerialism says is 'best'. Practice can never be fully described or prescribed in advance of its enactment in real time. It is the practices of particular communities, not generalised representations, that provide the conditions of intelligibility for ongoing action and explain why certain actions make sense and others do not (Gherardi 2009; MacIntyre 1984; Schatzki 2005).

French philosopher Deleuze (as cited in Foucault 1977/1980) said of the relationships between theory and practice:

> From the moment a theory moves into its proper domain, it begins to encounter obstacles ... *No theory can develop without eventually encountering a wall, and practice is necessary for piercing this wall*.... Representation no longer exists; there is only action....
>
> (pp. 205–207)[2]

This underscores theoretical and practical action as different facets of a single phenomenon and implies a generative tension between them. Deleuze (1992) argued representations become relatively impotent the moment they are brought into the specific living moments that constitute practice. Gabbay and le May (2011) emphasised that each practice encounter is a unique event that cannot be fully understood, nor specific action developed based only on abstract, universal guidelines. Practices continue to emerge in response to what happens moment by moment and the next steps can only unfold as practitioners engage in making sense of and improvising their way through their work together (Briggs 2012; Sandberg and Tsoukas 2011, 2020; Shotter 2007).

What practitioners ought to do ('best practice'), what it makes sense to do in the specific circumstance they find themselves in (what is 'fitting'), and what it is possible to do in the real time and space of practice (what practitioners 'actually' do) emerge in paradoxical, self-organising patterns. Because practices have a coherence that makes it possible for people to understand and make agreements about their work together, not just anything happens. Practice is not fully random but patterned and somewhat predictable; at the same time, practitioners cannot determine their actions solely based on a guideline or policy directive, nor can they definitively foresee the consequences of decisions and actions.

Tsoukas (2017) pointed out that practices consist of many elements that give sense and meaning to practitioners movements, actions, and discourse. As *moral, ethical, and social enterprises*, practices are directed toward particular ends, which Schatzki (2002) described as teleo-affective (i.e. guided by a *shared sense of what we intend to do and how we want to feel* as we work together to achieve the ends). Gherardi (2009) reframed Wenger's (1998, 2000) 'communities of practice' to the 'practices of a community' to position community as a local configuration of people and things rather than homogeneous entities that operate the same regardless of context. Context always matters and is always local. The practices of a given community *evolve in the context and relations of that community and are paradoxically both stable* (normative elements that help practitioners recognise and react predictably to the circumstances and develop identity); *and generative* (novelty can arise and be helpful, or not) (Gherardi 2009; Mowles 2015; Sandberg and Tsoukas 2011; Stacey 2005, 2007). *Paradoxical* tensions characterise the experience of practices (e.g. co-operation and conflict, stability and novelty, and reflexive and diffractive sense-making). Barad (2007) argued that reflexive understanding is grounded in representational thinking in which one looks back to discover truth; diffractive sense-making seeks to explore difference, that which is unexpected or puzzling. She suggests that diffractive thinking may be more likely to generate or signal novelty. Practices are *oriented to a particular moment in time, space, and history*, and, in this sense, they are always *stable and emergent, predictable and indeterminate*. Practices/practicing actively *resist the standardised, formulaic rules* set out by 'best' practice statements, guidelines, and algorithms (Scott 1998, p. 310).

How Knowledge/Knowing – and Practice – Is Understood

Where 'best practice' is generated through the scientific method and is thought to be objective and generalisable, the processes of knowledge creation in the facets of sense-making and improvisation happen in the local and real-time enactment of practices and focus on practical wisdom (phronesis), technical wisdom (techne), and metis (the ability to 'work the system' in a practical and even somewhat cunning way) (Benner et al. 2010; Scott 1998). Knowledge and knowing are understood to be embodied, performative and responsive in ongoing socio-material inter/intra-activity, occurring in time and place. Representational, received knowledge is not abandoned, but what is practical and makes most sense in the moment is negotiated through practitioners' immediate (inter)actions. This is necessarily a collaborative knowledge-generating process, and why reference to collaboration as if another way of being together were possible is not helpful. Collaboration may be understood as a knowledge-generating dialogue (Bleakley 2013; Bleakley et al. 2011). This is a useful way to think about the deep intersections of knowledge and knowing – through everyday interactions, practitioners continuously generate unique, context-dependent knowledge/understanding. The enactment of clinical, managerial, or consultative decisions may be grounded in what is already known in a general sense, but requires practitioners to make sense of and improvise their way through the expected and unexpected moments of their lived experience. In the complex, indeterminate moments of clinical practice, this requires collaboration (adaptive learning through knowledge-generating dialogue), co-ordination (sequencing agreements), co-operation (ceding our own priority to accommodate others), and communication (information sharing). These communicative and negotiated patterns require much more than following best practice protocols. Practice is more like the turning of a kaleidoscope, with glass bits that fall into new coherent patterns, thereby enabling or highlighting certain aspects of practice and hiding others until turning it again collapses and reforms another image (Weick 2017, p. xi).

Benner et al. (2010) wrote of developing clinical and moral imagination in professional practices. The tendency to think of anything that isn't objective truth as subjective and untrustworthy impedes practitioners, managers, and consultants from taking practical and even technical wisdom seriously and denouncing metis altogether as political manipulation (e.g. see Box 2.4). It is not only expert knowledge that guides practitioners in the moments of practice, even though 'the evidence' is helpful to practice and their defence if clinical practice is challenged (Barad 2007; Gabbay and le May 2004, 2011). Practical wisdom (phronesis) and technical know-how (techne) combined with a cunning sense of what matters most and how to move on in the moment (metis) also guide collaborative decisions.

Thought of in this way, all practices are both interprofessional and collaborative. Casting ICP as one form of practice has kept attention on more abstract ideals, including the effort to link change strategies such as Plan, Do, Study, Act (PDSA) Cycles, with outcomes such as earlier discharge, improved patient satisfaction, or reduced litigation.

> **BOX 2.4 LEADERSHIP TRAINING IS ON HOLD...**
>
> A healthcare organisation has 'leadership development' as goal in its current strategic plan. The plan calls for an external leadership consultant to provide formal training. This has been put on hold due to the demands of dealing with the coronavirus pandemic. The Board was asked to approve keeping leadership development on hold. Everyone had risen in extraordinary ways to the exceptional and unanticipated demands of the pandemic. Leaders and leadership are evident everywhere – 'leadership development' was certainly not on hold! But because development was 'only' practice-based, not based on external expert teaching *about* leadership, the value of this incredibly rich practice-based learning was not seen to meet the identified strategic goal. This demonstrates how strongly representationalism holds practitioners to value external expertise (one best way) over practice-based learning and how 'legitimate, expert' teaching separates out context and experience from learning.

Representative Artifacts and Processes of Sense-Making and Improvisation

Processes of sense-making often start from a consideration of the 'evidence', but practitioners quickly move this to the background. More than the technical translation of best-to-bedside, practice is a moral, social, ethical enterprise, guided by shared sense of what practitioners intend to do and accomplish, how they want to feel, and a general sense of 'how things are done around here' – habits and patterns that are not easily discerned or defined, but which nevertheless significantly influence what is and is not said and done. Rarely are these characteristics made explicit. When practitioners meet (i.e. team rounds, clinical hand-offs, administrative planning – really, any conversation), they are engaged in making sense of things in the moment. When practitioners act, it is always in the context of what is emerging in real time, and they adjust what they do according to the emergent circumstances and what works best now. What is 'best' (the guidelines, policies, professional regulations, strategic plans, and the ideals they represent) are interpreted and acted on only in consideration of the emergent context (real time, embodied, always interprofessional, and are always collaborative, yet not always in the ways people anticipate and hope for). The artifacts of sense-making and improvisation are conversations and the multiple and complex skills of human communication are its tools. Awareness, compromise, competition, rivalry, collaboration, laughter, anger, compassion, feelings of hope and hopelessness – the human aspects of practice that guide and express people's moment-to-moment experience. Power and how it is expressed in the practice environment is a particularly complex dynamic. Power is often misunderstood as something that one has – or not. Practice theorists point to a more complex understanding of power as a dynamic feature of all processes of relating.

Mead (1923) argued that fully attending to what is immediately around us – the present – necessarily includes the past and future:

> Reality exists in a present ... [that] implies a past and a future, and to both these we deny existence ... for that which has passed would not have ceased to exist, and that which is to exist would already be in that inclusive present ... *for that which marks a present is its becoming and its disappearing.*
> (p. 1)[3]

This idea is important as it underscores the importance of each lived moment as it comes and as practitioners negotiate their way through concrete, real-time, lived experience that we are mostly absorbed in and don't really notice. Practitioners are unselfconsciously caught up in 'the way we do things around here' and may be unaware of what constrains and enables choices people make. In other words, carefully designing a new and better future is not as important or impactful as fully attending to the immediate experience of practice and reflecting on whether and how the collective facets of practice support their teleo-affective goals. Figure 2.3 depicts in summary the three facets of the practices of communities.

How Ethics Comes into Play

Normative ethics tends to guide the conduct of researchers and research in rational science. Relational and pragmatic ethics are more prominent in the sense-making and improvisation facets of practice, respectively.

Relational ethics takes relational/cultural context of the circumstances to be a legitimate focus (Bergum and Dossetor 2005) in ethical discernment. Niebuhr (1963) argued for what he called an ethics of responsibility, in which action may be judged 'fitting' if it makes sense in the context of ongoing interactions of interdependent humans in particular contexts. Following Mead (1934), Niebuhr (1963, pp. 78–79) argued that fitting action is determined through understanding 'the ethos of society' and the ongoing

CALLS TO INTERPROFESSIONALISM 35

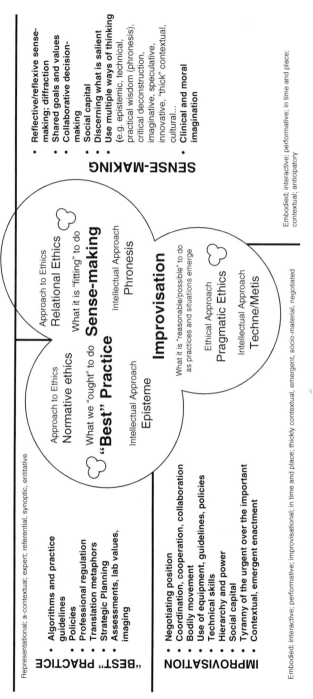

Figure 2.3 Co-Expressed Facets of Practice

interpersonal interactions. Just as clinical decision-making cannot abandon what science has to offer, relational ethics does not abandon ethical principles. Relational ethics simply holds in paradoxical tension what is 'right' and 'good' with what is most 'fitting' given all the circumstances and does not consider any given course of action to be final (ibid), since any situation will continue to unfold and may call for different decisions as this happens.

Serra (2010) explores pragmatic ethics through the writings of Peirce and Dewey, two major figures in the American pragmatist movement. For Peirce, ethics is about rational deliberation about how to act so that we might shape our lives to an ideal – one that is not fixed, but that continues to emerge in the context, habits, and conditioned practices of a specific community. Dewey focused on the deliberative processes in which actors imagine the consequences of various possible actions. 'For Dewey, there are no isolated moral subjects, but societies wherein agents interact' (Serra 2010, p. 5). Both Peirce and Dewey believed that meaningful theory (normative ethics) cannot exist apart from practice, and theorising is not prior to or independent of experience, but instead grows out of experience. So, pragmatic ethics rejects moral absolutes and determines how to go on together through engaged social deliberation, including imaginative projection of possible outcomes of moral judgments:

> Pragmatist ethics is teleological but in a special sense, where the end which is valued is neither imposed from without nor comes from within, but rather is discovered and developed in...human practices which constitute the moral life.
>
> (Serra 2010, p. 9)

Pragmatic approaches to ethical discernment are particularly fitting as actors improvise actions in the lived experience and moments of practice. Imagine for a moment that you are the manager in the scenario presented in Box 3. In that scenario, objectve application of normative ethics led to the actions that were taken in the immediate aftermath of this event. But the full story is much deeper than the individualistic approach where right and wrong seem clear and unambiguous. Further deliberation and sense-making using approaches grounded more in relational and pragmatic ethics leads to a more nuanced and helpful understanding the situation. This may lead to a deeper understanding of not only what happened but what the circumstances were in which the incident happened and how the actions each person took made sense to them in the moment. As courses of action are initiated, the situation will continue to evolve and further discernment and improvisation will be helpful. The commitment to and quality of this ongoing deliberation, how the moral and clinical imagination in ongoing intra/interactions matter to how the practices of this community will continue to evolve (Barad 2007; Benner et al. 2010). Staying close to what happens as decisions are enacted (and bearing in mind that we cannot know in advance what the consequences of our actions will be) and continuing the process of discernment, acknowledging there is no 'final' answer – just the next step – is what both relational and pragmatic ethics emphasises. Bergum and Dossetor (2005) referred to this engaged nature of relational and pragmatic ethics as 'close up ethics' – an apt image for how to discern what one ought to do in the face of true ethical dilemmas understood as uncertainty in the face of contradictory legitimate claims.

Vital Contributions

Modern rational science must be respected and taken very seriously. It has also been given a place of privilege and it is only the privileging of science over other forms of knowing and ways of being that I question. Schatzki et al. (2001, p. 12) said:

> Practices are the source and carrier of meaning, language and normativity. The generation, maintenance, and transformation of these phenomena are achievements ... realized in the public realm of actions and interactions that practices open up.

Stacey (2001, p. 98) described knowledge as:

> continuously reproduced and transformed in relational interaction between individuals. ... Knowledge is the act of conversing and learning occurs when ways of talking and therefore patterns of relationship change. ... The knowledge assets of an organization ... lie in the pattern of relationships between its members.

People's ability to make sense of and improvise their way through interactions in a way that enhances the chances of achieving meaningful teleo-affective intentions occurs within interactions and the patterns of relationships that exist in a particular setting and through relays between theory and practice. In other words, mutually intelligible courses of action emerge from conversation, relationships and how theory and practice work creatively together.

What practitioners know and how they know it; who they are and how their identity formed and reformed; how power is experienced in relationships, decisions, and actions; how conflict arises and recedes and what its impact is; and how they negotiate position and priority are some of the practice-based topics that are largely beyond the grasp or interest of rational science. Clinical practice guidelines do not consider the training, experience, mood, or enthusiasm of the practitioner using the guideline or the specific circumstances of a particular care unit. Guidelines cannot take the social processes into account by which practitioners make sense of what is happening or could happen, how they improvise in the living moments of practice, how they work together, what will prevent 'best' from happening, or what 'best' actually even means in specific circumstances. Even less attention is paid to experiences which might be considered 'negative' such as competition, rivalry, or power plays.

What practitioners know, they know in a context and through many avenues. People know through phronesis (practical wisdom) informed by experience; they know through intuition – the kind of gut feel that all practitioners are familiar with and learn to pay attention to; they know through metis how to navigate power plays; they predict through speculation and imagination informed by experience what might happen but remain alert to what does happen; and all of these ways of knowing and others are accomplished through the collective experience of their ongoing relationships with each other, and the objects, tools, and resources they have. All knowing emerges through this complex and responsive, socio-material participation in the specific communities in which people's practices are enacted. Practices are not random – not just anything will happen. All practices both resist and produce novelty (and sometimes that novelty improves things and sometimes it makes matters worse). The paradox of stability and change through the embodied, processual, dynamic intra/interaction among people within a local setting is perhaps the most important contribution of practice theory. This way of thinking opens important avenues through which to explore collective experience, avenues that include but go beyond representationalism and rational managerialism. By embracing and giving place to the human side of healthcare practices, the important role that leaders and consultants have to create and hold safe enough the space needed for conflict to be more fully experienced and explored would make it possible for practitioners to make sense of their experience, modify their shared teleo-affective goals, and consider what next steps make sense.

Key Limitations

The logics of practice risk to some extent creating an impression that science bears little influences on practice, since practitioners apparently do not read science, believe it only to the extent it matches their own experience, and act on it only to the extent it is consistent with the specific conditions of intelligibility in their own local context. I stress again that to ignore science and the value that it contributes to healthcare practices would be foolish and is not my intent.

Perhaps the key challenge that the practice discourse introduces is how complex it is – how difficult it is to grasp and to talk about with clarity and precision (something epistemic science is particularly good at doing). The practice discourse can be disconcertingly imprecise and frustrating as it resists the very thing that science values most – universal truth adduced through controlled experimentation. This can make practice discourse very challenging for those who are most comfortable in the epistemic world. Practice may seem anathema to science and science to practice, yet they are paradoxically related, generative, and interdependent.

The Challenge of Precision in an Indeterminate World

Breaking practices down to three facets – best (representational) practice, sense-making, and improvisation – is challenging, as I am arguing that these facets do not function independently or sequentially. They are always in paradoxical tension, transform past/present/future simultaneously, they are local, not universal, and are simultaneously predictable and unpredictable. Not just anything can happen; there is form and structure in each practice context that influences and makes actions intelligible within that community. Yet, what practitioners know and do, they can only know and do as practices are enacted, negotiated, and improvised in real time.

Lubinow (2002, p. 218) offered a helpful image. The indeterminacy of practice is characterised by 'sloping frontiers [rather than the] sharp boundaries' found in the determinate precision of positivism.

> [In practice we] reopen and renegotiate ... meaning as we deploy new evidence, or ... deploy old evidence in new ways ... indeterminacy ... [involves] oblique standards of conduct ... [not] explicit rules of behavior ... [and] from its own internal complexities, [practice produces] its own innovations.
> (Lubinow 2002, pp. 281, 226)

The discourses of practice generate evolving intentions, rather than a predetermined destination.

Weber (as cited in Geertz 1973) framed this idea beautifully:

> Man is an animal suspended in webs of significance he himself has spun. I take culture to be those webs, and the analysis of it to be therefore not an experimental science in search of law but an interpretive one in search of meaning.
> (p. 5)

Perhaps the effort to be precise about three facets of practice and differences in the logics of science and practice is not as contradictory as it might appear (even though achieving precision will continue to be elusive). The game is worthwhile precisely because people tacitly or explicitly agree to be transformed in some way by engaging with others in building a web of meaning through which they can try to understand what they are doing and who they are becoming as they enact their intentions.

What Are the Practical Implications of a Clear Focus on Practice in Healthcare?

The Challenge

It is ironic that the logics of practice are largely ignored in practice. The hegemony of rational idealism (representationalism) in healthcare practices makes it difficult to accord validity to and discuss a relational processual approach to practice. Most leaders and practice consultants are, like practitioners, comfortable in the familiar discourses of science and crave certainty in the life-and-death environments in which they work. They have much less experience and confidence in thinking or talking about the logics of practice described in this chapter.

Healthcare practitioners and leaders want to believe that the evidence speaks for itself, leaving nothing else to discuss (see Box 2), yet they know that sometimes, even if the evidence is pointing in one direction, another must be taken. Those who work in the field of healthcare are guided by the evidence, but also by practical wisdom (phronesis), technical wisdom (the instinctive touch), and metis (navigating ambiguous territory with cunning and intuitive precision). They are guided by normative ethics but also by relational and pragmatic ethics. This chapter imagines a world where there are rules and norms, but where relationships and what is practical can also be considered worthy topics of conversation and study. I argue the value of being more aware of the tender emergent interplay between what practitioners ought to do, what it is fitting to do, and what they actually do in the embodied, lived experience of the practices of their community. And most importantly, I am proposing that practitioners actually talk about and study all these influences and the interplay between them. These considerations would guide our attention to that which gets missed when science and evidence are the only sustained considerations.

The Opportunity

Taking seriously the logics of practice and considering all three facets of practice discussed in this chapter invites healthcare practitioners, leaders, and consultants to understand everyday experience as the foundation and building blocks of practices. The questions they ask in their inquiries about practices would shift away from 'what should we do'? or 'how do we enforce best practices'? toward starting points such as 'what is going on here'? or 'how do we consider the guidelines in our context and with these particular patients'? Healthcare leaders and consultants would function as engaged members of the team – not separate from them – and would become skilled in discerning and speaking with staff about the patterns revealed in each practice facet in each local context as the kaleidoscope of practice turns and one unique, multifaceted image temporarily comes into view. They would enable what Heidegger (1927/1966) called second-order breakdowns – a strategic continuance of first-order breakdowns that holds safe enough space open for deeper exploration of conflict and uncertainty to engage practitioners in discussion about practices and patterns normally not visible to them. They would enhance their comfort with inquiring about and supporting multiple ways of thinking such as epistemic, intuitive, speculative, imaginative, critical deconstructive, practical wisdom, and innovative. They would understand normative ethics, but also consider the full relational context and ensure pragmatic sense in the ongoing modification and enactment of ethical decisions.

Think of team rounds as a process in which the purpose is to make sense of how to provide the best possible care to a specific group of patients. Practitioners thinking in the ways I have been describing would interrogate aspects of team rounds like how decisions are made or what time rounds are held and why. Who is advantaged and who is disadvantaged? Who leads rounds? Is there an order in which people speak and offer their views? How do practitioners understand what guides the order – is it random or is something else at play? Have 'places' emerged where people habitually sit or stand in meetings – what do these places suggest about power and authority? How do individual members of the team feel about their participation and that of others? How are disagreements handled? Does the team welcome or experience discomfort in the face of disagreements? How are newcomers integrated into the team? What is professional development like for this team? How is social capital accrued and spent? Are multiple ways of thinking (e.g. epistemic, technical, practical wisdom, critical deconstruction, intuitive, speculative, imaginative) encouraged/discouraged, respected, or tolerated? Are certain ways of thinking more likely attributed to one team member and not another? How does hierarchy work and is it acknowledged? These kinds of questions interrogate practice, not evidence. They consider what practitioners' 'ought' to do but also focus on what they are actually doing. They invite reflective/diffractive consideration about the degree to which they assent to or dispute the actions taken and the values expressed in their practices.

As practitioners improvise, they might think about how they go about their day together, how they negotiate position and priority, organise, and use space, equipment, and technology. They might explore the tyranny of the urgent over the important and how priorities determined in team rounds, for example, give way to what is emerging in the moments of their practices. They might interrogate the affordances that allow or detract from policies and guidelines being followed. The generation and use of social capital come into play as practitioners improvise sometimes to their advantage, sometimes ceding their role or place or priority to another.

In other words, a focus on practices (inclusive of the impact on them of theory, science, rational logic, empiricism) invites practitioners to pay attention to perspectives usually ignored or even considered harmful because they are messy and subjective – prone to human judgment, values and therefore error. The multiple perspective-taking I advocate for considers a rich, thickly contextualised, close-up view of lived experience and elucidates many avenues of inquiry into practice that can help practitioners, leaders, and consultants to understand, make further sense of practices, and support improvisations, not toward an ultimate, fixed ideal, but rather toward the shared teleo-affective intentions for the practices undertaken in a particular community, context, and time (see Figure 2.3).

Stacey and Griffin (2005, p. 24) asserted the purpose of research – and I argue thinking aimed at understanding what is and could be going on in an organisation – is:

> ...not to solve a problem or make an improvement..., but to develop practitioner skills in paying attention to the complexity of local, micro-interactions [they are] engaged in, because it is in these [interactions] that wider organizational patterns emerge.

Without attention to complexity, the practitioner's gaze will be too narrowly focused on only one thing at a time – the latest evidence, team structure, power sharing, or quality improvement strategy. For example, professional development is typically focused on extending scientific knowledge in discipline-specific contexts. With a wider gaze, practitioners might use professional development to enhance their ability to feel comfortable in using multiple intellectual approaches (epistemic, phronetic, techne, and metis); recognise and develop the moral and aesthetic sensibilities (axiology) of their work together; explore and apply normative, relational, and pragmatic ethics; and be more comfortable and adept at welcoming and exploring uncertainty and conflict. In terms of conflict, practitioners might enhance their comfort and ability to deeply explore the broader issues it can reveal (e.g. aspects of the local habitus that are normally inarticulate – hidden from site) and give shape to, and form, subtly new ways of being together (Shotter and Tsoukas 2014, p. 2).

In other words:

> ...taking a performative approach [that] focuses on situational details, exploring felt emotions and the actions they prefigure, and looking for particular sequences of actions and how they interactively unfold – is more likely to...provide a richer picture of the exercise of judgment 'from within'.
> (Shotter and Tsoukas 2014, p. 3)

MacIntyre (1984, p. 216) made the point that discerning what practitioners are to do requires first that they understand the story they are in – in other words, how the traditions (habitus) of the groups they are part of shape their actions and responses. Much of what influences the interactions in a practice setting is hidden, except in times of conflict and breakdown. When they come into people's peripheral vision in times of conflict, they could be explored courageously and used to discern some of the influences that shape practices and responses (MacIntyre 1984; Polanyi 1966; Sandberg and Tsoukas 2014; Shotter 2007).

The turn to practice places embodied and performative aspects of practice clearly in focus (Barad 2007; Gherardi 2017). The practice focus is neither individual nor symbolic but storied – practices emerge in the lived, embodied, interactions between people in their stories. The opportunity for public sector leaders and consultants in taking a more practice-based approach rests in broadening what is considered not only a legitimate focus of inquiry, but a necessary one. Healthcare, all human services, are just that – human services. None are purely technical. None can be adequately explained, understood, studied, or changed without understanding that all practices (including scientific practices) are undertaken by fallible humans working together in generative ways. Context always matters. Practice is always local, never universal. It is contingent, not fully predictable, and it is coherent and intelligible because it expresses and recreates history *and* a possible future in 'the breath before each lived moment creates the world anew' (Barad 2007). If practitioners took the logics of practice more seriously, they would look more closely at what is actually happening and less closely on theory practice gaps. They would take as a key focus of their inquiries and actions how people are working together, what patterns of behavior they are expressing, and the degree to which they think these patterns will move them toward or away from where they want to be and how they want to feel on the journey. They would recognise that it is in their interactions – by whatever name they choose to label them – that their experiences are created and emerge in both habituated patterns and novel ways. If practitioners do not take a practice-based approach in leadership and consulting practices, they will continue to work hardest at implementing guidelines, inventing evermore effective sticks and carrots, but with the same result – a frustrating experience of almost (but never quite) failing and of almost, but never quite succeeding.

Practitioners are neither failing nor succeeding – they are simply practicing together, moment by moment – each moment significant and worthy. In each moment, practitioners compete and co-operate, resist and assent, express dynamic relations of power, and form and reform professional and personal identity, all in full measure. It is vital to more generously welcome, accept, and explicitly animate the many ways in which knowledge is co-produced between researchers, practitioners, leaders, and service users in local contexts (Redman et al. 2021).

Received wisdom and epistemic science are valuable. It is also vital to pay attention to the multiple logics of practice. To make explicit the teleo-affective intentions of practitioners as they work together, pay close attention to and make visible what is actually happening in the moment-by-moment interactions of practices; understand how context necessarily modifies generic 'best practice' guideline; enhance our comfort with and ability to explore what sense we make of our experience and how practitioners improvise; bring consideration of how practitioners feel in the moments of their work together as much to mainstream conversation as how patients/clients experience the health and social care systems; openly explore conflict with the intent to understand, not resolve, it. Crucially, practitioners and their leaders must pay attention to what 'ought' to happen, what is 'fitting' under the circumstances and what 'can' happen, when decisions are enacted in real time, not with the intent to implement another idealisation of what practice is, but with the intent to shift our focus slightly away from 'doing life right' and slightly toward simply understanding and fully experiencing life as it is.

Notes

1 The point-of-care staff who participated in my postdoctoral study found it more intuitive to understand this facet if I expressed it not as Representation but as 'best practice'.
2 Emphasis added.
3 Emphasis added.

References

Barad, K., 2007. *Meeting the universe halfway: quantum physics and the entanglement of matter and meaning.* Durham, NC: Duke University Press.

Beauchamp, T.L., and Childress, J.F., 1989. *The principles of biomedical ethics.* 3rd ed. New York: Oxford University Press.

Benner, P., et al., 2010. *Educating nurses: a call for radical transformation.* San Francisco, CA: Jossey-Bass.

Bergum, V., and Dossetor, J., 2005. *Relational ethics: the full meaning of respect.* Hagerstown, MD: University Publishing Group.

Bleakley, A., 2013. Working in 'teams' in an era of 'liquid' healthcare: what is the use of theory? *Journal of Interprofessional Care,* 27(1), 18–26. https://doi.org/10.3109/13561820.2012.699479

Bleakley, A., Bligh, J., and Brown, J., 2011. *Advances in medical education for the future: identity, power, and location.* New York: Springer.

Bourdieu, P., 1980/1990. *The logic of practice.* Stanford, CA: Stanford University Press.

Briggs, M., 2012. *Complexity and the practices of communities in healthcare: implications for an internal practice consultant.* Thesis (PhD). University of Hertfordshire.

Briggs, M., and McElhaney, J., 2015. Frailty and interprofessional collaboration. In: O. Theou and K. Rockwood (eds.) *Frailty in aging: biological, clinical and social implications.* Basel, Switzerland: Karger, vol. 41, 121–136.

Canadian Interprofessional Health Collaborative, 2010. *A national interprofessional competency framework.* Available from: http://ICPontherun.ca/wp-content/uploads/2014/06/National-Framework.pdf Accessed 2020-11-18

Chia, R., 1996. *Organizational analysis as deconstructive practice.* New York: Walter de Gruyter Company.

Deleuze, G., 1992. What is a dispositif? In: T.J. Armstrong (trans.) *Michel Foucault philosopher: essays translated from French and German.* New York: Routledge, 159–168.

Dewey, J., 1958. *Experience and nature.* Mineola, NY: Dover.

Duffy, G.L., 2019. A systematic review. *Lean & Six Sigma Review,* 18 (3), 8–15.

Fenwick, T., Nerland, M., and Jensen, K., 2012. Sociomaterial approaches to conceptualising professional learning and practice. *Journal of Education and Work,* 25(1), 1–13. https://doi.org/10.1080/13639080.2012.644901

Foucault, M., 1977/1980. *Language, counter-memory, practice: selected essays and interviews.* Ithaca, NY: Cornell University Press.

Gabbay, J., and le May, A., 2004. Evidence based guidelines or collectively constructed 'mindlines?' Ethnographic study of knowledge management in primary care. *British Medical Journal*, 329, 1013. https://doi.org/10.1136/bmj.329.7473.1013

Gabbay, J., and le May, A., 2011. *Practice-based evidence for healthcare: clinical mindlines.* New York: Routledge.

Gabbay, J., and le May, A., 2016. Mindlines: making sense of evidence in practice. *British Journal of General Practice*, 66(649), 402–403. https://doi.org/10.3399/bjgp16X686221

Geertz, C., 1973. *The interpretation of cultures: selected essays.* New York: Basic Books.

Gherardi, S., 2009. Community of practice or practices of a community? In: S. Armstrong and C. Fukami (eds.) *Handbook of management learning, education, and development.* London: Sage, 514–530.

Gherardi, S., 2017. One turn … and now another one: do the turn to practice and the turn to affect have something in common? *Management Learning*, 48(3), 345–358.

Heidegger, M., 1927/1996. *Being and time.* Translated by J. Stambaugh. New York: New York State University Press.

Horsley, T., *et al.*, 2020. The use of BEME reviews in the medical education literature. *Medical Teacher*, 42(10), 1171–1178. https://doi.org/10.1080/0142159X.2020.1798909

James, W., 2004. *Pragmatism: a new name for some old ways of thinking* [Online]. Available from: http://www.gutenberg.org/ebooks/5116 [Accessed 28 November 2020].

Linker, B., 2005. The business of ethics: gender, medicine, and the professional codification of the American Physiotherapy Association, 1918–1935. *Journal of the History of Medicine and Allied Sciences*, 60(3), 320–354. https://doi.org/10.1093/jhmas/jri043

Lubinow, W.C., 2002. Making words flesh: changing roles of university learning and the professions in 19th century England. *Minerva*, 40, 217–234.

MacIntyre, A., 1984. *After virtue.* 2nd ed. Notre Dame: Notre Dame University Press.

Mead, G.H., 1934. *Mind, self, and society from the standpoint of a social behavioralist.* Chicago, IL: University of Chicago Press.

Mowles, C., 2015. *Managing in uncertainty.* Abington, Oxon: Routledge.

Nicolini, D., 2013. *Practice theory, work, & organization: an introduction.* Oxford: Oxford University Press.

Niebuhr, H.R., 1963. *The responsible self.* New York: Harper and Rowe.
Peirce, C.S., 1997. *Pragmatism as a principle and method of right thinking: the 1903 Harvard lectures on pragmatism.* Albany: State University of New York Press.
Polanyi, M., 1966. *The tacit dimension.* Chicago, IL: University of Chicago Press.
Redman, S., et al., 2021. Co-production of knowledge: the future. *BMJ,* 372(434). http://dx.doi.org/10.1136/bmj.n434
Sackett, D.L., et al., 1997. Evidence-based medicine: how to practice and teach EBM. *Canadian Medical Association Journal,* 157(6), 788.
Sameshima, P., 2007. *Seeing red: a pedagogy of parallax, an epistolary bildungsroman on artful scholarly inquiry.* Youngstown, NY: Cambria Press.
Sandberg, J., Langly, A., and Tsoukas, H., 2017. *Skillful performance: enacting capabilities, knowledge, competence, and expertise in organizations.* Oxford: Oxford University Press.
Sandberg, J., and Tsoukas, H., 2011. Grasping the logic of practice: theorizing through practical rationality. *Academy of Management Review,* 36(2), 338–360.
Sandberg, J., and Tsoukas, H., 2014. Making sense of the sensemaking perspective: its constituents, limitation, and opportunities for further development. *Journal of Organizational Behavior,* 36(S1), S6–S32. https://doi.org/10.1002/job.1937
Sandberg, J., and Tsoukas, H., 2020. Sensemaking reconsidered: towards a broader understanding through phenomenology. *Organization Theory,* 1, 1–34. https://doi.org/10.1177/2631787719879937
Schatzki, T.R., 2002. *The site of the social: a philosophical account of the constitution of social life and change.* Philadelphia: University of Pennsylvania Press.
Schatzki, T.R., 2005. The sites of organizations. *Organizational Studies,* 26(3), 465–484. https://doi.org/10.1177/0170840605050876
Schatzki, T.R., 2010. *The timespace of human activity: on performance, society, and history as indeterminate teleological events.* Plymouth: Lexington Books.
Schatzki, T.R., Cetina, K.K., and von Savigny, E., eds., 2001. *The practice turn in contemporary theory.* London: Routledge.
Scott, J.C., 1998. *Seeing like a state: how certain schemes to improve the human condition have failed.* New Haven, CT: Yale University Press.
Serra, J.P., 2010. What is and what should pragmatic ethics be? *European Journal of Pragmatism and American Philosophy,* II-2. https://doi.org/10.4000/ejpap.905

Shotter, J., 2007. Wittgenstein and his philosophy of first-time events. *History of Philosophy of Psychology*, 9(1), 1–11.

Shotter, J., and Tsoukas, H., 2014. Performing phronesis: on the way to engaged judgement. *Management Learning*, 45(4), 377–396. https://doi.org/10.1177/1350507614541196

Stacey, R.D., 2001. *Complex responsive processes in organizations: learning and knowledge creation.* London: Routledge.

Stacey, R.D., ed., 2005. *Experiencing emergence in organizations: local interaction and the emergence of global pattern.* London: Routledge.

Stacey, R.D., 2007. *Strategic management and organizational dynamics: the challenge of complexity.* 5th ed. Essex: Prentice Hall.

Stacey, R.D., 2010. *Complexity and organizational reality: uncertainty and the need to rethink management after the collapse of investment capitalism.* 2nd ed. London: Routledge.

Stacey, R.D., and Griffin, D., eds., 2005. *A complexity perspective on researching organizations: taking experience seriously.* London: Routledge.

Tsoukas, H., 2005. *Complex knowledge: studies in organizational epistemology.* Oxford: Oxford University Press.

Tsoukas, H., 2011. Foreword: representation, signification, improvisation – a three-dimensional view of organizational knowledge. In: H. Canary and R.D. McPhee (eds.) *Communication and organizational knowledge: contemporary issues for theory and practice.* New York: Routledge, x–xix.

Tsoukas, H., 2017. Don't simplify, complexify: from disjunctive to conjunctive theorizing in organization and management studies. *Journal of Management Studies*, 52(2), 132–153. http://dx.doi.org/10.1111/joms.12219

Tsoukas, H., 2019. *Philosophical organizational theory.* Oxford: Oxford University Press.

Weick, K.E., 2017. Foreword to foreword. In: H. Tsoukas (ed.) *Philosophical organizational theory.* Oxford: Oxford University Press, xi.

Wenger, E., 1998. *Communities of practice: learning, meaning and identity.* Cambridge: Cambridge University Press.

Wenger, E., 2000. Communities of practice and social learning system. *Organization*, 7(2), 225–246. https://doi.org/10.1177/135050840072002

3
THE DOUBLE BIND OF METRICS

Emma Elkington

Introduction

Until starting to undertake my doctoral research, I had never questioned the use of performance metrics, it was simply 'the way it is'. I had thought that if using metrics didn't work in the way I expected, it was either because I was not a good enough manager, or because others were 'misaligned to the goals of the organisation', or because the metrics had been interpreted incorrectly, and sometimes a combination of all three. My thinking had been heavily influenced by my experiences of working outside of Higher Education (HE). I had previously managed a regional office of a listed profit-making private education firm, which supplied accountancy and law training, and had received large bonuses based on achievement of a range of metrics. Prior to that, I had completed my early career training to be an accountant and then training accountants in one of the 'Big Four' accountancy firms.[1] In addition to my experiences of being managed through and managing others using metrics, I had been influenced by

DOI: 10.4324/9781003099925-3

management and accounting literature, which I was introduced to through my university education, accountancy training and management development courses. Advocates of metrics argue that focussing on metrics will lead to improvements in the object we are trying to measure (e.g. Taylor, 1911; Drucker, 1974; Peters, 1986). Drucker (1974) argues that a manager needs to establish yardsticks and have measurements available to them as the foundation for firm decision-making and Peters (1986) coined the phrase, "… what gets measured gets done". Accounting literature suggests that accounting is a method of furnishing unambiguous data to provide managers with evidence to make savings and rationalise efficiencies. 'Evidence' in the form of metrics then should put an end to disputes and is the best way to manage. If we assume that humans are motivated by achieving targets, then it is reasonable to assume that people need to be given 'a carrot' to try their hardest to achieve the results that the managers demand.

To illustrate some of the assumptions about the use of metrics in my own university, I recount the following statement, which was made at a recent all-employee welcome back meeting, by a senior member of the leadership team of my academic school:

> We use metrics to think about the right things. It gives us more information. Measuring performance is a natural outcome of wanting to excel. You would be disappointed if we managed just on gut instinct.

The assumption seems to be that only by measuring and providing metrics will staff and managers excel. This statement suggests that metrics are a more 'objective' and reliable basis for making judgements, presuming human intuition is 'subjective', unreliable and limited in its impartiality.

I recollect that as this statement was made I shuffled uncomfortably in my seat and scanned the large lecture hall to see who was going to object. Prior to my research, my response would probably be similar to that of the 100+ staff present in the large lecture hall, namely, to nod and smile. However, for reasons I will explain, I noticed instead how this statement caused feelings of unease and dejection.

This chapter first explains the context of HE in the UK before focussing on the proliferation of performance metrics used to measure the outputs of HE in the UK. It then explores the behaviours of myself and others in my business school when managed by and trying to manage with performance metrics and the feeling of unease and dejection I highlight above. The chapter then discusses the ethical concerns regarding feelings of lack of agency that may arise from an uncritical application of metrics.

Metrics in Higher Education

Whilst the traditional characterisation of a UK university sees university leadership and governance founded on principles of collegiality, whereby universities were run by academics who reached senior positions following selection by their contemporaries and decisions were reached by consent (Watson, 2011), university management nowadays increasingly resembles management in any other large business (Alvesson & Spicer, 2016:31). This means that universities have come to mimic private sector firms in introducing budgets, quantitative targets and techniques for punishment and reward.

In HE there has been a proliferation of metrics used to assess whether universities are 'good' at the same time as the pseudo-marketisation[2] of the sector. A key aspect of the metrification of HE attempts to measure whether students got a good experience, using survey-based rankings of satisfaction. There are two widely publicised metrics about whether universities are 'good' which are used to inform further rankings and to purportedly influence students' choice of university.

First, there is an annual survey of satisfaction named the National Student Survey (NSS), which asks final year students about their university experience. This survey is conducted by an independent market research organisation. The output of the NSS is used by many media outlets, who state that they are shining a light on student satisfaction levels. The NSS informs different published league tables such as the Guardian League tables (Guardian, 2021), The Times Good University Guide (O'Leary, 2018) and The Complete University Guide (2021). In addition, the NSS results are displayed when a student is researching their programme and institution on the Discoveruni website (Discoveruni, 2021).

Second, in 2016 the government introduced the Teaching Excellence Framework (TEF). TEF assessors, who are a panel of students, academics and widening participation experts and employers, are given information on universities to assess them for a bronze, silver or gold award. These awards are intended to reflect excellence across the universities teaching, learning environment and student outcomes. The aim is to "...provide clear information to students about where the best provision can be found", "...encourage providers to improve teaching quality to reduce variability" and to "...help drive UK productivity by ensuring a better match of graduate skills with the needs of employers and the economy" (The Department of Business, Innovation and Skills, 2016:5).

It is not uncommon to see NSS metrics or boasts of Gold TEF awards on university web sites, backs of buses, social media and on the email footers of academic staff along with being reported in the popular press.[3] It is presumed that a rise or fall in the NSS or awarding of Gold, Silver or Bronze in TEF could have significant consequences for a UK HE institution. There is an assumption that an increased NSS or TEF status leads to increased reputation in the domestic and international market, increases student numbers, makes it easier to attract top students (and therefore income) leading to improved facilities, teaching and research. Conversely, a fall could lead to decreased student numbers and ultimately, presumably, closure of the institution (Wilkins & Huisman, 2012).

It appears to me that seeking accountability in HE seems to have shifted from a legitimate demand that universities be accountable to society, to one where it appears that the only publicly acceptable way to measure 'quality' is through rankings of universities, using some of the proxy measures of quality or attainment such as NSS ranking tables. Under a marketised ideology, students must be able to have transparent information about the 'value' that they will individually receive from their education. In theory then, this requires students to ask, 'what am I paying for'? Indeed, since the introduction of the TEF there has been an increasing emphasis away from assessment of the teaching and learning environment towards 'student outcomes', that is, the type of work a graduate has and the salary they earn from doing this. More recently, the Office for Students (OfS) has published an experimental metric labelled PROCEED (Projected Completion and Employment from Entrant Data). This metric attempts to give incoming undergraduates an estimate of the likelihood that they will gain an award and progress to graduate-level employment. Whilst the government have stated that they have no immediate plan to use this data, there is a strong likelihood of these metrics finding their way into league tables and public discourse, with a potential knock-on impact on course and university viability.[4]

Ranking universities in league tables such as NSS and the use of output rankings of student experience in exercises such as the TEF are seen as a reasonable and useful thing to do in an environment in which the government, prospective and current students and senior leaders of universities see HE as a competitive market.[5] Providing performance data gives 'customers' the information they need to make judgements about what product to buy. Students are meant to be guided in their choice of HE 'provider' by using these ranking systems to inform their individual 'investment' in a university education. The metrics that are being used in HE are subsumed with the ideology that students are consumers of their education and that an education is a commodity that can be used to get value for money, in terms of higher salary, for each individual, post-graduation.

Metrics in My Business School

In my business school, metrics seem to be taken up in ways which reflect what is happening more generally in the HE sector. In my institution, there is an assumption that competition is the way that HE should be organised and is taken up, on the whole, uncritically among managers of the senior leadership team (SLT),[6] and in many cases re-enforced. Much of what happens in my institution focuses upon the metrics that measure student satisfaction and assume that the student is a consumer of their education and the ultimate arbitrator of what a good education is. Staff are considered to be resources; indeed, as a line manager of academic staff, I am referred to as a resource manager in many formal university meetings. There are also conversations about how we may compete with other universities to gain students, along with the feelings of existential terror that not attracting students may mean. I had previously failed to consider that the application of metrics was not something someone was 'doing to me' but rather something that we, as SLT, were also helping to form/reform in our conversations with one another, thus simultaneously reforming the marketisation and metrification of the HE sector within our business school.

I now see that the patterns of conversations that are happening in my school are not inevitable but rather are influenced from both the wider context of the metrification of HE, but at the same time are influenced by our personal backgrounds and the enabling-constraining nature of working together.

To give an example of these types of performance metrics in my university, students are surveyed in mid-semester, surveys to ask them if they are finding their teaching enjoyable, engaging and if they understand how they will be assessed. The feedback from these questionnaires is presented on a metricised scale of 1–5 (1 being poor and 5 being excellent) and summarised and presented to middle managers in Red-Amber-Green (RAG) traffic light systems, highlighting those teaching areas rated as above a targeted level (Green) and those below (Red). Middle managers are expected to discuss these RAG ratings with senior leaders of the school and are exhorted to take actions to ensure that they 'sort out' the red-rated modules. The practicality of such 'sorting out' may involve many different activities, such as removing those poorly rated modules and replacing them with others, by moving activities within modules to ensure the parts students struggle with come after the mid-semester evaluation is done and sometimes in instituting HR-approved process on managing poor performance with those leading the activities that had been rated red. Any of these activities may improve the metrics that we are being measured against (or may not) but very few improve the learning and teaching we are giving to students. In his book *The Tyranny of Metrics*, Muller points out how such activities are endemic in the US and UK across healthcare, police reform, overseas aid programmes and finance and refers to such activities as 'gaming the metrics' (Muller, 2018:24).

These same metrics of student satisfaction from these mid-module feedback questionnaires have also been presented at senior leadership meetings. At these, each of the subject areas of the business schools has had their data from the modules they deliver aggregated on a weighted average basis and then presented graphically against a targeted level, clearly showing those subject areas with modules on average outperforming the targeted 'satisfaction' and those subject areas that are on average falling below those levels. The use of these performance metrics and graphs has been presented in shaming and humiliating ways, with those middle managers responsible for the subject areas being expected to account to the SLT for their good performance or failure in their areas of influence, along with exhortations from those leading the school to make the target even higher, in the belief that this will motivate further improvement. In my research, I note how questioning whether an increase in targets is helpful or demotivating or, indeed, whether taking the opinions of our students is the only measure of whether we are 'good' leads to swift reprimands and shaming of those middle managers calling these into question, leaving them shocked, upset, silenced or defiant (and sometimes both silenced and defiant at the same time).

What motivated my research was noticing that despite what was promised in much accounting and management literature about how metrics could be used as a tool to make managing easier, this was not my experience. Instead, I noticed how the meaning of the performance metrics were sometimes contested, and there were times where there was denial of what the results meant when they reflected badly on individuals and conflicted with our views on our performance. I noticed that my colleagues and I appeared to amplify and dampen existing power relations, using the metrics as 'evidence' of how good we were, either by inflating our own sense of worth and value in collaborating with our allies or by diminishing the achievements of others who we are in competition with. I also recognised the feeling of being stuck that emerged when working with metrics, which led to feelings of helplessness, both with respect to my ability to argue about the use of performance metrics or to question what these were 'telling' us.

Datafication[7]

One of the reasons that metrics seem to be seeing a resurgence is based on a faith that they are objective, fair and logical, as Beer (2016:138), a professor of sociology, suggests. A number holds the promise of confidence, accuracy and neutrality. Power (2004:774) suggests that metrics hold out a Benthamite dream of ultimate commensurability and argues that metrification potentially reduces cronyism and bias. This assumption that measuring is objective and neutral and is the appropriate way to manage has its roots in the Enlightenment quest for rational knowledge in search of universal truths, where we privilege reason as a way of controlling our environment. In theory, metrics are convincing and leave little ground for any subjective response or reaction. This assumes that the relationship between metrified data and 'reality' is unidirectional; that is, metrics reflect and measure a pre-existent reality. While metrics are clearly not new, Beer argues that there has been a clear shift in recent decades towards measurement: "…as a replacement or substitute for more qualitative judgement" (Beer, 2016:23). In HE, measuring performance, in theory, makes the provision of education observable at a distance and enables managers to compare, rate and rank.

As a middle manager in a UK Business School, I am not arguing against the use of metrics. Political scientist Scott (1998) reminds us that measuring may be necessary when trying to manage at a distance. He depicts how much early modern statecraft was devoted to rationalising and standardising complex activities into legible and administratively more convenient formats to enable activities such as taxation, conscription and relief of the poor. Scott argues simplifications were necessary for social realities to be intelligible to state regulators who sit at a distance and explains that this simplification, abstraction and mapping are essential tools of modern statecraft (ibid.: 4). Stacey (2012), drawing on Foucault, points out that modern organisations may struggle to manage without such tools and techniques. Managing using metrics could be used to provide synoptic information to enable managers to focus efforts, which could help make managing easier and less contested. This may be valuable to help contain anxiety and to enable those with less experience to have procedures and create stability to enable them to carry out their work.

However, I am also opposed to the idea that all qualities that we are interested in can be summarised into quantities (and in this I am not alone – this has a long history back to the Romantic period). Metrics certainly provide a numerical score, which appears objective, but are arrived at through making judgements and assumptions. As Collini, a professor of intellectual history, argues:

> Asking users of higher education whether they are satisfied with the quality of the education they have received is likely to produce responses that are quantifiable but of little use, or responses that may be relevant to the activity but are not quantifiable.
>
> (Collini, 2018:40)

What appears to have been happening in my institution is that proxy measures, such as high student satisfaction scores, become a target to be aimed at rather than 'good teaching' in itself. Muller (2018) suggests that it is common that the proxy becomes the measure and the measure becomes the target. Muller argues that there are numerous unintended but predictable negative consequences of metric fixation (Muller, 2018:169).

As a middle manager in a UK university, I notice how the metrics we use have been changing the conversations that I have with my staff and between members of the SLT. In accordance with the arguments of Scott (1998), I contend that metrics not only measure but also help shape the things we are measuring in ways that may be both helpful and unhelpful. The metrics are not therefore simply measuring a 'reality' that pre-exists, but are changing the activities people undertake and conversations they have as they try to improve these metrics. Scott (1998:4) reminds us that when scientific knowledge is imposed on complex environments of societies, they are almost always at risk of being inefficient, inappropriate and at times dangerous. Similarly, Stacey (2012:67) points out that when we claim that the function of such management tools and techniques is solely to improve performance, we may fail to recognise their role as a technique of discipline and thus lose sight of our role in the ethical dimensions involved in their implementation.

In summary, metrics may be useful at an abstract level for managing at a distance when there are longer chains of command. The use of metrics could be used as a means of opening an exploration of what it is we do and what it is we value. However, my experience is that we are likely to privilege metrics significance when they accord with our preconceptions and we use them to support our ideological position. Where the metrics do not support our preconceptions, we are likely to downplay their significance.

The Double Bind[8] of Metrics

Much of the HE literature about the use of performance metrics privileges an idea of rationality and objectivity. In my research on how metrics were taken up in my organisation, I noticed how some metrics were used by people to blame and shame others for perceived failures, which provoked strong feelings and emotions and amplified the potential for stigmatisation and exclusion. Conversely, metrics were also used to recognise success and reward those for performance of certain activities which were valued by those setting the targets. This mixture led to 'high fives' and celebrations about 'good' results, as well as shame and anxiety about not doing one's job well enough. Some staff (myself included) experienced feelings of panic about potentially losing one's job and a lowering of status. Conversely, when the metrics for my area looked good, I felt a guilty pride in 'beating' my colleagues. I came to realise that there is never really a winner in the 'game' of metrics. For example, whilst the current metric regime may show me as 'good', it is difficult to boast about it because other metric regimes, or even the same metrics next time round, may show another outcome, thereby promoting uncertainty over time. Metrics appear to portray different people in different lights, not just as metrics change, but in response to the sense we make of them.

I suggest that managing using metrics seems to present middle managers with a double bind because when the metrics make us look good it seems to be hard to argue against their limitations, potentially because of feelings of pride, but also perhaps because we are grateful that we are the ones that will not be disciplined (on this occasion). It is not in our interests to question their success. However, if we perform badly, any critique of the use of metrics is often deemed defensive. So, when the metrics show us not to be doing as well, we may try to play down the value of those metrics, but this may be viewed by others as 'sour grapes'.

In order to explore patterns of blame, pride and shame when managing using metrics, I have drawn on a view of the individual based on Mead's ideas (1934) of how our minds and selves arise in interactions with others and Elias's (1994) ideas that we are constrained and enabled by our interdependencies with others. Elias also argues that engaging in interaction with people involves dynamics of inclusion and exclusion (Elias & Scotson, 1994) in and from a group. He suggests that there is a negotiating of who is 'in' and who is 'out', who 'we' are and consequently who 'they', the excluded, are. Those who speak out in this negotiation risk being excluded by expressing an opinion that differs from the majority. Taking up these ideas, if we derive part of our identity from the groups to which we belong, if we are then excluded from a group with which we want to identify, we lose a part of our identity, which immediately makes us feel insecure and vulnerable.

I contend that part of the double bind of being managed and managing using metrics means that even though we know that metrics are neither objective nor neutral, we continue to use them as if they are. It is seemingly easy to fall back into these same habitual patterns. In perpetuating a way of thinking that metrics are neutral, objective and natural and because we are enabled/constrained by each other, there is a risk of exclusion. This makes it more difficult to argue against the 'way things are'. I suggest that in using metrics to manage when they serve to raise our standing, we may self-silence any doubt about their use. I submit that we may perpetuate the use of metrics and/or not question them by colluding in their use, either as a means of aggrandising those who do well or stigmatising those who do not. For me, I realise I have suppressed concerns about the use of metrics, not only because I was worried about the risk of being critical, but also because I was simultaneously enabled and constrained by the image I had of myself as a loyal middle manager.

I, like colleagues, have previously fallen into the trap of lending metrics agency, as though they had some power over us, rather than being something that I and others were taking up in particular ways. I have come to see that rather than considering that metrics have agency over me, in a sense the metrics are socially constructed; that is, we are doing this to each other. Not to play the metrics game is to risk exclusion, but to speak out might prompt a similar outcome. I suggest the feeling of being in a 'double bind' that emerges when working with metrics means that we may feel helpless and without agency.

Stuck in the Middle

Much of the literature on middle managers suggests that their role is to take the strategic plans of those above them and deploy them by controlling and persuading those below them to carry out specific actions (e.g. Mintzberg, 1989; Huy, 2001; Floyd & Dimmock, 2011). In HE literature, there is a depiction of the middle manager as being 'stuck in the middle' between organisational goals and the expectations of the staff they lead, with a focus on the lack of formal training that middle managers in HE receive (e.g. Floyd, 2016; Gonaim, 2016) or listing out the activities and competencies middle managers in HE requires (e.g. Graham, 2013). Up to this point I have thought of my role as a middle manager as being caught between the directives that are being given from those above me telling me to 'sort it out' and having to implement these by persuading, cajoling or simply telling those below me what they need to do.

I believe this may be a recognisable feeling of many middle managers, and certainly this is part of the conversation in my institution. I had considered myself to be a good manager if I followed the directives of those 'above me' and applied the rules of the organisation. It had previously seemed to me that my choices fell into following the rules (which allowed me to abrogate myself from the responsibility for actions I was taking) or to flounce out of the organisation as there was no possibility of resistance from within (which I have come to realise is another form of abrogating responsibility). However, I have come to see that we are all middle managers in some ways, or at least in processual terms this is how it feels. The Dean has expressed how his 'hands are tied' by the requirements of the Vice Chancellor.[9] I am also aware that the Vice Chancellor feels he must account to the Board of Governors, and they in turn to the OfS. Simultaneously, it feels as if the Dean is powerless to get anything done unless I acquiesce to persuade my staff, and nor can I in turn achieve much without the compliance of my staff.

I now recognise that it is not simply that I am being subjugated by the senior leaders of my school and in turn subjugate my staff, but also that there are times where I (and others) also try to overtly or covertly constrain the Dean's actions which in turn he tries to resist. I also notice there are times when my staff also carry out acts that constrain my actions and could be considered petty acts of resistance or non-compliance. I find Scott's 1990 study *Domination and the Arts of Resistance: Hidden Transcripts* helpful in understanding public and hidden features of subjugation and resistance. Drawing on Scott's work and Elias's work on inclusion and exclusion (Elias & Scotson, 1994), I suggest that whilst I have felt subjugated when others want me to do something I don't want to do and sometimes feel compelled to subjugate others when they don't do what I want them to do, I now recognise these as the enabling-constraining activities of working with others. This problematises the view of middle managers as simply being in the middle, whilst acknowledging that this is how it feels. Recognising that others in the organisational 'hierarchy' may be as enabled and constrained in working with others, as I have felt to be, has enabled me to think about my feelings of being stuck.

Taking a social perspective has enabled me to imagine the perspective of others and what might be going on for them. This, in turn, has provoked feelings of guilt, pity, shame (or blame), which have helped me to take a more nuanced judgement about what their motivations might mean. One person's subterfuge may be another person's subjugation. For example, it is possible that any attempts I may make to shield my staff from the metric regime that we are constantly exposed to may be seen by others as an attempt to keep information from them. In any situation, there are competing goods and negotiation of what 'good' is. As we functionalise our values in everyday work, we may both comply with and resist the dominant ideology and in that way influence (and are influenced by) shifts in what is discussed and actioned.

Metrics and Emotions

As I have stated above, many protagonists of the use of metrics suggest that they make the process of managing less emotional. The value attributed to numbers is that, as opposed to expert opinion, they are impersonal (Porter, 1995:32). The authority of metrics is not only vested in our sense of their accuracy as representing something we may not otherwise know, but also in their long and evolving association with rationality and objectivity (Espeland & Stevens, 2008:417). However, my experience of managing using metrics and of metrics being used to measure my performance has led me to challenge the above assumption. In my introduction to this chapter, I explained the feelings I had of dejection and a feeling of being stuck when it was claimed that metrics show things and we would not want to manage on gut instinct. My experience of being managed by and managing with performance metrics is feeling a range of emotions, including pride, joy, anger, shame, anxiety, fear, jealousy and relief. My doctoral research explored how this was often also the case for others.

Burkitt (2014) argues that feelings and emotions are how we orientate ourselves within a situation and to others (Burkitt, 2014:8). He sees emotions as the outcome of moral evaluation that we apply to other people's behaviour (ibid.: 5) and that we interpret this behaviour in ways that are "…socially and culturally meaningful" (ibid.: 66). Burkitt argues that we have a certain disposition to act according to our feelings, but disagrees with the more traditional theories on emotions, which state that this disposition equals a "…determination to act" as though pointing to a linear correlation between our emotions and our reactions (ibid.: 16). He rather understands this disposition as a "…tendency to act in particular ways", as habitual patterns dependent on the social context, which in themselves are "…sedimentations of past patterns of relationships" which must adapt to the situations we are confronted with and where we bring our own biographies to life in the emotional response (ibid.: 7). I take this to mean we will not all react in the same way to the same stimuli, but we will be affected by our past experience – which is why we may experience different emotions to the same situation. Burkitt (2014:55) suggests that our responses come from others' gestures and depend on the specific context, past experiences, personal interests and how we anticipate the chances of a likely outcome.

Beer (2016:194–195) in a coda to his book *Metric Power* draws on the work of Wetherell (2012, 2014) to link emotions to metrics, making the case that there is a link between metrics and uncertainty. He draws on the work of Davies (2014), on neoliberalism, concluding that the purpose of measuring is not to achieve a peaceful consensus but to nurture existential anxieties. He argues that metrics, in their role as facilitators of competition, are central to the production of uncertainty and claims that this uncertainty evokes emotions. He suggests that what makes systems of measurement powerful is the affective responses that they provoke (ibid.: 211). He contends that a key factor in how metrics "…produce outcomes, behaviours and practices is how they make us feel" (ibid.: 212). Beer's work claims that it is our *expectation* of what the metrics may capture and how we may be compared that provokes emotions. In my research, I recognise the links between metrics and the creation of uncertainty and provocation of an emotional response.

However, Beer acknowledges that this chapter is only included to bridge to future works on the way metrics make us feel (ibid.: 212). Building on Beer's work and drawing on the work of Burkitt, I contend that what I experience as 'my' feelings and emotions are influenced by my intellectual assumptions and personal history of being managed and managing using metrics and the enabling/constraining relationships within the SLT where I now work. For example, I grew up thinking that showing strong emotions was a sign of weakness and that for me to operate properly as a 'good' manager required me to retain a sense of control and to behave in a non-emotional way that others (and I) would expect. In my formative work experiences, I felt proud when 'exceeding expectations' but also afraid of failing against the targets set. These experiences have the potential to influence how I am interacting with others in the present and the sense I am making of managing using metrics and the emotions I feel. In my current context in HE, my experience has been of constantly feeling I am being judged through the use of metrics. I argue therefore that, after Burkitt, our emotions are influenced by the context and socially shaped past experiences in anticipation of our expectation of recognisable social patterns. I therefore contend that there are both general and particular responses to metrics. On the one hand we feel anxious and judged or proud when metrics come into play, and I argue this is a general phenomenon, because others have told me they feel this way too. However, because of our particular histories, our responses to being scrutinised by metrics may evoke even more amplified feelings in some of us, as they have for me. Thus, I argue that it is not the metrics that make me feel proud, ashamed or angry, but it is my expectation of how those metrics may be used in the current context, based on my previous experiences. I now see emotions as being constituted within a social situation, reflecting power relations as the enabling and constraining activities of others. My experience has shown that metrics appear to evoke the very emotions protagonists of metrics claim they are designed to prevent, possibly even amplifying them, because it feels so hard to argue against them. I argue that this is partly because of the double bind I describe above.

Agency

I now acknowledge that taking the perspective that metrics show us things and that as middle managers we need to simply translate the directives of those above us has some advantages. I suggest that the use of metrics and standardised procedures may mean middle managers feel that we don't need to take responsibility for the actions we take. For example, in instigating poor performance management processes with staff who are 'red' module leaders, it is possible to point to the metrics to show that any judgement of their performance is 'the truth'. On reflection, I realised that this was a way of avoiding a more difficult conversation with a colleague about the specific concerns I had about their teaching skills. I could follow standardised, sanctioned procedures to demonstrate to the staff member, and myself, that I am simply doing is what is expected from me and therefore the 'right' thing to be doing, and in this way abrogate myself from the responsibility of the actions I was taking.

However, I now realise that losing sight of the fact that metrics are abstractions risks us losing sight of the human beings involved and the consequences of what we are doing together. What may then happen is that people can be dehumanised and thought about as 'categories' (e.g. 'red' or 'green') or that we come up with solutions like 'removing failing activities', disregarding the consequences for the people being 'removed'. I contend that the idealisation by many of the 'objective' nature of metrics may make it even harder to talk about emotions, relationships and vulnerabilities.

What I have become more alert to as a middle manager is the quality of my own participation in ongoing interactions and ways in which this may (or may not) be influential. Acknowledging now that claiming that metrics 'showed me things' and that just 'following the procedures' to discipline staff for poor performance is not necessarily as ethical as I had previously presumed it to be, has made it very hard to carry on in my supposition that it is possible to simply 'sort "it" [a red module] out' as advised by my managers.

Consequently, I now realise that this raises ethical and ideological questions about who we are and what we think we are doing, calling our values into question. What middle managers may then come to recognise is that there are ethical decisions to be made about what we question and how we may do that. For example, in my organisation, recognising that the dominant ideology that we operate under is one of marketisation and managerialism does not mean that I must acquiesce or agree, but nor could I expect to overtly critique this viewpoint without expecting to be excluded. Indeed, in other academic institutions in the UK, scholars and research areas who take a critical view of the marketisation of managerialism of society are being closed down.[10] So, whilst it is not possible to step outside the panopticon-like gaze of metrics (because we are all doing this to one another), I believe that recognising the 'feeling' of a double bind may enable us to act in political ways that are more nuanced and therefore transform (or not) how we might negotiate what we are doing together. As Mowles (2021) states: "however limited our actions may be in the web of other people's actions, to be aware of the limitations of individual choice is not the same as saying that that we have no agency". I have started to see that although the feeling of double blind makes it feel as if I am subjugated, I am not completely helpless and without agency, but rather, I have ethical choices to make about what I am being asked to do. As Burkitt suggests: "...to be part of a community to which we are answerable, to feel that we belong to, we must be capable of doing more than reproducing it in a routine fashion" (Burkitt, 2008:61).

I now recognise that a focus on metrics appears to be reducing both my own and my colleagues' capacity to engage critically with one another and with our staff about what we are doing together. Once it became clear to me that the use of metrics is a fundamentally social process, the ethical implications and possibilities of quantification have become more visible to me. I have been considering what it means to continue working in an organisation that sometimes takes decisions that I can see may do harm to those that work for and with me. I propose that acknowledging that managing using metrics may lead to emotional responses may help increase the capacity of middle managers to respond to these when they arise. I now believe that emotions are highly relevant and therefore worth paying attention to, because they offer people the opportunity to expand their awareness of what is going on in social situations, to become aware of their emotional tendencies and to reflect on our habitual responses in emotionally charged situations. I argue that the manager who is more aware of their emotional tendencies and can acknowledge that strong emotions are likely to emerge when managing with metrics may be in a better position to adapt to local circumstances and to consider their involvement in the enabling/constraining conversations in which they are engaged.

Acknowledging that managing using metrics means that middle managers are likely to encounter strong emotional responses and may present them with a double bind, which may then lead to feelings of hopelessness and subjugation, could enable middle managers to become more aware of their habits in response to these feelings and enable them to reflect upon them. Acknowledging these strong emotions and feelings of futility may help us increase our capacity for being able to cope with the sense of 'being caught in the middle' and may help middle managers to engage more imaginatively in how we might act.

For me, I find now that I am more attentive to my own behaviour and more ready to consider how we are all participating in interaction rather than (as previously) to assume that problems are located with individuals. My exploration has helped me better negotiate my way through my interactions with colleagues, showing a capacity for taking the attitude of others' and becoming more sensitive to "…inclusion-exclusion dynamics created by particular ways of talking" (Stacey, 2003:125). Being more aware of my emotional tendencies and acknowledging that strong emotions are likely to emerge when managing with metrics has helped me to consider how I am participating in the enabling/constraining conversations I am engaged in. In addition, paying attention to how resistance and conflict emerge in our everyday interaction as we explore our differences and similarities has enabled new patterns of relating to arise. Recognising such patterns has enabled me to increase my capacity to cope with the anxiety of the risk of being excluded.

I have also come to see that making alliances and acknowledging the importance of informal networks has enabled me to become a more politically astute middle manager. I have discovered more possibilities of working in a regime that sometimes makes me feel uncomfortable without retreating to either blindly following what has been asked of me or feeling compelled to leave the organisation. I have been having frequent conversations with senior leaders of the school about the impact that this relentless focus on metrics is having on me, my staff and our relationships. This may (or may not) be moving us forward to thinking about metrics differently. I believe, however, that I have developed my capacity to live with uncertainty that bit longer, to 'sit in the fire', explore and negotiate the next steps into the unknown.

Notes

1 The 'Big Four' refers to the four largest professional services networks in the world: KPMG, EY, Deloitte and PWC. Collectively, they are estimated to have around a two-third share of the global accountancy market. In the UK, the Economic Affairs Committee reported that the Big Four audit all but one of the FTSE100 companies and 240 of the FTSE250, an index of the leading listing companies (Economic Affairs Committee, 2011).
2 After Williams (2013:13), I have referred to the market in UK HE as a pseudo-market because it is not a perfect economic model. First, price is not set by the market itself but by the government by capping student fees. Supply is manipulated by bringing in new 'suppliers' by giving degree-awarding powers to new institutions, by attempting to lower costs and by increasing and/or reducing subsidies for certain courses. Similarly, demand is also somewhat manipulated. The government regulates the number of overseas students allowed to enter the UK through visa caps, offers cut-price places in further education (FE) colleges and has fined universities for over-recruiting students against targets.
3 This is especially the case where 'known' good universities were awarded bronze awards, such as London School of Economics (LSE) (*The Independent*, 2018). LSE accused the TEF as reporting '...subjective estimates'.
4 The PROCEED data was published in numerous newspapers on the day it was released.
5 Williams argues that the student has been recast as a consumer/customer of HE (Williams, 2013:2–15) and Biesta suggests that the conception

of a free market implies that 'customers know what they want' (Biesta, 2017:320).
6   The SLT of my business school is comprised of the Dean of school, Deputy Dean, six Heads of subject groups and a dozen Associate Deans of school with portfolios ranging from research to enterprise to teaching and learning.
7   Datafication is a term borrowed from Mayer-Schonenberger and Cukkier (2013:78), who use it to describe the contemporary phenomenon of quantifying aspects of life that previously were not measured numerically.
8   Mowles (2015:14) defines a double bind as two mutually exclusive negative consequences; neither choice being particularly palatable, either choice judged as 'bad'. A double bind has some of the qualities of a paradox but presents two negative choices with a further obligation to choose one of them. He also argues that there is no escape from it: a person is forced to choose between one and the other and this takes away all sense of freedom.
9   Of course, this could also be a rhetoric of blaming those above to get something one wants; a rhetorical ploy I recognise, because I have also used this at times myself.
10 At the University of Leicester in May 2021, the University closed the school of Critical Management Studies and Political Economy and enforced redundancies because their research interests were 'not primarily in areas aligned with school strategic priorities for research', a move widely criticised by academics from across the UK and learned societies such as the British sociological society (BSA Everyday Society, 2021).

References

Alvesson, M. & Spicer, A. (2016). '(Un)Conditional surrender? Why do professionals willingly comply with managerialism?' *Journal of Organizational Change Management.* 29 (1), pp 29–45.

Beer, D. (2016). *Metric Power.* London: Palgrave Macmillan.

Biesta, G. (2017). 'Education, measurement and the professions: Reclaiming a space for a democratic professionality in education'. *Educational Philosophy and Theory.* 49 (4), pp 315–330.

BSA Today (2021). *BSA President writes to Leicester VC on the Proposed Closure of Critical Management Studies and Political Economy.* [Online] Available at:

BSA President writes to Leicester VC on the proposed closure of Critical Management Studies and Political Economy – The British Sociological Association (britsoc.co.uk). [Accessed 25 August 2021].

Burkitt, I. (2008). *Social Selves: Theories of Self and Society*. London: SAGE.

Burkitt, I. (2014). *Emotions and Social Relations*. London: SAGE.

Collini, S. (2017). *Speaking of Universities*. London: Verso.

Complete University Guide (2018). *University League Tables 2021*. [Online] Available at: https://www.thecompleteuniversityguide.co.uk/league-tables/rankings. [Accessed 28 May 2021].

Davies, W. (2014). *The Limits of Neoliberalism*. London: SAGE.

Department for Business, Innovation and Skills (2016). *Teaching Excellence Framework: Technical Consultation for Year 2*. [Online] Available at: https://assets.publishing.service.gov.uk/government/uploads/system/uploads/attachment_data/file/523340/bis-16-262-teaching-excellence-framework-techcon.pdf. [Accessed 19 December 2020].

DiscoverUni (2021). [Online] Available at: https://discoveruni.gov.uk/. [Accessed 28 May 2021].

Drucker, P. (1974). *Management: Tasks, Responsibilities, Practices*. London: Heinemann.

Economic Affairs Committee (2011). *'Complacency' of Auditors Contributed to Financial Crisis*. [Online] Available at: https://www.parliament.uk/business/committees/committees-a-z/lords-select/economic-affairs-committee/news/big-4-auditors-inquiry-report/ [Accessed 26 July 2020].

Elias, N. (1994). *The Civilizing Process*. Oxford: Blackwell

Elias, N. & Scotson, J. (1994). *The Established and the Outsiders*. London: SAGE.

Espeland, W. & Stevens, M. (2008). 'A sociology of quantification'. *European Journal of Sociology*. 49 (3), pp 401–436.

Floyd, A. (2016). 'Supporting academic managers in higher education; Do we care?' *Higher Education Policy*. 29, pp 167–183.

Floyd, A. & Dimmock, C. (2011). "'Jugglers', 'copers' and 'strugglers'; Academic perceptions of being a HOD in a post-1992 university and how it influences their future careers'. *Journal of Higher Education Policy and Management*. 33 (4), pp 387–399.

Gonaim, F. (2016). 'A department chair: A lifeguard without a life jacket'. *Higher Education Policy*. 29, pp 272–286.

Graham, G. (2013). *Universities: The Recovery of an Idea*. Thorverton: Imprint Academic.

Guardian (2021). *University League Tables 2021*. The Guardian. [Online]. Available at https://www.theguardian.com/education/ng-interactive/2020/sep/05/the-best-uk-universities-2021-league-table [Accessed 18 May 2021].

Huy, Q. (2001). 'In praise of middle managers'. *Harvard Business Review*. 79 (8), pp 72–79.

The Independent. (2018). *Elite Universities Improve Teaching Scores after Requesting to Be Judged Again in Government Rankings*. The Independent. 6 June 2018. Available at https://www.independent.co.uk/news/education/education-news/university-teaching-scores-russell-group-improvements-government-rankings-tef-a8386321.html [Accessed 21 February 2020].

Mayer-Schonenberger, V. & Cukkier, K. (2013). *Big Data: A Revelation That Will Transform How We Live, Work and Think*. Boston, MA: Houghton Miffen Harcourt.

Mintzberg, H. (1989). *Mintzberg on Management: Inside Our Strange World of Organizations*. London: Free Press.

Mowles, C. (2015). *Managing in Uncertainty: Complexity and the Paradoxes of Everyday Organisational Life*. London: Routledge.

Mowles, C. (2021). *Complexity: A Key Idea for Business and Society*. London: Routledge.

Muller, J. (2018). *The Tyranny of Metrics*. Princeton, NJ: Princeton University Press.

O'Leary, J. (2018). *The Times Good University Guide 2019: Where to Go and What to Study*. Glasgow: Times Books.

Perrin, B. (1998). 'Effective Use and Misuse of Performance Measurement'. *American Journal of Evaluation*. 19 (3), pp 367–379.

Peters, T. (1986). *What Gets Measured Gets Done*. [Online] Available at What Gets Measured Gets Done – Tom Peters [Accessed 2 November 2020].

Porter, T. (1995). *Trust in Numbers: The Pursuit of Objectivity in Science and Public Life*. Princeton, NJ: Princeton University Press.

Power, M. (2004). 'Counting, control and calculation: Reflections on measuring and management'. *Human Relations*. 57 (6), pp 765–783.

Scott, J. (1985). *Weapons of the Weak: Everyday Forms of Peasant Resistance*. New Haven, CT: Yale University Press.

Scott, J. (1990). *Domination and the Arts of Resistance: Hidden Transcripts*. New Haven, CT: Yale University Press.

Scott, J. (1998). *Seeing Like a State: How Certain Schemes to Improve the Human Condition Have Failed*. New Haven, CT: Yale University Press.

Stacey, R. (2012). *Tools and Techniques of Leadership and Management. Meeting the Challenge of Complexity*. Hoboken, NJ: Taylor and Francis.

Taylor, F. (1911). *The Principles of Scientific Management*. New York: Harper & brothers.

Watson, T. (2011). 'Ethnography, reality, and truth: the vital need for studies of "How Things Work" in organizations and management'. *Journal of Management Studies*. 48 (1), pp 202–217.

Wetherell, M. (2012). *Affect and Emotions: A New Social Science Understanding*. London: SAGE.

Wetherell, M. (2014). 'Trends in the turn to affect: A social psychological critique'. *Body and Society*. 21 (2), pp 139–166.

Wilkins, S. & Huisman, J. (2012). 'UK business school rankings over the last 30 years (1980–2010): trends and explanations'. *Higher Education*. 63 (3), pp 367–382.

Williams, J. (2013). *Consuming Higher Education: Why Learning Can't Be Bought*. London: Bloomsbury Publishing.

4

WORKING WITH DIFFERENCE

The Emergence of Prejudice When Integrating Care in the National Health Service (NHS)

Fiona Yung

Introduction

When large public sector organisations in the UK contemplate change, they usually think about it as a planned, step-wise process dependent upon developing a sense of unity and harmony. I've been a manager in the National Health Service (NHS) for many years. I trained as a registered dietitian, but then broadened out into general management. As part of my leadership development journey, I acquired skills for managing change through orthodox management training courses and on-the-job learning. I never felt the need to question these approaches or how my own behavior would affect any outcome, even when my plans were not successful. However, this all changed when the organisation I was working for at the time merged with another organisation and I was expected to implement a strategic directive around 'Integrated Care' using a more conventional approach to strategic planning. This initiative was intended to address the increased demand on healthcare caused by an ageing population with more chronic disease. Patients that we currently see in the

NHS are increasingly complex with multiple illnesses that often impact on one another. When this is combined with social, psychological as well as physical healthcare requirements, it means there is a need for joined-up care that cuts across services and organisational boundaries. From a patient perspective, it is often frustrating to have multiple care providers who have variable access to information. This can lead to duplication of work or difficulties between clinical teams in finding out what the other has done. Ultimately, it's the patients who suffer when the disjointed care does not meet their needs. The ideal of integrated care is that hospital, community/social care providers and general practitioners (GPs) work together in a more efficient and convenient way that would benefit the patient. However, as I discover below, there is currently no standard definition of integrated care and therefore the process relies on the clinical context or the needs of a particular patient group to enable teams to describe and plan the care (NICE, 2018: 4).

Consistent with my training and the expectations of my organisation, my assumption was that all participants, despite their organisational backgrounds, would have similar values and therefore the same generalised notion and interpretation of the directive. To my surprise, differences emerged as a consequence of different values and beliefs about patient care delivery and prejudices held by different professional groups about each other, which meant things did not go to plan.

I present two very different events which demonstrate how people are able to collaborate in times of great pressure with unanimity in values and the opposite, where people struggle to find similarity with each other enabling their prejudices to surface and become apparent. Although these events are ten years apart and contrast, in the end there are interconnected patterns of behavior that lead to the same outcome as I hope to demonstrate.

Example 1 – Cult Values in a Pandemic

In March 2020, we were beginning to see large numbers of people being diagnosed with COVID-19 with severe breathing problems requiring hospitalisation. Our hospital was one of the first to be able to respond by expanding our intensive care units in order to treat very sick people. To do this, many staff had to be redeployed to support the expansion. This could only have been done with their support and dedication. We had surgeons supporting intensive care units, we had a dentist acting as a phlebotomist; we had finance staff supporting catering and portering. The groupings, divisional boundaries and tribalism that normally exist in any organisation seemed to be put aside. This mass redeployment in a short space of time stemmed from many volunteers offering to help and undertake roles that they were not employed to do or traditionally skilled to do.

There was also a directive from the chief executive officer (CEO) that we would stop the majority of our planned surgical work other than very urgent cases. This was a difficult decision to make for any hospital, because in cancelling patient surgery there would be a risk that patients' conditions could potentially worsen. We knew that we were setting ourselves up to have long waiting lists further down the line. Understanding that there would likely be a backlog of patients needing to be seen in the future, the senior leaders put out messages, a 'call to arms' and much of the communication to staff in those early days was to encourage everyone to play their part and put aside their practice boundaries and start collaborating together as one team. The 'one team' slogan started forming part of our daily communication briefs with staff adopting this term on social media and this gave rise to the term hashtag #OneTeam.

Sadly, many patients died during this period and we saw unprecedented numbers of deceased filling our mortuaries. When the media started to report the rising death toll in hospitals, this was exactly what frontline staff were witnessing, with many NHS hospitals running out of space to put the bodies. This was an extremely alarming and shocking experience for us all and was only worsened when some of our colleagues began to fall ill and subsequently die. Many of our staff were working under extreme conditions with an ever-present risk of catching COVID-19, either from our day-to-day contact with patients or from members of the public. Social distancing had not fully been enforced and face coverings were not mandatory at this stage. Clinical staff had to wear personal protective equipment (PPE), and each time they moved from area to area, they would have to change into new PPE which was time-consuming, extremely uncomfortable to wear over long periods and exhausting. Many people were putting in 12–14-hour shifts a day. Amidst the calamity and desperation of working under these extreme conditions, there was collaboration and camaraderie as people's differences were temporarily set aside with everyone, from my perspective, working together for a common purpose.

As all the clinical specialties put aside their differences, a feeling and a practice of #OneTeam emerged, reinforcing the value of saving lives. It gave people a sense that no matter what their job, they were all working to a common goal. This overwhelming purpose to preserve life is a fundamental principle for people working in the NHS and was amplified during this intense period. When coupled with more money and resources being made available to support frontline staff, it in some way eased the feelings of difference. When I talk about people that work in the NHS as having similar values, I mean that we all work together whether clinical or non-clinical to save lives. This is a powerful value above and beyond the narrow focus of the particular discipline one might be trained in. Values can be attractive and compelling in a voluntary and committed sense and can motivate us and open ourselves up to the opportunity of action (Stacey, 2010: 31). Mead (1934) describes how people have a tendency to idealise this unity of experience or collective which trumps all other motives. For me, #OneTeam held so much meaning, reinforcing all the good experiences I had about being part of the NHS such as teamwork, comradery, purpose and like many others it became a symbol of hope.

However, differences in interprofessional teams can never be buried for long. The idea of working together for a common goal can soon disintegrate when people anticipate change that threatens their previous ways of working and disrupts customs and practices underpinning their professional identity or sense of belonging to a particular group. In times of crises, people are more willing to put aside their issues with one another and more likely to collaborate and co-operate because the threat to life is more imminent.

Once the existential threat of the pandemic eased as we started to roll out the vaccines, #OneTeam felt more tenuous. People started to get back to their daily routines and differences re-emerged in contrasting professional opinions about how and where to deliver best care to patients and how best to reallocate resources. This mirrored the insights gained in my doctoral thesis, which I summarise below as a means of reflecting further on my central themes of integrated care, difference and prejudice.

I have shown how an intense period of co-operation and setting aside differences can happen in extreme situations, and this is an ideal that orthodox management aspires to for routine, day-to-day work. But far from viewing the exploration of difference as negative aspects of organisational life, the narrative I present to you in what follows is an autoethnographic inquiry that attempts to give an alternative viewpoint to the patterns of behavior that emerge when teams don't identify with one another and they are directed to define and work toward a common goal of Integrated Care (IC).

In contrast to my example of #OneTeam where a unity of values came from an extraordinary situation, I look at the ways we might respond to and think about prejudgment (prejudice) which emerges in our attempts to interpret and make sense of and functionalise values in the day-to-day, which invariably leads to conflict. I argue that prejudgment or prejudice often informs conflictual situations where opposing views can be understood as arising from our presumptions linked to our own self-interest. Our prejudgments are acquired from our uniquely different history, traditions and cultures.

Example 2 – Integrated Care and a Stakeholders Meeting Post-Merger

In 2010, the NHS community health organisation I worked for merged with a hospital. At this particular time, a number of NHS organisations were merging as a result of austerity measures brought about by the economic crash in 2008 (Nuffield Trust, 2012). This was characterised by the reduction in NHS spending budgets and increasing demand for health provision. By improving productivity and in some cases overspending, the NHS has managed to shield patients from the effects of the financial challenge (Kings Fund, 2017). Further pressures arose from a growing demand for healthcare staff to meet the needs of an ageing population that was growing in size and experiencing more chronic disease. This was further exacerbated by a disparity between health and social care budgets and the location of their services; that is, hospital provision is often more expensive than provision in community and therefore commanding larger budgets. To improve the situation and reduce the widening inequality, NHS organisations were encouraged to merge, the idea being that this would bring economies of scale and thereby improve productivity and provide more joined-up and seamless care to the population.

Prior to the merger, the two organisations had operated very differently and worked independently of one another. The hospital group had a tradition of having doctors lead their clinical pathways which determined patient care and was strongly dominated by them. In contrast, the community health group had nurses leading their clinical pathways and had a strong nursing identity. After the merger, my management role changed to leading services across both the hospital and the community. The first directive I was given was to try to join two respiratory services together and integrate their ways of working. I had been consulting with both services individually, who went along with the idea of integration despite both parties being cautious of one another's motives. I had organised a stakeholder meeting as a way of starting the engagement and enabling both groups to have time to get to know one another in order to build relationships and gain trust. The merger happened relatively quickly, and although a single Chief Executive had been appointed, the detail on how the teams were going to integrate had not been worked out. This was left to managers such as myself, who were expected to bring the teams together in the most expedient way possible using conventional change management processes aimed at reducing any kind of conflict or resistance.

The hospital group felt that there had been a 'takeover' by the community health group because almost all the new managers employed in the merged organisation were from community health backgrounds – including myself. There were concerns that by integrating services, their practices would be diluted and they might lose the specialist skills, of which they were proud. In contrast, the community health group talked about how difficult it would be to work with the hospital group. They had a perception that hospital staff always viewed themselves as superior to community health staff because the patients needing hospital care were much sicker and therefore needed more skillful specialised support that community health could not provide. Community staff also felt that they were always the poor relation to hospitals and perceived that hospitals 'hoovered up' resources, leaving very little to be invested in community health.

The stakeholder meeting was the start of a process of engagement, which is a well-established approach in organisational mergers to involve everyone. This is seen as an important step in minimising any resistance to change. I had a plan and an agenda which involved me facilitating discussions following a series of group presentations by certain stakeholders. I had invited hospital and community staff and a number of GP and a patient representative so that we could have a broader discussion and get many different people joining together to form what I expected to be a unified view. As a previous community health manager, I had made an effort to form a good relationship with the hospital doctors (not wanting to be seen as being biased toward community) by encouraging them to understand community health and to feel part of a wider merged organisation. I had asked them to lead the discussions on integrated care in the meeting and to present their thoughts on what an integrated respiratory service might look like.

On the day of the meeting, I chaired the start by opening with the usual PowerPoint presentation with ground rules for polite behavior, aims and objectives and an agenda and outlining the expected outcomes. This was intended to give the meeting structure and enable a more focused discussion. The meeting and presentations started off well with all parties listening politely and everyone putting on a great show of actively engaging with one another. I was feeling positive that we would get a good result and a plan of action for moving forward.

When it was the turn of one of the hospital doctors to present, they started off talking about all the good work they had done and how they had improved patient care. This was backed up by evidence of audits and research that had been carried out to support their practice. The discussion moved on to address who should lead clinical decision-making for looking after patients who were becoming acutely unwell. Unfortunately, one of the hospital doctors made a comment that the community respiratory team did not always provide the 'right care', because their service was not medically led and therefore they didn't have the expertise in treating patients that were very sick and probably needed to be in hospital. This was then followed by another equally confrontational comment from a doctor that sometimes community health practices were not always delivered in ways that gave the best quality outcomes.

A major argument broke out, with the GPs and community respiratory team uniting against the hospital's doctors, with both parties vehemently defending their territory. As the GPs and community respiratory teams felt they were being criticised, they attempted to defend their services strongly by retaliating with their own assumptions, which they labelled as 'evidence' alleging that hospital services always took all of the NHS resources and that they kept patients in hospital unnecessarily. The community team was angry about how dismissive the hospital doctors had been about the good work in the community, directing all their anger at the hospital doctor who had presented. All their prejudices around hospital ways of working poured out in public. We were in open conflict; people talked over one another, with comments becoming very personal. The hospital teams rallied to the defence of their colleague with a counterattack of more of their own prejudices around the lack of evidence for community ways of working.

It was clear my facilitation skills were unable to bring calm. The room was a cacophony of loud voices, snide remarks, sarcasm, heckling and a mixture of side conversations, perhaps more in keeping with parliamentary debate than in a local meeting of healthcare professionals intended to be collaborative. I felt I had lost control of the meeting. I loudly interrupted their arguments to bring order to the meeting and invited the patient representative to talk about their experience. The room descended into silence. Everyone immediately stopped what they were saying. They listened reverently to what the patient had to say, as if he were making a divine statement. When asked what kind of service he would like to see, he responded simply by saying:

> All I want is to have the right care when I need it, I don't want to be in hospital if I don't need to be, I would rather be in my own home but I want to know that I can get to a hospital if I need to.

To my utter relief, the room continued in silence for a couple of seconds, which gave me ample opportunity to summarise and close the meeting, thank everyone and inform them that I would get back to them all with next steps.

Reflecting on the Meeting

I took for granted that staff would naturally want to work together because integrated care was very much part of the national strategy to try to keep people out of hospital and support them more in their own homes. My assumptions were that 'buy-in' for this would come from appealing to staff's sense of valuing better patient care, and in managerial terms, this would be achieved by aligning values and setting common goals. I had not anticipated the subsequent conflict that arose as we all argued about what the term 'integrated care' meant to one another. However, with hindsight, it is not difficult to understand why my attempts to gain consensus at this meeting did not go to plan. Each group felt that their practices and ways of working were the right ones for developing this integrated respiratory service and were not prepared to compromise. They both had strong identities relating to their history and traditions in their previous organisational forms, which together with their professional and collegiate backgrounds formed the basis of their rationale. On reflection, I could see that they viewed working with each other as a potential threat to this. As the arguments started to get more challenging about each other's practice, and they defended their respective positions, they began to reveal their true feelings for one another and their prejudices began to surface.

In summary, my first example about cult values, that is, values which are powerfully expressed as a way of achieving an idealised sense of 'we', demonstrated co-operation in a crisis where matters of life and death made the difference to people's ways of working. Appealing to the 'cult' of #OneTeam made a difference to everyone's sense of purpose within the NHS at a critical time and meant differences were set aside. In my second example, using well-established change management methods, I tried to 'create the right conditions' for people to sign up to integrated care but it was much harder to achieve a common sense of purpose. Staff didn't perceive an imminent threat to patients' lives but did perceive threats to their own ways of working, which very much linked to the teams' identities.

The next section therefore considers how we might think about organisational life from a radically social perspective when trying to put into practice an ideal such as 'integrated care'. This is not with the intention of disregarding the importance of managers and leaders in implementing change but to bring in another way of thinking that enables us to understand differently how individuals and groups function. Rather than focusing on 'best practice', it concentrates instead on the relational side of our day to day interactions with one another.

Making Sense of Integrated Care

Although the term integrated care is commonly accepted in the NHS, there remains confusion about how it is defined with a range of definitions arising from different views of various stakeholders in care settings (Goodwin, 2016: 1) If we take the example of my stakeholders' meeting, there were differing viewpoints hospital versus community, GP versus hospital, nurses versus doctors, manager versus professional, all of which were contingent on the group's context.

The stakeholders' meeting was my attempt to enable a diverse group to articulate and agree a good enough consensus on what IC meant to them, with a view to then forming better working relationships to benefit patients. This was my ideal and I assumed that no one would oppose this in principle, at least in public, where everyone needed to present a good image of themselves. However, as the meeting continued, the threat to their existing ways of working made the mask slip and people were emboldened to say out loud what they were really thinking. In addition, the perspective of the patient had been completely forgotten until a patient was invited to speak and only then did the individual groups realise that their habitual ways of working did not always meet the needs of their patients. My point here is that the guiding principle of joined-up care may sound obvious and resonate with professional values advocating that patients are the central focus of our work, but the diversity of perspective and context made it extremely challenging to agree what this actually meant in practice.

Stacey (2012) has written extensively on organisational behavior in relation to the complexity sciences. He offers an alternative way of thinking which challenges managerialism by arguing the importance of taking seriously our own experience and that of others in everyday interactions. He believes we need to move away from considering leadership as an idealised and abstract practice located with an individual and think about it as a social activity which takes place in groups. Both Stacey and Mowles (2016) have developed a perspective they term *complex responsive processes*, the key tenets of which are set out in the preface to this volume, better to describe what happens in organisations when people come together to try to make sense of what's going on. The perspective problematises taken-for-granted notions in managerialism such as the predictability of planning and points out how little control over outcome anyone has (Stacey, 2012: 1), even though we may try to shape action through an appeal to organisational values, through the use of performance management or other change control techniques, in this instance, facilitation. A complex responsive process perspective assumes a more social understanding of organisational change, shifting the emphasis away from individuals and generalisations to one where local interactions are key (our relationships with one another). This, in turn, enables us better to understand how organisations are both sustained and changed at the same time by people's every day actions.

Local interactions could be described as 'particularisation', an explorative process of negotiating meaning of idealisations in a local context at a particular time (Stacey, 2010, 2011). This may happen through our own private conversation as we try to reason things out in our own minds or in conversations with others. It is when we are at odds with ourselves that we become aware of our private dialogue.

The way that we may interpret the abstraction 'integrated care' in our specific situation is dependent on our particular experiences relating to the idea. This may have little or no relation to someone else's experience and anticipation of the same idea (Stacey & Mowles, 2016). The process of making sense involves selectively interpreting what is relevant to us which fits with our view of what we are trying to achieve. It's inevitable that we will have our own views and prejudices and bring our own experience and self-interests into any decisions we make.

Returning to the stakeholders' meeting, we were all participating in the experience of attempting to apply the imagined whole of 'integrated care' to our own particular contingent situation and that of the group we belonged to. I was preoccupied with trying to ensure that I gained agreement from everyone that they would collaborate. As a facilitator, I was too involved in trying to get through the agenda and achieve an outcome and too detached from considering how they might be feeling about the newly formed organisation and suddenly having to work with groups that they didn't feel that they had anything in common with.

Elias (1987) makes the distinction between involved and detached participation as a different way of thinking about the usual dualism of being subjectively or objectively involved in social life. By being involved he meant more immersed, emotional participation and by being detached he meant feeling more distanced from what is happening. In conversation, we may shift between these two poles but never achieve either state in pure form. For Elias, we are always both involved and detached because there is no objective position outside the conversation (Stacey & Mowles, 2016: 348–349). Everyone at the meeting seemed to be going along with the ideals of collaboration and partnership at the same time as potentially holding personal commitments of not wanting to change any of their ways or working and not wanting to make too many compromises: in a way, people were cautious of one another. During the course of our interactions, our prejudices about one another started to surface as the conversation became conflictual because we were all interpreting integrated care in many different ways, but mostly in ways which were beneficial to our own 'side'. We were unable to concede any common ground that might affect our habitual ways of working.

Controlling Conversation to Manage Difference

Edgar Schein (2004) is a social psychologist and a leading authority on organisational culture and is often quoted when managers want to consider culture and change. He illustrates a way of thinking that at the time made sense to me as a way of structuring some form of process that would enable me to manage change. His ideas seemed particularly relevant in my efforts to control and influence the conversations at the stakeholders' meeting and even prior to that with the hospital doctors. Schein's perspective on how leaders can influence organisational culture locates actions of influence and change with individual managers and leaders and who use simple tools to understand the dynamics of organisations.

Schein is clear that people are unable to tolerate too much 'uncertainty or stimulus overload'. However, if they can somehow share collective meanings that can organise perceptions and thoughts of a group, then they can focus on what is important and discard anything that is not. In doing so, anxiety levels can be reduced, creating an environment for coordinated action. He goes on to stipulate that when forming new groups, members need to learn each other's meanings and understand each other's language; there is an important role for the leader to identify each group's categorisation of meanings in the group's actions, gestures and speech (ibid: 115–116). This provides a sense of commonality which is strengthened by what Schein attributes to an investment in special meanings and assumptions of what the words really mean; this, he believes, is what supports and maintains group culture. This resonated with all of us trying to define integrated care. In bringing different assumptions of meaning into the open, it is believed that they can be addressed in a consensual way if leaders acknowledge them, accept them and reframe interpretations in a way that will obtain consensus. Schein acknowledges the importance of leaders participating in the interaction but suggests that they must also be able to observe objectively in order to assess situations and intervene in the interaction therefore acting as both participant and observer.

Meanwhile Bret and Goldeberg (2017) in an article written for the Harvard Business review, discuss how best to handle disagreements in teams. They acknowledge that managers and leaders cannot remain neutral but rather try and control the process. They advocate taking the role of a mediator or facilitator for teams to learn and resolve conflict for themselves. They argue that research shows there are ways in which we can facilitate agreement or consensus. Again, and similar to Schein, they emphasise the individual's ability to control the process and use the right techniques to support teams to overcome conflict.

At the stakeholders' meeting, our differences could not be addressed in a unified way because they were so varied. And I could not coherently articulate my plans because of my own contradictory conflicting thoughts trying to surface my own motives which were very much linked to values as well as attempting to control what was going on, at the same time as beginning to recognise that my self-interests were affecting how I responded to the situation. I did not experience myself as being an objective observer in this situation.

Schein's arguments continue to hold great appeal in management discourse. Leaders are thought to be in a strong position to control and influence people, suggesting they can build trust in a group by independently and objectively improving what's going on, understood as system, from the outside. My experience in the meeting I described has caused me to challenge that assumption. I realised that my loyalties lay with the community team, which meant it was extremely difficult for me to remain objective.

Prejudice as an Aspect of Organisation

I mentioned earlier the significance of lived experience and I think little attention is paid to how we are affected by our histories in our day-to-day encounters and how it links to our own prejudices. At the stakeholders' meeting, a power struggle took place between hospital staff – in particular, the doctors – and community staff. I took this personally as a threat to my own previous 'community' identity and ways of doing things. This, in turn, prejudiced the way I was thinking and responding to others. My behavior betrayed my true allegiances at the time, when I felt that this meeting should be community focused and led. My attitude was a prejudgment and based on everything I had come to know about my years spent working in community health. But I didn't recognise this as such, and certainly if I had, I would not have wanted to acknowledge this publicly; so I justified my actions by ignoring the fact that I didn't agree with the hospital doctors and the impact that might be having on my sense-making, so committed was I to staying on track with getting the teams to work to a common goal. As I mention above, our lived experience is constituted from our interactions with one another. We recall our past experience as a means of making sense of the present in order to imagine the future consequences of what we are doing. This process inevitably draws in our prejudices both consciously and unconsciously, which invariably impact on our actions.

History and tradition are all part of culture in organisations and the basis for which teams develop their identity and it's useful to understand how both these concepts would have had an impact on how I was influencing and how others were influencing me at the meeting. Our views of other groups and people could be considered ethnocentric; that is to say, an individual places their own group at the center of their observations and the priority is given to the value, beliefs and attitudes of their own group above any other. (Northhouse, 2016: 428–429). For example, the doctors believed that their outcomes for patient care were better than those of the community teams. They were making a subjective and critical evaluation of another group by selecting out data from their own ways of working that would show them in the best possible light as a way of legitimising their own assumptions and prejudices. Northhouse (2016) believes that privileging one's own group can be an obstacle to effective leadership, in that it can prevent people from fully understanding and respecting others' viewpoints.

Prejudice follows closely on from ethnocentrism. Hans George Gadamer, the German hermeneutic philosopher, wrote *Truth and Method* (1975), in which his account of prejudice provides his interpretation of how the concept started to be used in negative ways. He writes that after the period of Enlightenment,[1] the word became discredited as a result of the scientific revolution that emphasised reason and objectivity as a means for gaining understanding rather than relying on traditional knowledge. From a management perspective in consideration of culture, prejudice is largely considered a fixed attitude or belief held by an individual about another individual or group and based on inaccurate or unsubstantiated information (Northhouse, 2016: 429). In my scenario, this plays out through the judgments made by each of the stakeholder groups about the other based on previous experiences each had of one another. Prejudice is often used in a pejorative sense in relation to race, gender, age, etc. but if we consider the term in its original form as a prejudgment, we are all prejudiced to some degree, and this enables us to hold onto partially formed views without the need to challenge or question within our own groups. It is an affirmation of group identity and gives us a sense of belonging. All of us at the stakeholders meeting had strongly held views and beliefs and differences about the way we worked as a means of being able to interpret our observations of others and as a way of making sense through our own experiences, rightly or wrongly.

Difference, Conflict and Prejudice

Douglas Griffin (2002), author of *The Emergence of Leadership* also contributed to the perspective of complex responsive processes and believes that there is very little tolerance for difference or diversity in organisations. He attributes this to the dominance of systems thinking, where individuals are understood as parts of the system – so that in extremes, difference can be understood as dysfunction. Systems thinking focuses on ensuring that parts of the organisation and the interaction between those parts work in harmony to serve the complex whole and takes a reductionist approach, meaning that if we take organisations down to key interactions and processes that can be analysed, they can be resolved (Jackson 2003). This reductionist approach informs organisational thinking in the NHS and explains why managers have adopted systems thinking into many areas such as quality and safety, managing risk and even leadership because it is seen as providing a systematic way of managing and controlling complex situations:

> In organisations, we attempt at all costs to avoid any sort of conflict, and focus on uniting the parts of the system to conform to some abstract sense of a whole, rather than of self.
>
> (Griffin, 2002: 202)

Griffin suggests that conflict, characterised as antagonistic relationships between people or hostility, fighting, lack of co-operation (Stacey & Mowles,

2016: 195), is necessary in the transformation of identity (although it is only an aspect of identity formation). We either acknowledge difference through conflict or we collude or deny difference as a way of protecting identity (Griffin, 2002: 198). The community and hospital held opposing views and in the meeting. A power struggle occurred with our own competing priorities and self-interests motivating each group to take up and defend their points of view.

The reliance on systems thinking in the NHS encourages leaders and managers to seek to resolve problems without recognising the potential for transformation when encountering difference or diversity. Prejudice is generated from many social exchanges of every day conversational exchange where we encounter different and diverse intentions. This might be better understood as a *process* that can give rise to conflict and at the same time shapes the nature of that conflict. In bringing teams together, people's prejudices were exposed as the conversations became conflictual and where the hospital and community teams began talk more openly of their values and the importance of their own practices. These assumptions became amplified where individuals and groups perceived a threat to their existing ways of working and their professional identity, as power struggles began to emerge between the different factions.

I ignored the emerging difference, still convinced that I could remain objective and we could get to consensus without having to address people's views, which could otherwise be considered sensitive. I found myself in a contradictory situation of trying to convey a sense of unanimity, even though I had my own prejudices about hospital ways of working. This raises a question for me as to how else might I have thought about prejudice in a way that would not have paralysed my ability to function with the group when confronted by this.

Prejudice as Process

Gadamer argues that prejudice (prejudgment) is needed in the process of understanding. In other words, you have to have a view, an opinion or a preconceived idea about something before you can judge. He attempts to retrieve both a positive and open conception of what he terms a 'legitimate' use of the word. Instead of thinking about prejudice as 'opinion formed without reason', he suggests we think of it as an opinion formed before all the elements that determine a situation have been finally examined. Therefore, we can only base our understanding and prejudgments and decisions on past references or lived experiences, which will only be a version of the truth. For example, the hospital doctors believed that the quality of care in the community was questionable, which they perceived to be the truth. However, their opinions may had been formed based on very little or anecdotal evidence which over time had successive affirmation from their own group and very little challenge from outside. In other words, prejudice can also be described as our expectations of meaning (presumptions), assumptions and our anticipations.

Gadamer proposes that prejudice emerges in a dialectical movement[1] that arises as we are involved in conversation such as an argument, discussion or debate – the way in which our presumptions and assumptions 'open' us up to the issues in such a way that they have the potential for revision. This enables us to gain understanding. All interpretation could be considered as prejudgmental, in the sense that it is always based on our expectations formed from our history and traditions but orientated or adjusted in our present experience. In the course of conversational exchanges, meaning arises in this dialectical process and at the same time changes the prejudgment and contributes to a revised understanding. This prejudicial character of understanding means that whenever we try and make sense of something, we are involved in dialogue that encompasses both our own self-understanding and our understanding of the issue. Simultaneously we become aware of our prejudices, which offer the potential for us to become more receptive to what we are trying to understand. Thus as our prejudices are revealed to us, they can at the same time also become the focus of our questioning.

There is a strong argument for not avoiding or shying away from the idea of prejudice as a way of enhancing our understanding. I now understand that taking prejudice seriously enables us to have greater perspective of ourselves. This is important for managers to acknowledge when bringing diverse groups together. From a social perspective, we would consider conversation as a useful means for provoking us to better identify those prejudices that create a problematic influence on our understanding. Not taking them seriously and inquiring into them can all too easily polarise and close down discussion by excluding or invalidating prejudgments of others which feel unfavorable or uncomfortable toward 'us' or by amplifying our own to discredit 'them'. Assuming that prejudice has no place in organisations or denying the fact that we all have prejudices could limit our potential for developing new meaning and mutual acceptance if we do not enable them to be revealed, realised and revised in relation to the prejudices of others.

When I discussed how leaders can influence culture change, I referred to the fact that the NHS managers are encouraged to follow more managerial ways of thinking about organisations informed by systems thinking. Systems thinking positions the leader outside the processes of change as if they themselves are independent of the process, but as I have just described, my own prejudices in the meeting between two teams shaped my intentions and steered them toward a particular set of actions to encourage a shared vision of integrated care in this newly merged organisation. This is in contrast to the insights provided by the perspective of complex responsive processes which, as I said previously, advocates taking seriously these microprocesses of relating to one another and which are not understood to form any system, and, in my view, gives a more reality-convergent picture of organisational life that acknowledges the significance of subjectivity.

However, prejudices are not just simply subjective interpretations of the meaning of actions of others' social norms; they illustrate the extent to which all our anticipation and expectations of meaning are linked to the experience we acquire from our history and how our self-interests develop. I describe in my narrative how both hospital and community groups had very different ways of delivering healthcare that evolved from differing cultures. Their perspectives on integrated care would have been very different. My own strong managerial history with community meant that I felt more sympathetic to and familiar with their ways of working. So, in effect, my prejudice emphasised the extent to which my presumptions and assumptions of 'integrated care' were embedded in my expectations that the hospital doctors would agree that we could enhance the care of patients in the community if they could come out of the hospital and work with the community teams seeing patient at home.

In general, our presumptions and assumptions comprise our current familiarity with a subject we are trying to understand. Second, they reflect the culture and traditions we have been exposed to and have participated in throughout our lives. This provides some sort of framework in our attempts to realise and make sense of experience. Our presumptions and assumptions provide us with an expectation of what integrated care might look like, but that expectation changes with each successive encounter or conversation we have with each other, so that our interpretation of the aspects of integrated care and our sense of its whole meaning are subject to a continuous process of revision and change, if we open ourselves up to consider alternatives.

What can managers and leaders learn from this? As mentioned previously, it is important to recognise that any understanding is inevitably prejudiced. Nonetheless, in the process of understanding others' views in relation to our own, we may find ourselves undertaking evaluation with others of which aspects are important and which are not in our developing an understanding of integrated care and how we should go on together. We may re-evaluate aspects of our understanding by exposing ourselves to those who think differently or who have different ideas to ourselves. This can take place through everyday conversation with one another and can enable us to explore and negotiate our presumptions and assumptions in the course of our interactions. We orientate ourselves to particular meanings, but when we start to challenge or question these, meanings can be revised. So, understanding develops when we reflect and refine our assumptions in ways which allow for different (interpretative choices) about how best to act.

I therefore emphasise the importance of managers and leaders paying attention to the influence of our customs and practices and to acknowledging the history of our assumptions. As a rule, we are not aware of our own prejudices until we encounter a difference of opinion. If we are not prepared to understand each other's perspective, as in the case of the participants at the meeting, conflict can arise because our own assumptions are challenged or called into question. Prejudices become apparent in the process of trying to understand the motivations for our actions and it's important to be aware that they are often unknowable even to ourselves. Therefore, to better understand ourselves and our prejudices involves taking risks and engaging fully with each other about these in reflective and critical ways.

Reflections and Considerations for Managers and Leaders

My narratives reflect how in times of crisis, groups with strong identities can set aside their difference to work together when threats to life are imminent. They are able to improvise in new ways to get things done, even if it impacts on their traditional ways of working. However, in my second narrative about the merger, when different teams from hospital and community healthcare backgrounds came together to functionalise an ideal of integrated care, differences were less easily set aside, conflict emerged and prejudices about what each thought constituted 'best care' for patients became apparent. We were unable fully to detach ourselves from our history and traditions and custom and practices of the particular groups with which we identified. They are part of who we are. Adopting a prejudicial approach serves to affirm our sense of self, our identity and belonging with 'our' particular group, often to the exclusion and/or denigration of 'others'. This has helped me to see that when managers rely too heavily on managerial approaches to change management which privilege consensus and harmony, they may end up missing the opportunity for conflictual conversations which may, in turn, subvert the very change they aim at bringing about.

Understanding prejudice when bringing different teams together is therefore helpful in so far as it is a thematic pattern of process that structures our experience of being together with the potential to shift the way we think and understand the world around us, particularly when we try to operationalise ideals of 'best practice' such as in the example of integrated care. In this context, prejudice is not something we should fear in the workplace or seek to ignore. Managers and leaders undertaking change of the order I describe in the preceding paragraphs can anticipate provoking strong feelings of group identification in the form of prejudice. Acknowledging such differences can allow for difficulties and conflicting points of view to be explored. It may mean that we are less likely to treat prejudices (prejudgments) as facts or a version of truth with which to categorise or stereotype. In addition, being receptive to questioning our own prejudices in relation to other people's views when we become aware of them and endeavouring to keep our emergent thoughts continually open to challenge and change can be a useful management practice.

I have suggested that it is not always possible to predetermine an outcome as suggested in managerialism and that locating change solely with individual managers or with a change in the 'system', suggesting that this obscures our capacity to understand the processes of organisational change in the much wider context of broader social processes. *Prejudice as process* can be productive and generative to our understanding if we take it to encompass our expectations of meaning and assume it is connected to our self-interest. By remaining open to exploring, challenging and negotiating meaning means that we allow ourselves to learn constantly from our day-to-day interactions. Being aware of our own prejudices is important and being able to constantly revise our current interpretations of what these might mean can enable us to acquire a much more nuanced appreciation of our relationships with one another when evaluating whether or not we are providing our patients with good care.

On a pragmatic note, I am not suggesting it is feasible to relinquish current management discourse in favor of a more micro-social focus. This is because I find I cannot readily abandon the familiar practices and traditions that have influenced my ways of working in the NHS. They have contributed to who I am and many have served both me and my patients well. Managerialist theories that focus on the individual and/or the system continue to be prominent in organisations, not least because they present an illusion of control in uncertain times, which can be a useful salve for our anxiety when we find ourselves in situations of uncertainty. However, I am calling into question our tendency to assume that this is the *only* way to make sense of organisational change. Managers need to be alert to the ways in which some popular theories can marginalise or gloss over differences, ignoring or problematising its existence, while at the same time asserting a singular perspective that limits our ability to explore different perspectives with one another. The value of working as #OneTeam felt good in so far as it enabled different teams to work together and put aside their differences under extreme conditions, but those differences are still present in our work and have since re-surfaced in different ways.

Accepting this broader definition of 'prejudice' and the way it functions in groups may help managers to gain a wider understanding of how organisational change can emerge through our exploration of difference and similarities in the workplace. I argue that change is an everyday occurrence, and in a more virtual world of work, I perceive that there will be more emphasis on teams being able to work together in different ways than we have otherwise been used to. More importantly, paying attention to our different values and beliefs about what constitutes 'best care' (especially in a context where it may not always be possible to provide care to a standard that meets the ideals we strive for) would enable us to observe the changing nature of prejudice.

As we enter the 'the recovery phase' post COVID pandemic, one of the things we have learned in health and social care is that there is an even more need for people to have joined-up care across large geographical areas.

There is a growing pressure to accelerate integrated care, not just between teams or organisations, but across regions and also internationally (as in, e.g., the need for well co-ordinated worldwide vaccination programs) to ensure we are prepared for any future challenges. The pandemic has highlighted the best aspects of the NHS such as the #OneTeam, but it has also exposed continued deep-rooted differences in the way we provide care. What I experienced in 2010 is still present in 2021 and with very little past experience post COVID to draw upon, limited information and the luxury of hindsight, I suggest that many of those same prejudices will continue to exist. I hope that these prejudices may be examined more productively in the forthcoming public enquiries and pandemic debriefings that are planned in ways that might enhance present and future working practices.

Maybe it's also time for leaders and managers to reflect on the past events in the light of a pandemic and to question how this has changed us all in our relationships with others. This can only happen if we demonstrate our intention to build trust by taking risks in speaking out, being honest about how we feel, to challenge and provoke and, importantly, to remain curious. It is a genuine risk because there are no guarantees that working in this way will always be successful. It takes time and practice and, as my narrative shows, skill on the part of the facilitator to be able to dwell with the ability to be more open about our own prejudices and assumptions, may allow us to engage in potentially more meaningful conversations. To do so would involve greater commitment to spontaneity and creativity; this requires us to not be quick to problematise issues by polarising discussions. We should try to stay in difficult conversations in which we have to discuss how we might best make unpalatable choices which conflict with our deeply held values. Holding the tension in a conflictual argument is extremely difficult. If we achieve this, then we can open possibilities of transforming ourselves in relation to others – and, through this process of mutual meaning-making, potentially transform our organisations.

Note

1. Dialectical movement implies our process to understanding or knowledge is a back and forth movement, graphically similar to a downhill skier weaving from side to side as they head downhill. Philosophically, it is an exchange of argument and counterargument resulting in a synthesis of opposing arguments to form new understanding. Http://newworldencyclopedia.org/entry/Dialectic. Accessed 27 September 2020 at 10:45am

References

Bret, J.M. and Goldeberg, S.B. (2017) How to handle a disagreement on your team. https://hbr.org/2017/07/how-to-handle-a-disagreement-on-your-team accessed 23 January 2022 at 12:39pm.

Elias, N. (1987) *Involvement and Detachment*. Oxford: Blackwell.

Gadamer, H.G. (1975) *Truth and Method*. New York: Continuum.

Goodwin, N. (2016) Understanding integrated care. *International Journal of Integrated Care* 16(4): pp. 1–4, 6. http://dx.doi.org/10.5334/ijic.2530. Accessed 3 May 2021 at 12:50pm.

Griffin, D. (2002) *Leadership and Ethics*. London: Routledge.

Jackson, M.C. (2003) *Systems Thinking*. West Sussex: John Wiley & Son LTD.

Kings Fund (2017) Understanding NHS financial pressure, how are they affecting patient care. https://www.kingsfund.org.uk/sites/default/files/field/field_publication_file/Understanding%20NHS%20financial%20pressures%20-%20full%20report.pdf. Accessed 12 September at 16:00.

Mead, G.H. (1934) *Mind, Self & Society*. London: University of Chicago Press.

Mowles, C. (2015) *Managing in Uncertainty*. London: Routledge.

NICE (2018) https://www.nice.org.uk/guidance/ng94/evidence/38.integrated-care-pdf-172397464677. Accessed 3 May 2021 at 15:00.

Northhouse, P.G. (2016) *Leadership, Theory and Practice*. 7th Ed. London: Sage.

Nuffield Trust (2012) *A Decade of Austerity*. https://www.nuffieldtrust.org.uk/files/2017-01/decade-of-austerity-full-web-final.pdf. Accessed 12 September at 14:09.

Schein, E. (2004) *Organisational Culture and Leadership*. San Francisco: Jossey-Bass.

Stacey, R.D. (2010) *Complexity and Organisational Reality*. London: Routledge.

Stacey, R.D. (2011) *Strategic Management and Organisational Dynamics: The Challenge of Complexity*. 6th Ed. London: FT Prentice-Hall.

Stacey, R.D. (2012) *Tools and Techniques of Leadership and Management: Meeting the Challenge of Complexity*. New York: Routledge.

Stacey, R.D. and Mowles, C. (2016) *Strategic Management and Organisational Dynamics: The Challenge or Complexity to Ways of Thinking about Organisation*. 7th Ed. Harlow: Pearsons Education Ltd.

5

TRUST, METRICS AND COMPLEXITY IN MEANING-MAKING

Sara Filbee

Introduction

It is important that those involved in the development of policies and programs in the public sector are able to explain what they are trying to accomplish and how well they have done what they set out to do. This is not a simple task. In our highly complex, interconnected and dynamic world, we often encounter many conflicting expectations and demands from the public and key stakeholders. At the same time, we often lack sufficient information to make informed decisions or the data we do have is ambiguous and contradictory.

This chapter explores this challenge. As the editors have already discussed, the generally accepted managerialist and individualist approach in Western countries has led to increasing emphasis on accountability, transparency and results (usually quantified) in government. Each of these is clearly an important value; however, this approach has both advantages and disadvantages in a complex environment.

DOI: 10.4324/9781003099925-5

In my experience of over 18 years in senior management in the Canadian Federal Government, I have noted how increasingly our work is required to be 'evidence-based'. As a public servant, I feel I need to be accountable for my decisions and to base them upon the best evidence I can find with a view to creating value for the taxpayers and for the Country. However, a naïve understanding of *evidence-based* can be problematic and lead to a heavy and non-nuanced reliance upon quantitative information. This chapter explores this dynamic tension.

To provide context, I share a couple of my experiences as senior executive head for one of four regions of a large department in the Canadian Federal Government. I consider the interplay of complexity and uncertainty, their effect on our processes of working together and the way we make sense of what is going on for us (what I refer to as meaning-making or sense-making). I argue that the uncertainties we face and the perceived high stakes in the event of failure can be conflictual, identity threatening and anxiety creating. We seek to manage this anxiety by seeking 'certainty' and reducing complexity through reliance on our relationships and on selecting information or evidence which justifies our actions and proves we have made the 'right' decisions. I examine the complex patterning of our trust relationships with each other from the perspective of complex responsive processes of relating, a way of thinking about complexity, and how such patterns of trust relating affect our work to make meaning. I then address the issue of the use of quantitative information and what I suggest is a problematic relationship between patterns of trust relationships and our use of metrics in meaning-making. In conclusion, I propose a number of implications for leaders based upon my research and experience.

The narrative which follows relates to a national meeting at the senior management level related to the delivery of direct services and benefits to Canadians. While most senior leadership engaged in policy and program development are based in headquarters, management of service delivery operations occurs largely in the four regions. A significant aspect of our work together involves our attempts to integrate the general and theoretical with the ongoing and detailed 'in the weeds' world of service delivery and management. The following is one meeting (among many) in which we sought to come to grips with how we understood what was going on and how we could demonstrate we were delivering upon our mandate in an environment marked by anxiety and uncertainty.

Productivity Woes

This was an in-person meeting to respond to concerns my boss, Robert, had expressed about recent numbers purporting to measure productivity of our Employment Insurance processing operations.[1] At a previous meeting (attended by one of my staff), a first draft had been introduced by an official working in the Employment Insurance area. They had claimed that these metrics demonstrated that only 63% of regional staff were working to 100% productivity (calculated by output per productive time). Robert, who later described this revelation as a moment 'when the top of his head had blown off', had demanded site-by-site numbers for comparison to explain what was going on. This morning's meeting was to review these numbers. Presented in complex, formula-based tables, we had only been given them the night before. I, along with my regional colleagues who were also present, had received a hurried brief from our staff shortly before the meeting.

The numbers purported to measure work to process applications and adjudicate applicants' entitlement to Employment Insurance benefits. If they meet regulatory requirements, applicants start receiving benefits. If not, they may appeal. The numbers we were looking at were mostly based on the number of work items (of which there might be several in a claim) completed over a given period and came from work site records used by local managers to determine individual staff performance. Additional measures included the cost per work item used to measure how well we manage our finances. Measuring productivity is not easy. The numbers were gathered on a site-by-site basis by hand and as such were difficult to compare, had significant and untested assumptions buried in them and were potentially open to gaming. Increasing automation and work practices designed to be client-focused means the work is more complex and time-consuming, and targets based on work pre-automation, in my (and others') view, were suspect. Certain types of necessary work were not reflected in the numbers presented, further understating staff efforts. Quality of work, fundamental to sustainable excellence in service delivery, was considered separately. The efforts of staff from other parts of the department, which significantly affect citizen experience (and effectiveness) of benefits delivery, were not considered. Finally, budgets available for processing used in calculating work item costs were treated differently across regions. For example, our region received an investment in the second half of the year to hire staff to increase production. As it takes time to get new employees up to speed, their productivity was lower and our results worse. Similar investments other regions received later in the year were, however, not included. None of this mattered when these numbers were used to manage individual performance, as managers could apply their judgment and awareness of the individual situations. However, I believed their usefulness was limited for the purposes being proposed, namely both as a final judgment on productivity and as a way of comparing work sites across the country.

I was perhaps particularly conscious (and cautious) about the quality and usefulness of numbers produced by departmental colleagues because of my past experience. As I prepared for the meeting, I recalled how early in my tenure in the department, headquarters' analysts had estimated that 'X' thousand workers in one of our provinces had claimed Employment Insurance benefits and reported this data to the Minister. The implication was that these workers should have been working in a local processing industry instead of the rather large numbers of temporary foreign workers actually employed. There was no consideration of their suitability for this work, whether they were within reasonable commuting distance or whether they were in a category known as 'working while on claim', in which they would have filed claims at the commencement of the season which would remain inactive, only generating benefits, if there was an industry downturn. Although we immediately protested that the numbers were significantly overstated, this information reflected the ongoing 'social narrative' about our region which suggests significant abuse of this particular benefit program. Further, the numbers had been produced by colleagues from headquarters who had strong relationships and credibility with the Minister and the Deputies. The Minister had already used the data publicly and as a basis for policy decisions that adversely affected an important regional industry. In the process, the pre-existing social narrative was further strengthened and to this day several years later, the impacts from this poor piece of analysis continue to reverberate in the region.

The meeting started and Sonia took us through the document. When she had finished her presentation, Robert asked for comments. I responded with the usual compliments about their good work and then referred to the first discussion question, labelled 'How to resolve the Productivity Problem'? I suggested it might be premature to conclude there was, in fact, such a problem and noted it was not yet clear that the numbers, and the methodology with which they were developed, were sufficiently robust and reliable either to determine what the issue was or to use for comparison purposes. Given my doubts and experience of how easily social narratives could affect analysis, I was hesitant to document as fact something that might actually not be correct. More importantly, I worried such a rush to conclusions might preclude a deeper exploration about what was actually going on.

Robert responded immediately. Looking directly at me and holding up the report, he said that the numbers were indisputable proof of a productivity problem. He looked to Sonia for confirmation, who quickly repeated his statement, almost word for word. Everyone else remained quiet.

I was completely taken aback. I had assumed we all recognised that the numbers were questionable but a good starting point for dialogue and exploration. Instead, it appeared Robert and Sonia had already made up their minds and saw further discussion as unnecessary. A rush of anxiety washed over me, and I wanted to disappear into the ground. I instantly regretted having spoken and feared Robert would presume I was not on board or on top of my areas of responsibility and was being naïve and obstructive. I was concerned I was at risk of not being considered part of the team.

In retrospect, I might have stood my ground and questioned the basis for Sonia's assertion that the productivity problem was indisputable and tried to convince them of the need to investigate the issue further. However, I realised that to do so, I would have to be critical about the analysis and results of my colleagues' work in order to justify my concerns and might thereby be perceived as 'throwing them under the bus'. This is never a good career move and particularly ill-advised when these colleagues have significantly more political capital than I. Robert and I had a rocky relationship and I felt he didn't have much faith in my abilities. I later realised that he was very selective in who and how much he trusted, and I was not the only person around the table that felt he didn't have their backs. However, in my anxiety and in that moment, I neither trusted my ability to convince him of anything nor that it would be *safe* to even try. Instead, I sought to find a way to retract my comments, which was, of course, impossible. I agreed there was an issue – although I wasn't yet convinced of this or, perhaps more accurately, of *what* it was – and went on to say that because it was early days and the numbers were still unreliable, we couldn't really know what they might be telling us. I hoped that this addition to my initial remarks would shift attention away from my unhelpful opinions and me and back to Sonia's agenda. The conversation continued for a few minutes longer as I attempted to undo the damage I felt my remarks had caused and to negotiate myself back into the group and my boss's good graces. I was relieved when he redirected his attention to Sonia and my colleagues, and the discussion turned to what we could do to solve this indisputable problem of productivity.

What Was Going On?

In reflecting on what had been going on in the meeting, the words that most resonated with me were *respect, safety* and *trust*. Would my colleagues listen to me? Did they trust me? Believe in me? Respect me? Would they give me the benefit of the doubt? Was it safe to continue with my intervention? I did not feel my doubts or concerns were welcome, nor that I was respected or trusted enough to be listened to. I felt unsafe and as a result, felt it was unwise to pursue my line of inquiry.

Upon reflection, I can see that it wasn't just me and that there was more than enough anxiety, conflict and emotion to go around. Robert and Sonia were justifiably concerned about the need to deliver on our commitments to the department and Parliament as the numbers suggested we were not doing so. In my anxiety, I may also have expressed myself poorly. My comments could also have been interpreted as saying I could not be counted on to help address this problem. After all, how could I be trusted if I did not 'get' the seriousness of the situation?

From my perspective, I realised that I experienced the meeting as I did and thus acted as I had because I did not feel trusted and in return did not trust my boss, which led me to an exploration of the concept of *trust*.

Trust

Scholarly interest in the concept of trust has increased significantly since the 1960s,[2] with many exploring its importance in the functioning of our society and organisations. Defining it, however, is not easy, given that the word is used in so many ways and for so many different purposes, for example, in legal terms, as a noun and a verb, to connote aspects of how we relate to each other and so on. An in-depth review would take more space than I have available, so for the purposes of this chapter, I draw on Larue Tone Hosmer's (1995, p. 381) extensive review of the literature on trust. Restating his and others work, I have adopted a definition of the term trust as a felt confidence that an individual and/or group will meet our expectations about a particular outcome.[3]

Hosmer's review actually identified five different contexts: *individual expectations, interpersonal relationships, social structures, economic exchanges* and *ethical principles*. I focus on the first three, as they are more germane to the understanding of trust and meaning-making, and in my view, inseparable.

In coming to an understanding of trust, I draw upon the perspective of complex responsive processes of relating (Stacey and Mowles, 2016). Whether or not we trust someone is situationally constructed and thus highly particularised, as scholars who take an approach based on individual expectations highlight (Luhmann, 1979/2017, p. 25; Hardin, 2006, p. 19; Hurley, 2012, p. 353). However, trust is also determined by our history and past experiences and informed by our anticipation of the future. It is experienced in localised interactions between individuals and groups, which also means it is interpersonal and thus necessarily social (Putnam, 1993, 2000; Hosmer, 1995, p. 388; Fukuyama, 1996; Misztal, 1996, pp. 206–207; Sztompka, 2006, p. 4). Our actions, decisions and acted-upon emotions, however particular they feel to us, are socially formed as each of us in our interactions is affected by and at the same time affects the other(s). As we attempt to make sense of what is going on and how we will or will not act in response, we do so in the context of networks of interdependent individuals enabling and constraining each other in ongoing processes of inclusion and exclusion and configuring of power relations. From the ebb and flow of these processes, themes (or patterns) of trust relating emerge that organise our experience of being together. Trust is thus paradoxically both individually particularised and generalised and socially constructed all at the same time.

In the above highly charged narrative, we each brought different histories, experiences, capabilities, reputations, concerns and emotions into our interactions as we individually and collectively made determinations as to what was and was not right and whom we should believe and whom we could trust. We acted and reacted to each other's determinations and actions in a dance affected by the ever-evolving figurations of power relations and dynamics of inclusion and exclusion, out of which trust emerged as a complex, recursive and iterative patterning of themes organising our experience of being together. While I experienced and particularised this situation as an individual, it was also (and simultaneously) socially constructed and generalised. In the result, my history with Robert and other colleagues, our different roles and responsibilities and perceived expertise, the power dynamics and my fears of exclusion all led to the emergence of patterns of trust relating that did not make me feel I could *safely* continue with my attempts to question the data.

Key Aspects of Trust

Before I continue, I want to highlight a couple of aspects of trust from the literature, which I view as important in understanding how or why we trust another – and, in turn, how that may affect our work to make meaning together.

First, it is impossible to separate mind from body and emotions from the cognitive or rational, and thus, trust is both rational and emotional. Recent research by Portuguese American neuroscientist Antonio Damasio (2019), based upon his study of brain lesions, suggests that the two are physiologically intertwined making it impossible to consider that one can be present without the other and therefore there is no 'neutral, non-personal, unemotional way of engaging with the world' (Burkitt, 2014, p. 21). This means that in our decision-making, we must take into account not only what might be considered to be objective, but also the emotions, past experiences and personal circumstances of those engaged in the discussion.

Second, a number of scholars (Putnam, 1993, 2000; Smith and Berg, 1997; Sztompka, 2006) have proposed that trust is reciprocal and that if I do not trust you, you are unlikely to trust me and vice versa. Trust is therefore a mutual affair and thus easily lost in situations where the multiplicity of perspectives, beliefs and concerns and divergent power dynamics of those interacting means that they may well have conflicting objectives and concerns that are inconsistent with one another.

Third, I adopt the approach of sociologists Barbara Misztal (1996) and Niklas Luhmann (1979/2017), who argue that trust is fragile in nature and easily lost. The reciprocal nature of trust means that it does not take much to introduce uncertainty as to whether another will 'have our back' in stressful circumstances because our objectives are different and perhaps conflicting. Given such an uncertainty, we are unlikely to feel confident that we can rely upon, and thus trust, each other.

Some Thoughts on How We Work Together

Before proceeding further, a few words on the work we do in organisations that, in turn, becomes the subject of measurement or assessment. We work in a complex environment, ostensibly in the pursuit of our collective organisational goals. Taking the perspective of complex responsive processes of relating detailed elsewhere in this volume, everything that is going on is the result of multitudes of local interactions of individuals, affected by power dynamics, emotions and evaluative choices such as norms and values. Out of these many, many interactions, population-wide patterns emerge which organise our experience of being together (Stacey and Mowles, 2016). Even independent contributors are themselves interacting in one way or another with and interdependent upon others. This work of working together, of 'figuring out' what to do and then doing it, is referred to in many ways. We 'make sense of what is going on' or we engage in 'problem-solving' or 'decision-making'. A commonly used term for this work, *sense-making*, was introduced to organisational studies in the 1970s by organisational theorist and psychologist Karl Weick (1995) to describe the processes of making sense individually and in groups (pp. 4–6), and for the purposes of this chapter, I have adopted this term. There are two elements that I highlight as key to how I understand the word *sense-making*.

First, I have frequently heard colleagues comment on the importance of keeping emotions out of our discussions when we are working to solve a problem. As already discussed, however, recent sociological and neuroscience research are making it increasingly clear that this is not possible. Second, my use of the term *sense-making* is not meant to imply agreement. Instead, I argue that meaning emerges from our interactions whether or not we agree or even share the same understanding or awareness of the outcome(s). Sense-making is both an individual and collective activity, as through our interactions we are affected by our ever-evolving experiences, histories, emotions, values and norms and power relations and through that process, we create meaning.

In my work experience, I have often found the activity of *sense-making* to be exciting: a coming together of the team and affirmation of our collective identities, as we seek to find a way to go on together. It can be rewarding, as we feel we have instituted an agreed-on order to the puzzlement of our existence. This was recognised by the great American pragmatist John Dewey (1929/1984), who used the term *productive doubt* to express the view that the disciplined mind would delight in and enjoy the doubtful or as he termed it 'operations of infinite inquiry' (p. 182).

Our work together to make sense of what is going on, however, is (in my experience) often difficult, anxiety provoking and destabilising as it is necessary because something has gone wrong and/or disrupted our expectations (Weick, 1995, pp. 4–6; Brown et al., 2015, p. 266). I have many times heard Deputy Ministers say categorically that we were in a 'no surprises' environment and it was our job to keep it that way. We needed to be 'in control' and 'on top of what was going on'. When we were unable to prevent such disruptions, there was always the risk of second-guessing and blame-laying with possible consequences for our organisation and careers.

In a complex world where we can neither predict nor control what will happen, surprises are an inevitable part of our daily reality. These are often anxiety-creating and unwelcome in the workplace. They are contrary to what was 'supposed to happen', making nonsense of our plans and hopes for success and cause us to doubt our capacity to know what is going on. Our engagement with difference in meaning-making thus necessarily involves conflict, due to the breakdowns resulting from our encounters with differing expectations. In fact, not only is conflict inevitable, I argue that difference and dissent are necessary for collaboration and sense-making in the exploration of a diversity of perspectives and to make productive use of doubt. We are in a difficult situation. We fear and try to avoid conflict, but it is inevitable in the processes of negotiating how we might go on together. We thus need to find ways to explore how we can manage this conflict so that we are able to stay in relation with each other despite our differences (Griffin and Stacey, 2005, p. 149; Mowles, 2015, p. 128).

Finally, in my experience of the give and take of meaning-making, my sense of who I am and my values or assumptions as to what 'I know' to be right and true are often challenged. Process sociologist Norbert Elias (1987/1991) suggests we continually renegotiate our identities as we form and, in turn, are formed by the reactions and actions of others (p. 316) in the ebb and flow of the patterning of our power relationships (1908/1978, p. 131). Canadian philosopher Charles Taylor (in Malpas et al., ed., 2002) similarly argued that we cannot understand each other without a changed understanding of ourselves (p. 295). Our very sense of our self and our sense of each other is therefore continually challenged in our work to make meaning.

I therefore suggest that anxiety is inevitable in our work together and needs to be taken into account. While I may be perceived to have accused John Dewey of idealising the joy and delight of inquiring into productive doubt, in fact he wrote eloquently on the challenging nature of problem-solving. His book, titled *Quest for Certainty* (1929/1984), considers how this continual 'quest' is driven by our anxieties and fears of risk and uncertainty.

In my experience, we develop many ways of coping with this anxiety. We do so by attempting to reduce complexity and simplify what is going on. We gather support for our point of view from those in whom we have confidence, that we trust and often that are like us. We sometimes pretend that it is possible to be in a 'no surprises' environment. We insist on a 'bias for action' and accuse others of analysis paralysis. Alternatively, we seek information and data as evidence for our decisions, sometimes to the point of analysis paralysis. We may even lay the responsibility on others by demanding that they provide the 'right answer', the 'best options' and do so professionally and based upon authoritative analysis. Then, we will be certain that we have it right!

Trust and Sense-Making

Having explained how I think of and define trust and the sometimes challenging nature of sense-making, I now consider its effect upon this work. Trust is often idealised, and it is assumed that the more we trust each other, the better. I argue however that patterns of trust relating can both enable and constrain a productive exploration of what is going on in our work.

Patterns of trust relating can help us stay in relation with one another, thus enhancing our ability to engage with productive doubt, despite the anxiety involved in meaning-making. Asking a question or raising a different perspective might be felt as making oneself vulnerable and at risk of exclusion. Such interventions, however, can also be a source of novelty and bring a perspective another might miss. Where an individual doesn't feel safe because they don't trust colleagues, particularly those with more power chances, they may be unlikely to engage. This was seen in the way in which the meeting I describe developed. My anxieties led me to feel unsafe and unable (or unwilling) to continue my questioning of the data. As 'novelty and innovation arise not from conformity and unity, but from engagement with difference' (Mowles, 2011, p. 165), disincentives to raising different views can obstruct innovation and engagement. Such a challenge is all too common in organisations, such as evidenced in the above narrative. Ironically, these are often the very same organisations whose leaders decry the lack of innovation and creativity in the workforce.

Strong patterns of trust can also, however, constrain individuals and groups in their work to make meaning. Where our identities and/or values are strongly held, patterns of trust relating can also lead to a failure to explore *productive doubt* as we are unable to safely challenge such identities and values. Indeed, these norms and values can be so strongly ingrained that it never even occurs to us to challenge them. It is just 'the way we do things around here' and habitual. We don't challenge because we don't even see them. An excellent example of the negative effects of trust is what psychologist Irving Janus (1982) called 'groupthink', a term he coined in his study of the Bay of Pigs and other high-profile disasters in American public policy to describe how perspectives, which challenge strongly held *we-identities* and values, are not raised, as they might jeopardise relationships with colleagues and lead to exclusion. In the narrative, we saw how strong convictions about, and thus trust in, the data (and arguably also the source of the data) meant that it was considered indisputable and any questioning unwelcome.

I have explored the sometimes challenging and anxiety-creating nature of our work and the relationship between *trust* and sense-making to provide context for the next discussion considering the reliance upon metrics and quantified data in analysis and policymaking.

Metrics: Evidence-Based?

The concept of evidence-based practice originated in the field of health care in the early 1970s through the work of epidemiologist Archie Cochrane (1972) but increasingly gained traction in medical practice and other fields such as management and public policy in the 1990s.

This approach has been adopted enthusiastically by the Canadian Public Service, which prides itself on being *evidence-based*. While clearly an important principle for practitioners seeking to serve the public in an accountable, transparent and effective way, its implementation in the often high-stakes, high-anxiety game of politics and policymaking can be problematic.

I have already discussed the destabilising nature of meaning-making, which makes it understandable that we seek to achieve a sense of control and objectivity to demonstrate we have made the 'right' decision. Science historian Theodore Porter in *Trust in Numbers: The Pursuit of Objectivity in Science and Public Life* (1995) examined the prevalence of quantification in the workplace and noted that it is often demanded for its presumed objectivity or precision where there is an absence of trust (Porter, 1995, pp. 97, 100–101, 152). He suggested that relationships of trust take time and experience that may not be available in a bureaucracy (p. 194). It is, therefore, not surprising in a bureaucratic world such as the government in which 'evidence-based public management' is expected that quantitative information is used to ensure evidence is sufficiently objective. I agree with Porter that this often prompts the use of quantitative methods as numbers are considered precise and beyond negotiation – or, as my boss put it, 'indisputable'. Targets and numerically expressed outcomes are assumed to be objective and allow us to 'prove' the effectiveness of our actions and show cause and effect for our decisions. They provide simple and direct evidence we can use to demonstrate we are 'in control' and 'on top of things' and achieving results, thus providing us with a way to manage the ever-prevalent anxiety of working in an uncertain, sensitive and high-risk environment.

This heavy reliance upon quantifiable data was criticized by some academics as early as 1956 (in a paper by V.F. Ridgway titled the 'Dysfunctional Consequences of Performance Measurements') and its quantitative bent critiqued in what became known as the McNamara (or quantitative) fallacy, named after Robert McNamara, the US Secretary of Defense from 1961 to 1968. It describes where decisions are made based solely on quantitative observations or metrics and all other information is ignored because these other observations cannot be proven. This fallacy was rather cynically described by Daniel Yankelovich (1972) as follows:

> The first step is to measure whatever can be easily measured. This is OK as far as it goes. The second step is to disregard that which can't be easily measured or to give it an arbitrary quantitative value. This is artificial and misleading. The third step is to presume that what can't be measured

easily really isn't important. This is blindness. The fourth step is to say that what can't be easily measured really doesn't exist. This is suicide.

While trust in data may help assuage our collective and individual anxieties, I maintain that a non-nuanced approach to metrics can cause as many problems as it solves. One result, particularly when tied into career advancement and status, can be the gaming behavior that measuring things and rewarding the fulfilment of targets calls out. While space does not allow me to explore this in detail, Robert Jackall's book *Moral Mazes: The World of Corporate Managers* (1988) is a fascinating exploration of this dynamic in the corporate environment.

For the purposes of this discussion, I focus upon two reasons why this approach can be problematic. First, data are trusted as objective information, despite being socially determined and enabled by patterns of trust relating; and second, its use is potentially destructive of trusting relationships, and in particular, trust in practical expertise in the workplace. This, in turn, further strengthens our trust in and reliance upon the use of numbers.

First, metrics are trusted because they are considered objective and precise in comparison with other forms of knowledge. I would argue, however, that as we saw in the narrative, quantitative information is itself socially formed as metrics are developed based upon assumptions and upon what can be quantified and sometimes even 'constructed', as was the case in my narrative. There are choices made about what gets counted and how and, I would argue, these judgments are often ideologically informed. Other considerations that are not counted (or even countable) are completely missed, and as the saying goes, 'What is counted counts'. Further, metrics often rely, in the words of Porter, on 'institutional or personal credibility even to produce impersonal numbers' (p. 214). Numbers or metrics do not emerge magically from the ether. As Dewey (1929/2015) suggested, data are not 'given' but 'taken' as they are '*selected* from … original subject-matter which gives the impetus to knowing; they are discriminated for a purpose' (pp. 142–143). Numbers gain in persuasiveness based on their source and/or where they are published (i.e. if the source or publication is *trusted*). We need to know an authority has blessed the numbers, else the data cannot be credible and trusted for use in meaning-making. It is thus socially formed and enabled by patterns of trust relating.

In the introduction to the narrative, I refer to an experience in which erroneous numbers were accepted and successfully defended from criticism both because of the reputation and status of the experts who had prepared them and the prevailing social narrative which fueled assumptions made about abuse of the benefits program. This resulted in an unquestioning acceptance of significantly overstated numbers, which were, in fact, not evidence-based. The assumptions were not made explicit and those engaged in this situation were likely not even aware of the role the social narratives had played in their decision-making and recommendations. In that high-stakes, high-anxiety situation, this caused a further strengthening of the social narrative. I suggest this probably happens more often than we would like to admit. Further, assumptions that are not made visible and cannot therefore be challenged can later blindside us when events turn out differently than had been assumed.

The numbers that indicated our 'productivity problem' were selected and calculated based on assumptions by headquarters colleagues who were trusted to prepare the numbers. The 'trust in numbers' was thus arguably trust in the *source* of the numbers. This is problematic; knowledge assumed to be objective is meant to be 'knowledge that does not depend too much on the particular individuals who author it' (Porter, 1995, p. 229). And yet, this was precisely what underpinned the credibility conferred on the numbers in this narrative.

Above, I suggested that numbers are considered necessary because we lack trust in practical judgment and require objective evidence to help us manage our anxieties. I claim that a simplistic reliance on quantitative methods can be problematic in terms of its impact on our working relationships. Porter noted a move to almost universal quantification in social science and applied disciplines and a 'push for rigor', in part as a result of the distrust of 'unarticulated expert knowledge' and 'suspicion of arbitrariness and discretion' that has shaped political culture, arguing this has led to a distrust in personal judgment (pp. 199–200). The American political scientist and anthropologist James C. Scott in his book *Seeing Like a State: How Certain Schemes to Improve the Human Condition Have Failed* (1998) argues that in complex environments, practical expertise and judgment is fundamentally important. And yet a distrust of practical experience may prevent those whose expertise is not valued from contributing to the discussion and thereby reduce our capacity to explore helpful perspectives. In the narrative, I felt that there was an underlying message that we were 'being held to account' and that the numbers showed 'problems' with the productivity of our workforce. I did not feel that the practical knowledge of what was going on which might have been helpful was welcome. Instead, my attempts to invite the group to engage in a more nuanced exploration of the numbers was met with the assertion that the conclusions were 'indisputable'. In this meeting I felt that my practical judgement was devalued, and in turn, I felt that both myself and my team had been disrespected. I have noticed how this reaction often created a pattern for them and for me, in which I became loath to make similar interventions in meetings. Ironically, it is my experience that when things go wrong, the very same people who had been silenced are often blamed as they are the ones that 'should have known' what was going on. Note the negative self-reinforcing cycle, in which reliance on metrics to the detriment of practical knowledge further reduces the likelihood that those whose expertise is disregarded will feel trusted or trust others, making metrics increasingly our only common ground. After all, one cannot argue with the numbers!

Above, I note the importance of reciprocity in trust (Putnam, 1993, 2000; Sztompka, 2006) and how if you do not trust me, I will probably not trust you. As I did not feel trusted, recognised or valued by my boss, I increasingly distrusted him. I experienced the disregard of my concerns in the productivity discussion as disrespect of my, and my team's, practical knowledge and experience. Thus, while most decision-makers will readily agree that the frame of reference matters, in this narrative, this context had disappeared and the metrics were all we had. In dismissing my concerns out of hand, I was left feeling shamed, excluded and not trusted. All the benefit of the doubt was accorded to the numbers, none of it to me. In the result, in the absence of trust relations, particularly in the high-anxiety/high-stakes world of politics, the siren song of numbers becomes almost irresistible with its promises of safety and certainty leading to a reduced capacity to explore productive doubt.

I do not argue against the use of quantitative data or metrics. In fact, I suggest that in a complex multispecialist world, numbers can be functionally useful, providing a common language and helping to manage our anxiety and increase our capacity to achieve mutual understanding and explore differences. They can also help make it *safe* for those with fewer power chances to bring up puzzling developments for collective exploration and problem-solving. The challenge, however, is that a nuanced and critical approach to their use is required.[4]

Conclusion

In this chapter, I have explored a narrative about processes of sense-making. In my experience, our work to address workplace issues can be destabilising as it often arises due to unwelcome surprises, frequently challenges our collective and individual identities and inevitably involves conflict. I define trust as a felt confidence that an individual and/or group will meet our expectations about a particular outcome. As we seek to manage our individual and collective anxieties, trust in each other can both enable and constrain us in our exploration of difference. I also suggest there is a problematic relationship between trust and metrics or quantifiable data in that numbers are assumed to be objective and certain while they are actually socially determined and maintained. Further, reliance upon them reduces our trust in practical knowledge, thus further cementing our dependence upon numbers to support our work and reducing our ability to draw upon the practical expertise of our colleagues.

It is, of course, important to try and make decisions upon the best information that we can find and then to understand whether the course of action we have agreed upon has been successful or not. Questions such as these are critical, especially in times of high complexity such as today, when innovation and creativity and new perspectives are needed more than ever. However, there is a well-known saying, which I paraphrase as 'no plan survives first contact with the enemy'. We need our teams to be able to surface and explore productive doubt – at all stages of the discussion and throughout implementation. These discussions can be conflictual and invoke strong emotions. This means we as leaders need to make it safe for our teams to engage in challenge and debate despite differing power chances and status and wary of closing down debate prematurely and/or seeing certainty where there is merely a yearning for it! Where our identities or corporate values are strongly held, we need be vigilant that they do not become idealised and stifle useful debate. In practical terms, we need to ensure there is sufficient time and 'space' for team members to raise their concerns. One approach I have found useful is reserving open agenda time in meetings for individuals to raise whatever issues they feel we need discuss as a team. My experience, and the feedback I have received, is that these 'agenda items' are often the most helpful parts of the meeting.

Quantitative data will always be important in our processes of making meaning. However, I recommend a nuanced approach to its interpretation, which incorporates the richness of practical expertise of practitioners and tries to explore the assumptions and factors that may not be able to be reduced to numbers, thus preserving our ability to engage in the exploration of John Dewey's *productive doubt*.

Final Thoughts for Managers

Our relationships are continually evolving, as we form and are formed by our interactions with each other, and thus how we work together today will affect how we will work together in the future. Our relationships with each other are important, and as they are fragile and reciprocal, they are easily damaged. An unfortunate and perhaps unintended off-the-cuff comment can be extremely destructive to our working relationships. A phrase I have coined elsewhere, *buffering conversations*, refers to the one-on-one conversations held outside formal meetings. They can assist by explaining or softening interventions in meetings and in repairing or maintaining relationships and expectations as we continually negotiate our understanding of whether we can trust each other (Filbee, 2019). This came from an interaction I observed prior to another in-person meeting. One of my colleagues, Charles, sidled up to another and said that he hoped his comment in a recent session was okay as what he was trying to do was introduce another concern he thought was important. When his colleague agreed that that made sense and of course he had understood it that way, the anxiety I had seen on Charles's face disappeared. I watched with interest, noting the importance of such conversations in *buffering* and sometimes mending relationships that may have been put at risk in an interaction. While with the increase in remote working due to the COVID-19 pandemic, these types of face-to-face encounters may be less and less common, or even possible, the need to continually nurture and protect our trusting relationships with colleagues remains fundamental to our ability to successfully work together.

In closing, I recognise the appeal of 'certainty' – of 'getting it right' – that one action or decision is better or worse than another; that there is a 'right' or a 'wrong' thing to do; or that numbers are precise, objective and beyond debate. I suggest, however, that such an approach is what I refer to as 'pseudo-certainty' and wishful thinking and in our highly complex world, problematic (and argumentatively, more than a little delusional!). Our view on what is the *right* way inevitably depends on who is making the judgment – and when they are doing so. What is a triumph and good decision today may be a debacle tomorrow. What I think is a great idea may be unacceptable to another. Instead, G.H. Mead (1938) proposed that the question is not whether there is a right value or a wrong value at stake, but 'a question of finding the possibility of acting so as to take into account as far as possible all the values involved' (p. 465). This approach is directly contrary to the search for a 'right' answer or the perfect numbers and seeking rules or predictions which will invariably apply. It is rather a pragmatic approach in which we see *right* as the best we can do in the circumstances in which we find ourselves today, to seek out a *good enough* step to take together *for now*, acknowledging that tomorrow 'we may be facing a completely different set of problems' (Mowles, 2015, p. 144).

If there is no right or wrong, does anything go? Clearly not, and this is where the advice of Mead (1938) and Mowles (2015a) is so useful. Taking their pragmatic approach, I argue our objective should be to seek out how we can stay in relation sufficiently to allow a collective exploration of different values, perspectives and concerns and thus make productive use of doubt, as advocated by John Dewey, so we can figure out what to do next. In my view, both trust and metrics have a role to play in our processes of meaning-making. Such an approach does not deny the inevitability of conflict and anxiety, but rather explores different ways we can seek to manage it together and make better sense of it rather than submitting to or avoiding it.

Notes

1 This program, governed by federal legislation, is intended to support unemployed workers.
2 In a blog, *Trust in Organisations*, Ralph Stacey illustrated this point with the results of a Google Scholar search on trust, organisations and leadership. It registered a few hundred entries per annum in the 1960s, a few thousand in the 1970s and 10,000 in the 1990s, before jumping to an average of 40,000 articles per year in the early 2000s. (Stacey, 2012).

3 While I acknowledge the connection between trust and distrust (you cannot have one without the other), my focus is on the former for the purposes of this discussion.
4 For more discussion on this issue, see Historian Jerry Muller's book *The Tyranny of Metrics* (2018).

References

Brown, A.D., Colville, I., & Pye, A. (2015). Making Sense of Sensemaking in Organization Studies. *Organization Studies*, 36(2), 265–277. https://doi-org.ezproxy.herts.ac.uk/10.1177/0170840614559259

Burkitt, I. (2014). *Emotions and Social Relations*. Los Angeles, CA: SAGE Publishing.

Cochrane, A.L. (1972). *Effectiveness and Efficiency. Random Reflections on Health Services*. London: Nuffield Provincial Hospitals Trust. ISBN 978-0900574177. OCLC 741462.

Damasio, A. (2019). *The Strange Order of Things: Life, Feeling, and the Making of Cultures*. New York, NY: Vintage Books.

Dewey, J. (1929/1984). *The Quest for Certainty: The Later Works, 1925–1953*. Carbondale: Southern Illinois University Press.

Dewey, J. (1929/2015). *Experience and Nature*. New York, NY: Dover Publications, Inc.

Drucker, P. (1974). *Management: Tasks, Responsibilities, Practices*. London, UK: Heinemann.

Elias, N. (1987/1991). *The Society of Individuals*. Oxford, UK: Basil Blackwell Ltd.

Filbee, S. (2019). *Trust and Its Consequences: A Regional Senior Manager's Experiences of Meaning Making in the Canadian Public Service*. Doctor of Management Thesis. University of Hertfordshire, Hatfield, UK.

Fukuyama, F. (1996). *Trust: The Social Virtues and the Creation of Prosperity*. New York, NY: Free Press Paperbacks.

Griffin, D., & Stacey, R., (Eds.). (2005). *Complexity and the Experience of Leading Organizations*. Oxford, UK: Routledge.

Hardin, R. (2006). *Trust*. Cambridge, UK: Polity Press.

Hosmer, L.T. (1995). Trust: The Connecting Link between Organizational Theory and Philosophical Ethics. *The Academy of Management Review*, 20(2), 379–403. https://doi.org/10.2307/258851

Hurley, R. (2012). *The Decision to Trust: How Leaders Create High-Trust Organizations.* San Francisco, CA: Jossey-Bass.

Jackall, R. (1988). *Moral Mazes: The World of Corporate Managers.* New York, NY: Oxford University Press, Inc.

Janus, I. (1982). *Groupthink: Psychological Studies of Policy Decisions and Fiascos.* Boston, MA: Houghton Mifflin.

Luhmann, N. (1979/2017). *Trust and Power.* Cambridge, UK: Polity Press.

Malpas, J., Arnswald, U., & Kertscher, J., (Eds.). (2002). *Gadamer's Century: Essays in Honor of Hans-Geor Gadamer.* Cambridge, MA: MIT Press.

Misztal, B.A. (1996). *Trust in Modern Societies: The Search for the Bases of Social Order.* Maldan, MA: Blackwell Publishers.

Mowles, C. (2011). *Rethinking Management: Radical Insights from the Complexity Sciences.* Surrey, UK: Gower Publishing Limited.

Mowles, C. (2015). *Managing in Uncertainty: Complexity and the Paradoxes of Everyday Organizational Life.* London, UK: Routledge.

Muller, J.Z. (2018). *The Tyranny of Metrics.* Princeton, NJ: Princeton University Press.

Porter, T.M. (1995). *Trust in Numbers: The Pursuit of Objectivity in Science and Public Life.* Princeton, NJ: Princeton University Press.

Putnam, R.D. (with Leonardi, R. and Nanetti, R.Y.). (1993). *Making Democracy Work: Civic Traditions in Modern Italy.* Princeton, NJ: Princeton University Press.

Putnam, R.D. (2000). *Bowling Alone: The Collapse and Revival of American Community.* New York, NY: Simon & Schuster.

Ridgway, V.F. (1956). Dysfunctional Consequences of Performance Measurements. *Administrative Science Quarterly,* 1(2) (Sage Publications, Inc., September, 1956), 240–247. https://doi.org/10.2307/2390989, https://www.jstor.org/stable/2390989

Scott, J.C. (1998). *Seeing Like a State: How Certain Schemes to Improve the Human Condition Have Failed.* Durham, NC: Yale Agrarian Studies Series.

Smith, K.K., & Berg, D.N. (1997). *Paradoxes of Life: Understanding Conflict, Paralysis, and Movement in Group Dynamics.* San Francisco, CA: Jossey-Bass.

Stacey, R.D. (2012). Trust in Organisations. Retrieved from https://complexityandmanagement.com/2012/11/23/trust-in-organisations/

Stacey, R.D., & Mowles, C. (2016). *Strategic Management and Organisational Dynamics: The Challenge of Complexity to Ways of Thinking about Organisations* (7th ed.). London, UK: Pearson Education.

Sztompka, P. (2006). *Trust: A Sociological Theory.* New York, NY: Cambridge University Press.

Weick, K.E. (1995). *Sensemaking in Organizations.* Los Angeles, CA: SAGE Publishing.

Yankelovich, D. (1972). *Corporate Priorities: A Continuing Study of the New Demands on Business.* Stamford, CT: Yankelovich Inc.

6

CORPORATE SOCIAL RESPONSIBILITY (CSR) IN THE UK UNIVERSITY

From Idealism to Pragmatism

Jana Filosof

Introduction

We have been concerned about our impact on the environment, both social and ecological, since biblical times. The industrial age saw the rise of the corporation, which gained a legal personhood status in the 19th century, and with this the corporation also 'inherited' the rights of individuals. Although some wealthy individuals (e.g. Cadbury in the UK, Carnegie in the US or Dunant in Switzerland) engaged in philanthropy, the discourse of the social responsibilities of corporations did not enter the public domain until after WWII. The notion of Corporate Social Responsibility (CSR) came into focus with the publication of Bowen's seminal book *Social Responsibilities of the Businessmen* in 1953.

For decades, interest in CSR was directed at corporations and other large business firms. Due to the nature of public sector institutions – organisations providing public goods to wider society – the idea of CSR in the public sector may have seemed redundant. It can be argued that, by definition, public sector organisations engage in CSR, which is understood as the organisational duties to society (Van Oosterhout and Heugens, 2008). Yet, New Public Management (NPM) ideas contributed to increased managerialism – focusing on business and management practices, rather than on social value – of the public sector in the UK. With the introduction of various business practices, the advent of NPM also led to a greater interest – public and academic – in the ways the public sector operates and how it addresses responsibilities beyond the business aims. And so, towards the end of the 20th century, the CSR discourse extended to other sectors of society – small- and medium-sized enterprises (SMEs), not-for-profits and public services (see Gindis, 2009; Micklethwait and Wooldridge, 2003).

As a part of the wider public sector in the UK, Higher Education (HE) wholeheartedly adopted NPM assumptions and aimed to become 'much more "business-like" and "market-oriented", that is, performance-, cost-, efficiency- and audit-oriented' (Diefenbach, 2009: 893). While some NPM tools and techniques may be necessary to manage complex organisations 'at a distance' (Scott, 1998), the wholesale translation of private sector recipes into public sector organisations may lead to clashes of public sector values, such as pluralism, egalitarianism and citizens' voice and participation, with private sector management rationality based on standardisation and reporting in the service of profitability (Simonet, 2013). And, as many of us working in the public sector would attest, market rationality often wins. Various aspects of managerialisation in HE have been a topic of discussion by many writers. This would come as no surprise to anyone working in a UK University. In the decades since joining the HE sector, I have witnessed a massive increase in bureaucracy and centralisation within my University. Similar to Parker's experience (2008), the route to promotion in my institution is almost always through administrative roles. We are encouraged to think of our 'students' as 'customers'. Describing our University as 'the UK's leading business-facing university and an exemplar in the sector' is an example of the senior managers' NPM attitudes, which are summarised by Brown and Cloke (2009: 479) as follows: '(w)hilst UK Universities may not be accountable to shareholders or driven only by the profit motive, they are increasingly operating as if those were their chief considerations'.

Universities' unique position, as both practitioners of and educators in CSR, draws attention from practitioners and academics alike. There is a plethora of research looking into CSR education; however, the research into the practice of CSR in Universities is lacking. In this chapter, I reflect on my own experiences of practicing CSR in a UK University, which included involving our students and staff in the local community, volunteering, assisting not-for-profits with our expertise and encouraging 'greener' practices. This experience also included standardising and measuring of the CSR practice. My reflection draws attention to the intertwining of intentions, histories and experiences of many interdependent players that led to the adoption of CSR-related managerialist practices in my institution. Reflecting on my practice of CSR, I suggest that focusing on the metrification of what is understood as organisational ethical obligation to society, which I believed was impervious to quantifying and measuring, emphasises the extent of the phenomenon in the public sector. I hope my experience described in this chapter may resonate with those of other practitioners in the public sector and encourage further discussions about CSR in our everyday practice.

Limitations of the Mainstream CSR Discourse

Prior to joining the University, I worked in a highly competitive media industry. As a planner in an advertising agency, I was making media purchasing decisions based on aggregated data about the media channels' users. Later, as a senior manager for a marketing arm of a TV network, my mornings would start with reviewing the previous day's TV ratings, which dictated the price of commercial airtime we were selling. Ratings were my employer's raison d'être, and my livelihood depended on them. Those ratings were collected by an independent research organisation using 'people-metres' (seeing the words in black and white makes me chuckle) and presented us with data, which we would slice and analyse according to various variables. We never thought about the human faces behind the data, they were unimportant. We would decide where to place a commercial for a product based solely on what type of TV programmes the viewers consumed. I hated the fact that my role was reduced to crunching numbers in order to present our channel as the lucrative alternative to our clients and to meeting monthly sales targets. I began resenting that job and became disillusioned with marketing. At the first opportunity, I left both the job and the media industry.

I joined HE hoping to serve a different purpose, to get away from what I understood as the exploitation of consumers I came to identify with commercial enterprise. I was not so naïve as to expect a career in the public sector to be devoid of managerialism and its tools and techniques. But I also did not expect the proverbial tail of reporting to wag the education dog. After experiencing various forms of 'the tyranny of metrics' (Muller, 2019) in the many roles I undertook in the University (e.g. lecturing, research and learning and teaching), I became a very vocal critic of the culture of 'If It Moves, Measure It' (Bond and O'Byrne, 2016). My interest in CSR expanded beyond research and teaching. When a Unit engaging in social responsibility was created in my Business School, I saw this as an opportunity to formalise my fragmented engagement in this sphere of action. And, selfishly, I hoped to avoid measuring of and reporting on what I believed to be unmeasurable – the quality of social interaction.

Mainstream CSR theories are rooted in the wider mainstream organisational theories, which adopt a systems perspective of organisations. The limitations of systems thinking are discussed in the introduction to this volume. Exploring those limitations in relation to CSR, I argue that by adopting a systemic understanding of organisation, one presumes that outcomes of social activities can be predicted and that managers can (and must) carefully choose the right action to arrive at the desired outcome. This approach disregards the interdependence of intentions and histories of many actors that participate in any act of CSR. This conventional systems-based understanding of CSR has led to a stream of research, the intention of which is to establish a (positive) relationship between social activities and financial performance, as a means of lending legitimacy and attractiveness to employees and other stakeholders. And in order to demonstrate this link, those social activities must be accurately measured. This literature is rooted in a 'paradigm that tries to uncover correlations and causal relationships in the social world by using the empirical methods of (natural) science' (Scherer and Palazzo, 2007: 1096). According to this perspective, CSR is perceived as an object created by managers, which is subject to managers' manipulations. As a result, in conventional management thought, the aim of social responsibility is to create an effective 'CSR system' that will assist in achieving one or more of the organisational strategic aims.

Another limitation of the orthodox CSR discourse is the tendency to conceptualise CSR as a generalised abstract idea, thus occluding particular experiences of CSR practitioners. This may lead to the appropriation of CSR as yet another management tool, in which the interest in considering the social and often immeasurable consequences of our actions diminishes. Adopting CSR as one of the tools in the managers' strategic toolbox can be understood as a Weberian 'rational action', one that is 'directed by the strategic, instrumental, calculated pursuit of a specific goal' (Bond and O'Byrne, 2013: 139). In light of the widespread acceptance of NPM by senior managers in HE, it is not surprising that this 'strategic' approach to CSR has also spread into the discourse of social responsibilities of Universities (see Hayter and Cahoy, 2018).

Placing CSR within a managerialist framework can be seen as a significant contributor to 'instrumental CSR', a dominant strand of CSR theories. This approach to CSR led to the 'corporate social responsibility is good for business' narrative, rooted in the neoclassical economic discourse. The idea of 'doing well by doing good' has been heavily promoted by Western corporations, non-governmental organisations (NGOs) and governments in the developing countries. This popular saying refers to the belief that socially responsible behaviour (doing good) leads to increased profits (doing well). Several years ago, I conducted a study of how CSR is understood and practiced in Ukraine. I interviewed executives from large commercial organisations, business owners and academics. I was struck by the disparity between their practice and rhetoric. Many of the executives interviewed mentioned 'business case' as the main motive for adopting CSR, even if the practice discussed had no apparent economic benefit for their organisation. But more surprising was the instrumental approach to CSR by the academics. Perhaps, following 70 years of the Soviet rule with its economic rationale, anything remotely associated with socialism is rejected in favour of capitalist vernacular. One of the study participants aptly noted that 'CSR is capitalism's mechanism to win over socialism'.[1] It is, therefore, possible that by adopting CSR rhetoric, those executives aim to align themselves with what they perceive as a 'proper' capitalist discourse. It is not surprising then that one executive explained his understanding of CSR as:

> the means for the company to contribute to the community, where we live and work, in a way that also has, of course, *a benefit for the company*. What is said at any CSR conference? 'If you're not doing this, if it has no way to contribute to your business, it's not CSR, it's philanthropy.' (my emphasis)

It is also possible that interviewees exhibited a 'Hawthorne Effect'.[2] They might have given the answers they thought I expected. In either case, the market rationalisation of their socially directed activities demonstrated an overwhelmingly instrumental approach to CSR. Speaking to both academics, NGO managers and corporate executives, I became aware how deeply ingrained in their thinking the mainstream management discourse on CSR had become.

There is very little dissent from this instrumental approach to CSR. One school of thought that provides an alternative understanding is Critical Management Studies (CMS). CMS scholars are not a monolithic block. Some focus on the mainstream CSR rhetoric as perpetuating the capitalist discourse, while others question whose interests are served by social actions and their underpinning motives. Kuhn and Deetz (2008: 191) suggest that 'many critical theorists are sceptical of common CSR interventions and corporations' claims of virtue'. Banerjee questions for whose benefit the CSR research is undertaken, highlighting that the majority of CSR research focuses on the CSR 'providers', leaving the 'consumers' of that research – the practitioners – in the dark as to how CSR initiatives affect society (Banerjee, 2010: 265). A unifying thread across CMS approaches problematises the uncritical acceptance of CSR as a management tool and challenging the managerialist approach, which 'incorporate[s] citizenship activities in order to benefit corporate agendas' (Nyberg et al., 2013: 433).

Although critical of enlisting CSR in the service of the large corporates, CMS scholars share some of the shortcomings of the dominant CSR discourse. First, both address CSR and related concepts from a systems perspective – discussing CSR as an object separate from the people who practice it and managers as its outside operators. Second, similar to the critics of managerialism in public sector, both mainstream and critical writers tend to discuss CSR in abstract terms, favouring generalisations and avoiding specifics. What is lacking in both camps are reflective accounts of CSR practice.

To summarise, so far I have argued that the demand for CSR metrics has increased in order to demonstrate a specific and measurable contribution to organisational strategic objectives in keeping with the dominant discourse of managerialism. Public sector organisations are not exempt from 'neoliberal anxieties' (Morrish, 2014), their senior executives have enthusiastically adopted NPM ideas 'inspired by the private sector' (Hyndman and Liguori, 2016: 7), including tools to aid management in the standardisation of and reporting on CSR.

But how is a practitioner to choose amongst the many assessment tools on offer? Theoretically, she can select an instrument (e.g. triple bottom line [Elkington, 2018] or ISO 26000) and apply it to her organisation. However, applying any of the management tools to a particular practice is problematic. All assessment schemes are generalised and ambiguous, and issues 'often arise at the interface of general ideas and local practice' (Jutterstrom and Norberg, 2013: 166). So far, little attention has been paid to how a practitioner deals with the issues that may arise in the particular adoption of general ideas. Despite increasing concerns by academic writers and practitioners alike about the Universities (and other public service organisations) falling victims to the NPM mentality, less attention has been paid to the processes in which this managerialisation arises and quantification of the public services takes place. In the narrative below, I explore being in the midst of attempts to standardise my practice and reflect on how and why a particular metric was adopted to assess the contribution of the CSR Unit I managed to the university's strategic plan.

To Measure or Not to Measure?

After years of sporadic and dispersed contributions to the social issues in the community, which mainly focused on volunteering, the Business School Dean decided to set up a Unit dedicated to organising the efforts of social engagement under one roof. When the role of the Director of the Unit was advertised, I felt it was written for me. I had lectured in CSR, in my teaching I was engaged with the local community, which I considered an example of CSR, and outside of work I engaged in volunteering and other civic activities. After the interview I was told that my passion for the topic was palpable, and I was appointed to the role.

Like any job descriptions, which are generalised aspirations about the specific role, this one was vague enough to allow individual interpretation regarding particularising of the general 'engaging with the community'. I became excited about the opportunity to 'consider potential developments in the Business School curricula that may involve charitable organisations' (Taylor, 2009). Encouraged by this and other initiatives, such introduction of Social Responsibility as one of the six graduate attributes,[3] I interpreted the new role as the opportunity to finally include social, not just economic goals, in the Business School provision. Having understood the role in such lofty terms, I started with eagerness and enthusiasm, idealism and naiveté. Having previously managed a sales and marketing department in the private sector, I was familiar with, and expected, the game-playing and politics of organisations. I had not expected that the Dean's excitement for CSR during my interview would quickly wane as it became yet another managerial initiative. I was hoping that as a member of a university, a public service organisation, I would be able to contribute to the betterment of the community. After all, I perceived the very existence of the Unit as demonstrating the Business School managers' commitment to social responsibility. I had not expected the University's senior managers narrowing perspective of CSR, something which I perceived as a moral obligation of managers and employees in any organisation in any sector of the economy, to what I felt was a more cynical manipulation of something I held dear, in the service of NPM.

I also had not expected to take an active part in this transformation. I had always been a vocal critic of managerialism in general and in HE in particular, which often leads to a demand for measuring and quantifying, a desire for standardising and creating reporting processes and procedures which aim to homogenise highly diverse and creative activities in order to manage at a distance. Starting the new role, I was hoping to create a unit in which like-minded colleagues would seek creative ways to support our community. I was not as naïve as to ignore the need to demonstrate that the work of the Unit was closely aligned with the aims of the university. But I was naive enough to believe that the Unit, which had been created to contribute to the community, would not be assessed only by narrow metrics. Being idealistic, I was more concerned with doing good, rather than with doing well. I aimed for the work of the Unit to contribute to the community and was not overly concerned with returns, monetary or reputational. The Dean left me to manage the Unit as I thought fit. I chose to understand this lack of interference as an expression of trust and not of lack of interest. Leaving me to my own devices also meant I had to initiate the monthly reporting meetings. Those meetings included productive discussions, during which we considered projects and activities we were involved with, deliberated future possibilities and explored the resources we may require to continue our work. When colleagues asked (admittedly, not too often) about the financial contribution of the Unit, I would jokingly say that it was the only Unit in the business school whose role is to spend and not to earn money.

In anticipation of being accused of riding the proverbial high moral horse, I would like to emphasise that I did not object to public scrutiny, nor to the managerial oversight of my work. Throughout the years of managing the Unit, I also welcomed the opportunity to regularly discuss with colleagues, beneficiaries and other stakeholders the proposed ways to develop the Unit. Often, my suggestions were challenged, and although bruising to my ego, I learned to accept the majority of those challenges as constructive engagement rather than as affront to my professionalism and moral stance. My criticism of standardisation of work in the community stems from my objection to short-termism and narrow focus on metrics, while ignoring the long-term impact of social engagement, which often could not be reduced to numerical data. Not being involved with activities regulated and monitored by the Higher Education Funding Council for England (HEFCE), which sets metrics of achievement for all UK Universities, resulted in a lack of close attention from the managers; and being a new initiative, I had very little guidance, which allowed me to explore various ways of working. Immediately after being appointed to the new role, I met with the newly appointed Pro-Vice Chancellor (PVC) responsible for Community Engagement. This role was also new, and he seemed very excited about the creation of the Unit and the ways I proposed to develop it. Within a short period of time, the work of the Unit was being appropriated by him whenever there arose a need to demonstrate entrepreneurship and innovation – often, I would be asked to talk to the visitors or write a 'case study' for a press release about our work.

In hindsight, my insisting on monthly meetings with the Dean was a wise decision, as the bliss of working without using measurement tools to assess our social contribution turned out to be short-lived. I had not heard from the PVC for several months after our initial meeting. Until one day I received an e-mail asking me to comment on the Unit's part of the first annual Community Engagement Strategy draft. Seeing the Unit placed first on his six Key Areas was very flattering, especially his adopting my description of the Unit and our goals almost verbatim. But as I read the next paragraph, alarm bells went off in my head:

PERFORMANCE INDICATORS:

> the number of charities being supported each year;
> the total value of fundraising carried out for those charities through the Unit.[4]

During the first year of managing the Unit, I was not concerned with measurements and metrics. Being naively idealistic, I believed that contributing to the community should not attract numerical values. I thought that by trying to measure the 'value of fundraising' in monetary terms, the social value of such activity – not only to the benefactors of the fundraising, but also to the organisers, the participants and the wider community – would be lost. On seeing the e-mail, I felt extremely disappointed. After a year of engaging with several organisations in the community, embedding projects involving social responsibility into the taught modules for undergraduate and graduate students, creating spaces for co-operation between various not-for-profits, facilitating volunteering and placements, raising awareness amongst colleagues – I felt annoyed that the value of all this work was to be measured solely by the number of charities supported or pounds raised. But realising this was the institutional game, I felt I could either play it or I could quit the role. I loved my role, so decided to play the game. Another realisation was that I would also have to try to have some influence over the rules. I was going to raise the Unit's (and consequently my own) profile, so if the managers wanted 'performance indicators', I was determined to try to exercise some control of what those indicators might include. For the monthly meetings with the Dean I had prepared a short summary of the work, and those reports were easy to retrieve. So, I replied with the following suggestion:

> Dear Stewart,
> I've been considering your question about performance indicators and I think I have a solution. We still put a 'social impact' indicator in the document, but the way to measure it is 'value added' to the organisation. E.g. if we produce a report – the value added would be the cost of buying that report at a going market rate from a consultancy. If the students raise money (fundraising) – that would be the value added. Facilities provided for community events – we will show how much that would cost if they had to hire the venue, etc. So actually we can start measuring impact in money terms, but that way we can measure all output, not just fundraising.
> I'd be happy to hear your thoughts about it.

I felt smug – I avoided a simple reductionist representation of the year's work and at the same time I provided some indicators – coming up with what I believed a win-win solution. Stewart was happy and I managed to promote the Unit without compromising my commitment to avoid reducing our work to a set of performance indicators. In the words of a Russian proverb: 'The wolves are satiated, and the sheep are intact'. What, in my self-righteousness, I failed to realise was that I adopted the very logic I was indignant about – I created a metric, albeit one that suited my purposes. I had begun measuring my activities and those measures addressed the managerialist requirement – narrow, specific and detailed. This method produced a very impressive depiction of the Unit's work, so I did not dwell further on the implications of its use.

The next year, Stewart asked for another brief summary. He remarked how impressed he was with the previous year's method, and I was so flattered that at the first reading, I nearly missed the last sentence:

> I would be able to tell the Board that you will calculate the figure for last year's work and will then use that as a baseline for setting targets.

How could I provide targets? I was not producing widgets or selling cars. I brokered co-operation between people in several organisations. I was building trust, as many of them, having had previous experience with UH, and its bureaucracy, were sceptical of my motives and abilities. Having earned their trust, I was inundated with requests from other organisations referred by them. I was being very careful with promises, and often the engagement would result in a mutual agreement to continue a dialogue rather than in a measurable outcome. How does this way of working align with targets?

I decided to ignore the last statement of that e-mail, hoping the following year Stewart and the Board would forget the targets, in the meantime continuing working as I thought appropriate. Was I discounting the future? Probably. I was overestimating the current convenient way of working and underestimating the possibility of tightening the boundaries of the work of the Unit in the future. After all, disagreeing with a PVC is not a best way to gain friends in the high places.

Another year passed without excessive managerial intervention. The Dean was happy, I gained the promotion I was hoping for, more projects were brokered, more contacts made. I was content with the work progress. Not being particularly fond of reporting, I forgot about the customary timing of the PVC's requests. When it arrived, I was not prepared:

> Many apologies for the short notice, but could you possibly send me a brief update on what the Unit has achieved over the past academic year. If you already have a report which you've produced for other purposes that would be great – I can easily extract what I need. **Ideally** [emphasis in original] a few figures such as number of projects supported, number of students involved, number of client organisations, and total commercial value of the work the Unit has done (as a measure of impact).

I was in the midst of balancing a research project, marking a particularly challenging set of assignments, designing a new module, in addition to the unrealistic demands of the workload – I was too busy, and frankly, not inclined to argue with Stewart. I was content to accommodate this request:

> The Unit supported at least 45 projects/40 client organisations
> Over 250 students involved
> I really struggle to estimate the commercial value of our support to the community, but I guesstimate that it is similar to last year's, so if you are pressed for a figure, I'd say £80,000.

He was pleased:

> That's just right for this level of report.

I breathed a sigh of relief. But at that stage, I started thinking about the need for coming up with a way of reporting that would reflect the quality, not just the quantity of the work. If I failed to do so, I expected that the metrification of the work would continue.

Another year passed, and at the end I was not surprised to see Stewart's e-mail in my Inbox.

> We could probably make the report a bit shorter this year, but the Governors always like to see numerical data, so please don't be afraid to bore them with such information!

I felt like crying and laughing at the same time. I was indignant with the demand for 'numerical data' only. At the same time, I could not stop myself from feeling self-righteous for anticipating this development. I began realising that by acquiescing to the request for standardising, I played the game by the rules I had intended to modify. Stewart and I only communicated by e-mail, so my prompt responses to his reporting requests could have been interpreted as agreeing or even being enthusiastic about quantifying my work. I had never openly objected to this, nor had I attempted to open a discussion about different ways of understanding the work of the Unit. It was easier to be indignant about Stewart's requirements than to acknowledge my contribution to the emerging managerialist discourse.

So this time, still uneasy to ignore what Governors 'always like' and at the same time not happy with reducing the work to an even 'shorter list', I compromised. This time I was aware of the potential implications of this compromise for maintaining the quantifying culture. But I still used the method of the previous year, adjusted for inflation and had arrived at yet another impressive figure, albeit a little lower than the one in the previous year. But I did not produce a shorter report, I itemised the activities. Was I worried about blatantly disregarding the plea for a 'shorter report'? Of course I was, but I was ready to defend my decision. So when the response came, I apprehensively opened my e-mail, only to be surprised by the congratulatory language. The e-mail went to all the contributors to the PVC report, and not only did it not mention my small act of rebellion, it singled out my contribution:

> The Board liked the way in which the financial impact of the Unit had been calculated, and were impressed by the resulting figures. Perhaps we should see if this approach could be applied in other areas of activity. One Board member asked if we knew how much our community engagement costs, and I said that there would be figures for each area of activity, but they hadn't been drawn together. I think we all agreed that this wouldn't be an exact exercise, given the problems of attaching costs to things like voluntary work, or staff who do a range of activities; but I think it would be interesting to get a 'ball park' figure for next year.

So, my not challenging the rules, my attempt to 'modify' them slightly, came back as a boomerang in the form of tighter rules. And even more so, those tightened rules, my creation, are now to be extended to other areas of the University. The transformation from 'let's see how we can measure what you do' to 'we should now apply the rules you set to other areas' was inconspicuous, happening over several years. And I contributed to for this transformation, not just Stewart, or the members of the Board. My responsibility for transforming, what I had perceived as '[a] Unit contributing not only to the charity sector, but to the experience of our students, to the community and creating synergies that will enable us, the BS staff, to give back to society more than any of us, as individuals, can ever hope to' (from my application for the role) into the reductionist management tool was evident. Reducing the stories of human interactions into a set of figures became easy, once the method was created. My responding to Stewart's reporting request by producing a concise set of guidelines was a way of keeping the managers happy and achieving their recognition and praise, allowing me to continue working with minimal managerial intervention. But this way of my responding to Stewart's gesture also led to a standardisation of my reporting and subsequently of the work itself. Reflecting on the previous year or two, I realised that I had begun focusing less on activities which could not be included in the report, prioritising more 'prestigious' engagements.

Having gained an insight into my own contribution to enumeration of what I had considered unmeasurable, I decided to avoid the temptation of continuing to play the game by the same old rules. So the following year, I produced a set of 'highlights' rather than a numerical report. This was a way, albeit minor, to stop my colluding with the managerialist approach to CSR at UH. The amended format of mine was not a full-blown rebellion, as I still couched the narratives in a language palatable to the Board members, but I could not un-realise what I had realised the previous year – my reports were contributing to the UH narrative, and if I wanted to change that narrative, I had to start with my own contribution. I was not a passive victim of the 'system'; I was an active participant in the interactions in which the reporting arose. I had great hopes that my gesture would result in a conversation about the meaning and value of CSR in the UH. So, I was anxious to see what response sending 'Highlights' instead of a report would elicit. A week later, Stewart's e-mail landed in my Inbox:

> The report will be in a new format, at the request of the Chairman of the Governors, so won't need much text. It will relate everything to the 2012 update of the UH Strategic Plan and, in particular, the KPIs on page 55 of that plan. I am hoping that you can give me updated figures and/or brief information about the following (covering the most recent 12 months for which you have data):
> 'Providing support for third sector organisations equivalent to at least £60k per year.' Because of the new format I won't have room for much

text, so will just need to have your estimate of the overall value of the work of the Unit and perhaps a couple of 'highlights' to illustrate its impact on the community – I know it will be hard to choose from all the good examples!

'My rebellion is quashed' was my initial thought reading it. There is no way I would get away from reducing my work to a set of figures. On a second reading, I saw what I missed. It was there, green shoots of success – 'perhaps a couple of "highlights" to illustrate…'. I managed to introduce a small change of tenor to the University reporting. Perhaps not all was not lost.

At the end of that summer, Stewart retired. With his retirement, the role of PVC Community Engagement was retired as well. There were no subsequent requests for annual reports on the SEU activities, so I could not avoid thinking that CSR was being pushed further down the University managers' agenda. For me, it meant progressively small budgets and workload allocations, and several years later, having tired of fighting the windmills, I resigned as well.

The ten years of managing the Unit were challenging and exhilarating. I felt I was doing something valuable, helping those in the community that had been previously overlooked by us at the HBS. I also gained an invaluable experience and insight into what it means to 'manage CSR' in practice.

My Understanding of the Events

Before I proceed making sense of the events, I'd like to provide further context to my narrative. The e-mail exchange took place over five years, and a whole year lapsed between each annual e-mail exchange. Managing the Unit was a fraction of my role, and reporting was a very small part of it. Despite each exchange causing me some annoyance, being busy with teaching and research, and actually promoting and engaging with CSR, my irritation would subside very shortly after each exchange.

Reflecting on my experience brings two things into focus. First is the tendency I am aware of and which comes across clearly in my narrative as well – overwhelming dismissal of my own achievements. I recognise this 'disposition' as perfectionism, 'striving for flawlessness and setting high standards of performance, accompanied by tendencies toward overly critical evaluation of one's behaviours' (Stoeber et al., 2015: 171). In-depth exploration of perfectionism is beyond the scope of this chapter. The reason I highlight it here is the implication of overly critical assessment of one's behaviour to disproportionately highlight what is perceived as negative outcomes and to obscure achievements. Those whose role involves community engagement and promotion of social responsibility may recognise this tendency to insist on the need for defending, what is understood as moral high ground. Taking this rigid moral stance may obscure the everyday politics of organisational life and risks perceiving any compromise as a loss.

Rereading my narrative, I relive the increasingly crushing weight of desperation I felt upon receiving Stewart's e-mails. My emotions spanned from surprise and disappointment at receiving the initial request for producing CSR measures, to self-righteous indignation at 'their' demand for target-setting and 'numerical data', to lamenting my contribution to 'tightening the rules' and finally to exasperation, leading to my leaving the role. What this narrative underrates is the significant contribution to social causes I achieved in the years of managing the Unit. To reiterate, I believe that in my perfectionism, by setting myself an unattainable generalised goal of embracing CSR as part of the Business School everyday activities, an aspiration which may resonate with others in the CSR field, limited the opportunity to appreciate less than grandiose achievements. Focusing on the perceived 'failures', in my case not being able to change the Board members' focus on the numerical outputs of the Unit, also occludes an appreciation of our being astute in navigating the organisational game. Reflecting on the events, I understand my responses to the Board's metrification requests, not only as yielding to their demands, but also as responding in a way that allowed me to continue to do the work I deemed important. Belittling successes obfuscates not just what is actually achieved, but also diverts attention from the processes in which these achievements arise.

The narrative also draws attention to the potential of both amplification and dwindling of many of our actions. In human interdependence it is impossible to predict which initiatives and activities will amplify and take hold in the organisation and which will dissipate. Despite resources allocated to the Unit and significant attention devoted to its reporting, the Unit no longer exists and the few remaining projects are taken up by individual members of staff with no co-ordination between them, nor guidance from the managers. And what seemed at the time as an insignificant chat with two colleagues has expanded into a major presence of a suicide prevention charity in secondary schools in Hertfordshire. At the time of being caught in the multiple conversations related to the work of the Unit, there was no way to anticipate the demise of the former or the incredible success of the latter.

Both successes and failures arise in interdependence of numerous intentions, beliefs, past experiences and future expectations of many actors. This narrative focuses on the negative experiences in order to explore my own participation in the processes of standardisation of social interactions. I chose to reflect on this narrative as the juxtaposition of my general idealistic position (rejecting standardising of CSR) and pragmatic behaviour.

Being caught in the hustle and bustle of work, I became alarmed about CSR reporting only when Stewart mentioned the Board singling out my contribution. Despite finding that e-mail very flattering, it was a defining moment for me. I was shocked into finally realising that I was playing a role in sustaining the standardisation of CSR in my institution, I was contributing to turning what I set out to achieve – a Unit working for the good – into a managerial tool. This development happened slowly enough for me to initially ignore it. In the early stages of managing the Unit, I was indignant about 'their' demands. I was too preoccupied with building my reputation with the senior managers, I was working towards promotion, I was busy. To some readers, these may seem like excuses. But in the midst of being preoccupied with daily routine of work, these were the realities I experienced. The commendation by the Board jolted me to recognise that in the previous years I had failed to acknowledge my lack of reflexivity. I was also caught up in the institutional game. Rereading the e-mail exchange allowed for a detached involvement with the events (Elias, 1956). Exploring my own participation in those events can provide insights into how processes of managerialisation are being developed, sustained and expanded in the organisations.

Although the narrative alludes to enabling constraints of developing the Unit, not having initial guidance about its working, including establishing reporting practices, and indeed without CSR being previously included in the University strategic plan, my experience provided me with a unique opportunity to reflect on the early stages of standardising CSR in a public sector organisation. My active participation in and contribution to the shaping of the reporting is undeniable. What is also undeniable is that the development of measurement activities and the decision about which narratives to include in the reports has been a highly social process.

Metrification as a Social Process

As highlighted previously, in the mainstream literature CSR is addressed as a system subject to managerial manipulation, and consequently CSR reporting is discussed as a system independent of the authors of those reports. For example, in a recent study, Diaz-Carrion et al. (2021) developed an index to compare responsible practices in several countries. The authors describe the criteria for inclusion and weighting in the index, but they do not acknowledge that the criteria itself is socially constructed. They do not reflect on their own interdependencies in choosing the criteria. To emphasise, I do not challenge their methodology; I draw attention to any index being socially constructed. By 'social' I mean recognising that the authors belong to various social groups and their ideas arise in the interactions with different people in those groups. The indices are constructed in the living present (Stacey, 2007) – a subtle, often unrecognised, interlinking of the authors' biases, interest, beliefs and aspirations. However, this social nature of CSR metrics remains undiscussed in the conventional literature. CMS scholars emphasise inevitability of a social context for any idea to take hold. Their critique of the reification of ideas or framing the ideas as independent of processes of human interaction focuses on the embedding of the ideas in organisations. In their analysis, however, the processes of the ideas' emergence remain obscure.

CSR development and CSR reporting in the mainstream literature is theorised reflecting a *homo clausus* (the closed man) approach to social interactions. Western thought privileges this understanding of a person as an isolated creator of knowledge, according to Elias (1956). His idea of the evolution of knowledge is based on understanding people as *homines aperti* (open people), individuals that are interlinked with each other. *[N]o person's knowledge has its beginning in him or herself*. Our thoughts ideas, understandings – all our experiences are extensions of the thoughts, ideas and understandings of many others. We stand on the shoulders of others – giants and dwarfs alike. The narrative in the previous section points out to that interconnectedness, not just of Stewart, the Board members and myself, but of our previous experiences and future expectations, which influences our decisions. Mine were influenced by my previous interactions with senior managers in this and other institutions, in which I learned what is valued and accepted as evidence of work completed, by my expectations of promotion and what this may depend on and from my inability to divorce from the managerialist way of thinking, which had been developed through many years of working and studying in that tradition. I can only attest to my own attitudes, but it is safe to assume that others' attitudes also arose in previous experiences. Understanding the development of the CSR reporting as happening in the living present means accepting that I did not divine my suggestion for reporting, but it evolved in the processes of interacting with others and recognising what might be important for them (or not!) and to me. The narrative highlights our being caught in these processes arising in mutual interdependence:

> more and more individuals, tend to become dependent on each other for their security and the satisfaction of their needs in ways which, for the greater part, surpass the comprehension of those involved.
>
> (Elias, 1956: 232)

Our interdependence with others is inevitable, and the constraints arising in this interdependence are often felt like an external force. In our everyday life, we 'cannot help being preoccupied with the urgent, narrow and parochial problems' (ibid.). And this being caught up in the immediate, often blinds us to our participation in this 'external force'. Being deeply involved with various demands of my job, reading the annual e-mail from Stewart landing in my Inbox, my immediate reaction would be becoming annoyed with 'them' – the Board, the managers, Stewart – for being so narrowly focused. Being preoccupied with addressing the immediate pressures, needs and expectations, it was difficult to take a more detached stance and to appreciate my contribution to the processes of standardising and measuring my practice. On reflecting with others on my practice, I have come to appreciate that I was not the victim of others' doings. Neither was I a villain in this narrative. I was a player in the organisational game, being influenced by its rules and influencing them at the same time.

Drawing on the insights from the perspective of complex responsive processes of relating, I understand the processes reflected upon in the narrative, not just as a response to a request from a senior manager, but as our way of making sense of the aims and the work of the Unit. It is plausible that similar pressures were experienced in some form by the Board members too, as they had to demonstrate efficiency while developing University processes and procedures. These processes are social and political. They are social because no single individual was acting independently of the contemporary, future and historical others. Emirbayer and Mische (1998: 963) argue that the action of the individual can only be understood in the social and temporal contexts as a:

> temporally embedded process of social engagement, informed by the past (in its habitual aspect), but also oriented toward the future (as a capacity to imagine alternative possibilities) and toward the present (as a capacity to contextualize past habits and future projects with the contingencies of the moment).

They are political, in the sense of being concerned with power relations, because power 'is a characteristic of human relationships – of *all* human relationships' (Elias, 1978: 74, emphasis in the original). My experiences of creating the Unit's 'Key Performance Indicators' is congruent with Sethi's (1972) insight into the social auditing process that acknowledges the political nature of any such endeavour.

As alluded above, it is not difficult to imagine that my experience of the demands for standardising was not dissimilar to the experiences of others. Reflecting on the period of serving as a school governor, I gained useful insights into the pressures of reporting processes from a board member's perspective. Shortly after becoming a Director of the Unit, I volunteered to join a Board of Governors of the local primary school. For five years, I served as a Community Governor (similar to an independent member of a University Board of Governors, having no prior vested interest in the school), and in that role I participated in discussions related to the setting of goals and objectives for the school and establishing policies and targets for achieving those objectives. Although it was only a small school (fewer than 200 pupils), our discussion could not focus on each student and every activity – it was not in our remit. We had to take a 'global perspective'. Our discussions were on 'aggregates', for example, the school SAT achievements or the teachers' reports on the entire year group and the short- and long-term targets for the entire school. In his book *Seeing Like a State*, anthropologist James C. Scott describes how taking such perspective requires simplifications, and those simplifications 'are observations of only those aspects of social life that are of official interest' (Scott, 1998: 80). He identifies five main characteristics of those simplifications, which are often represented as facts. Those facts are utilitarian, documentary, static, aggregate and standardised. Reading Scott's description, I felt he was talking about my experience:

> The process by which standardized facts susceptible to aggregation are manufactured seems to require at least three steps. The first... is the creation of common units of measurement or coding ... In the next step, each item or instance falling within a category is counted and classified according to the new unit of assessment. Each fact must be recuperated and brought back on stage, as it were, dressed in a new uniform...One arrives, finally, at synoptic facts that are useful to officials.
>
> (ibid: 80)

The further the 'official' is removed from the 'field', the more the details are blurred, until they are finally dispensed with. As a school governor, an 'official', I was a party to 'inflicting' standardisation on the teachers. In this process, the pupils were classified according to their achievements, their belonging to a demographic group and other impersonal categories. And because the goals and objectives were considered on aggregate, we, the governors, were interested in the aggregated reporting. I should not have been surprised, then, when, as the Unit director, I was at the receiving end of such standardisation. But, as already stated, at the time I was too involved in the immediate actions to reflect on the parallels between the two roles.

Reflecting on the experience of responding to requests for standardised, enumerated reporting and drawing on the ideas of James C. Scott provides an insight into how the demand for counting and measuring of social activities is arising. Globally renowned indexes, similar to the more local measurements of social activities, are always created locally, in microinteractions. These measurements, which can be understood as themes and patterns of relating that have emerged, are likely to constrain and enable people who are acting locally.

As the measurements arise in processes of co-operation and competition, the players constrain and enable each other through power relations and make arguments to persuade each other to take one course of action or another. The course (or courses, in case of CSR indexes) of action that emerge may be experienced by individual practitioners as externally imposed, but this conduct can only exist if we, in our local interactions, continue to sustain it.

Summary

In this chapter, I draw attention to my experience of participating in the processes in which the measuring of CSR has arisen in my university. The aim of turning the spotlight on myself as a participant in the processes in which reporting on the Unit I managed arose is not self-flagellation or self-aggrandising. Although my narrative focuses on a somewhat narrow area of practice, I believe that my reflection will resonate with other managers in the public sector, who would be able to relate to the experience of being caught in, and the need to navigate, organisational politics.

The political nature of working in organisations may seem counterintuitive to practicing CSR and working in public sector, especially in organisations whose moral aims and values we espouse. Having some of CSR initiatives rejected might be perceived as rejection of the organisation's moral aim. And engaging in political games to sustain those values might seem an affront to morality, resulting in petulant withdrawal. Becoming more reflexive might help practitioners mature politically, in order to continue engaging with those whose particularisation of generalised organisational moral aims differs from ours.

I have been an ardent opponent to the managerialisation of HE in general and in CSR in particular, expressing this view in my teaching and my research; however, when faced with the reporting requirements, I ended up sustaining the very patterns of interactions I have been so vehemently criticising. Although I professed to hold an idealised notion of CSR, my actions have exposed me as a pragmatist. And being pragmatic meant adapting to the rules of organisational game and adapting these rules at the same time. Scott's (1998) discussion of how the drawing of the maps impacts reconceptualising of reality resonates with my practice. My focusing on the activities that were easier to measure is an example of how standardisation of reporting also impacts one's understanding of reporting and one's practice.

I recognise that there is more than one way of interpreting the email exchange introduced in this chapter. One can read it as self-righteous responses to legitimate requests of the Board as refusing to play by the rules of organisational game when it does not suit one's own goals. Multiple interpretations of events are inevitable and support a call for becoming more reflexive.

By being reflexive, I suggest others can benefit from my experience and recognise sooner when they are being drawn into managerialising their practice. Rather than feeling powerless and being done to, by being reflective, managers would be able to recognise that like other managerial processes, quantification of and reporting on their practice arise in interdependence of many organisational players. We may not be the main perpetrators, but we are also not helpless victims. Our actions matter, and although we cannot predict their outcomes, we cannot expect management practices to change, if we collude with those practices by not challenging them.

Notes

1. Bowen claimed that the 'assumption of social responsibilities, therefore, is at least a partial alternative to socialism' (1953: 28). The participant, by his own admission, had not read Bowen.
2. 'Hawthorne Effect' refers to studies' participants responding to being observed rather than to various stimuli (Landsberger, 1958).
3. At the time the Unit was established, the University published the list of the 'graduate attributes' – a set of attributes all our graduates are supposed to develop during their studies 'to equip them for life in a complex and rapidly changing world' (UH, 2021).
4. In this narrative, all quotes are from internal correspondence between the PVC and me are verbatim, except the identifying names and titles.

References

Banerjee, S. B. 2010. Governing the Global Corporation: A Critical Perspective. *Business Ethics Quarterly*, 20, 265–274.

Bond, C. & O'Byrne, D. 2013. If It Moves, Measure It: Taylor's Impact on UH Higher Education. *In:* Evans, C. & Holmes, L. (eds.) *Re-Tayloring Management: Scientific Management a Century on*. Farnham: Ashgate Publishing Ltd, 137–153.

Bowen, H. R. 2013/1953. *Social Responsibilities of the Businessman*. IowaCity: University of Iowa Press.

Brown, E. & Cloke, J. 2009. Corporate Social Responsibility in Higher Education. *ACME: An International E-Journal for Critical Geographies*, 8, 474–483.

Diaz-Carrion, R., López-Fernández, M. & Romero-Fernandez, P. M. 2021. Constructing an Index for Comparing Human Resources Management Sustainability in Europe. *Human Resource Management Journal*, 31, 12–142.

Diefenbach, T. 2009. New Public Management in Public Sector Organizations: The Dark Sides of Managerialistic 'Enlightenment'. *Public Administration*, 87 (4), 892–909.

Elias, N. 1956. Problems of Involvement and Detachment. *The British Journal of Sociology*, 7, 226–252.

Elias, N. 1978. *What Is Sociology*. London: Hutchinson & Co (Publishers) Ltd.

Elkington, J. 2018. 25 Years ago I Coined the Phrase "Triple Bottom Line." Here's Why It's Time to Rethink It. [Online] *Harvard Business Review Digital Articles*. Available: https://web-s-ebscohost-com.ezproxy.herts.ac.uk/bsi/detail/detail?vid=8&sid=6f79e883-a080-4504-bc52ad4d29124a70%40redis&bdata=JnNpdGU9YnNpLWxpdmU%3d#AN=130449047&db=bth [Accessed 7 December 2021].

Emirbayer, M. & Mische, A. 1998. What Is Agency? *American Journal of Sociology*, 103, 962–1023.

Gindis, D. 2009. From Fictions and Aggregates to Real Entities in the Theory of the Firm. *Journal of Institutional Economics*, 5, 25–46.

Hayter, C. S. & Cahoy, D. R. (2018) Toward a Strategic View of Higher Education Social Responsibilities: A Dynamic Capabilities Approach. *Strategic Organization*, 16(1), 12–34.

Hyndman, N. & Liguori, M., 2016. Public Sector Reforms: Changing Contours on an NPM Landscape. *Financial Accountability & Management*, 32(1), 5–32.

Jutterstrom, M. & Norberg, P. (eds.). 2013. *CSR as a Management Idea: Ethics in Practice*. Cheltenham: Edward Elgar.

Kuhn, T. & Deetz, S. 2008. Critical Theory and Corporate Social Responsibility: Can/Should We Get beyond Cynical Reasoning. *In:* Crane, A., Mcwilliams, A., Matten, D., Moon, J. & Siegel, D. (eds.) *The Oxford Handbook of Corporate Social Responsibility*. Oxford: Oxford University Press, 173–196.

Landsberger, H. A. 1958. *Hathorne Revisited*. Ithaca: The New York State School of Industrial and Labor Relations.

Micklethwait, J. & Wooldridge, A. 2003. *The Company: A Short History of a Revolutionary Idea*. New York: Random House.

Morrish, L. 2014. *Institutional Discourse and the Cult(ure) of Managerialism* [Online]. Discover Society. Available: http://www.discoversociety.org/2014/05/06/institutional-discourse-and-the-culture-of-managerialism/ [Accessed 19 May 2014].

Muller, J. Z. 2019. *The Tyranny of Metrics*, Princeton, NJ: Princeton University Press.

Nyberg, D., Spicer, A. & Wright, C. 2013. Incorporating Citizens: Corporate Political Engagement with Climate Change in Australia. *Organization*, 20, 433–453.

Parker, L. 2008. Old Professors Never Die. *Accounting, Auditing & Accountability Journal*, 21, 753–754.

Sethi, S. P. 1972. Getting a Handle on the Social Audit. *Business & Society Review/Innovation*, 31.

Scherer, A. G. & Palazzo, G. 2007. Toward a Political Conception of Corporate Responsibility: Business and Society Seen from a Habermasian Perspective. *Academy of Management Review*, 32, 1096–1120.

Scott, J. C. 1998. *Seeing Like a State: How Certain Schemes to Improve the Human Condition Have Failed*. New Haven, CT and London: Yale University Press.

Simonet, D. 2013. The New Public Management Theory in the British Health Care System: A Critical Review. *Administration and Society*, 47(7), 802–826.

Stacey, R. D. 2007. The Challenge of Human Interdependence: Consequences for Thinking about the Day to Day Practice of Management in Organizations. *European Business Review*, 19, 292–302.

Stoeber, J., Haskew, A. E. & Scott, C. 2015. Perfectionism and Exam Performance: The Mediating Effect of Task-approach Goals. *Personality and Individual Differences*, 74, 171–176.

Taylor, M. 2009. Email to bs-school@herts.ac.uk list, 28 May 2009.

UH 2021. *University of Hertfordshire Graduate Attributes.* [Online] Available: https://www.herts.ac.uk/about-us/student-charter/graduate-attributes [Accessed 21 July 2020].

Van Oosterhout, J. & Heugens, P. M. A. R. 2008. Much Ado about Nothing: A Conceptual Critique of CSR. *In:* Crane, A., Mcwilliams, A., Matten, D., Moon, J. & Siegel, D. (eds.) *The Oxford Handbook of Corporate Social Responsibility.* Oxford: Oxford University Press, 197–223.

7

REFLECTIONS ON HOW DIFFERING VALUES AND POWER RELATIONSHIPS IMPACT ON THE LOCAL IMPLEMENTATION OF CENTRAL POLICY DIRECTIVES IN THE UK NATIONAL HEALTH SERVICE

Sheila Marriott

This story begins when the Trust Chief Executive Officer (CEO) asked the Director of Nursing, Jane, to 'do something' about the Children's Directorate in a large teaching hospital trust in the UK. The Directorate was consistently overspent, missed surgical waiting time targets, and the CEO was exasperated. Given their repetitive justifications for poor performance and his knowledge of how the ever-tightening noose of missed targets had damaged many an up-and-coming Chief Executive, it was unsurprising that the CEO was concerned.

I was working as a healthcare consultant when Jane contacted me to discuss their concerns. Although there was no evidence that the quality of care was poor on the children's wards, she was concerned about their management.

She asked me to help understand why targets were being missed, the budget was overspent and why nurse recruitment was poor, the latter leading to low staffing levels. We had worked together before, and she knew that my style of work was to reflect on what was happening in the day-to-day functioning of the workplace rather than producing improvement and development plans. My previous assignments involved talking with staff to help understand how they were making sense of the situations they found themselves in. I was clear that there was no 'magic bullet' about the way I worked. Nevertheless, Jane had noticed that the conversations I was involved in encouraged staff to reflect on their contribution to the issues, which sometimes presented opportunities for more creative ways of working together.

Jane described the relationship between the directorate manager and the lead registered nurse (RN) as 'working from different value bases'. I explored what she thought this meant. She described the primary motivation of one staff member as focused on achieving their key performance indicators, particularly waiting times for surgery. The other was more motivated by the need to provide a child and family centred clinical environment. The Clinical Director, in charge of the unit, rarely appeared to get involved in the day-to-day management of the service. Jane invited me to meet the staff and visit the Children's Directorate to try and understand what the problems appeared to be.

I met the Directorate Manager Tim, an enthusiastic young man who had responsibility for the waiting times for operations. This was a key performance indicator for the CEO, as part of the overall performance of the Trust in line with national targets. Tim raised concerns about the ability of his Nurse Manager colleague, Helen, who he felt was a competent clinical nurse and a very kind and caring person, but not a good manager. These shortcomings had led to staffing shortages due to poor recruitment practices. This resulted in bed closures with an adverse impact on the length of the waiting lists for surgery, which, he added, was not good for the well-being of sick children. He had tried to help by devising action plans, but nothing seemed to improve.

Tim confided that this was impacting on his personal reputation with the CEO, and although he didn't say it out loud, it was apparent he was concerned about his career prospects. He got on well with the Clinical Director, who left him 'in charge of things' he said. This was an interesting comment as his role was of equal seniority to Helen's.

Helen was a registered Children's Nurse who had qualified at the local university and been in the role for many years. When the staffing numbers were low, she worked clinical shifts resulting in being unavailable for some directorate meetings, which annoyed Tim. She described Tim as an ally and thought he had tried to help her, but his focus on planning had left her feeling subjugated, powerless and inadequate. She also did not trust him. She conceded that his plans were sometimes useful but did not associate Tim's plans with improving the care of children. The disparity between the two managers about the way in which they perceived 'improving the care of children' appeared to be a significant factor.

Finally, she stated, with considerable energy, that she was sick of all the changes that were constantly being imposed, she was 'not a bean counter' – concluding that she was not interested in meeting targets to make the children's unit look good, saying, 'My focus is to make sure that children get properly looked after'. As she dashed off to solve another staffing crisis, I was mindful of the paradox between her description of Tim as an ally, yet at the same time she felt dominated and powerless. After meeting the two managers, Jane's comments about their differing values were becoming more apparent and these were evidently causing considerable conflict within their relationship.

My initial thoughts were that both managers believed that they had the children's interests at heart. Long waiting times were a problem that both would agree needed addressing. The challenge appeared to be how the performance management ideologies were taken up using metrics and league tables in unhelpful ways. Stacey (2003) argues that idealised or cult values become functional values, made concrete, in the everyday interactions in the workplace. In the health service, a cult value would be 'family centred care' or 'improving quality and outcomes', to which workers would be expected to conform. The operationalising of these cult values brings conflict and uncertainty into the workplace as people interpret them in differing ways.

Tim showed me around the unit as Helen was busy and took me to visit a separate surgical Day Care unit shared between adult and children's services. Working within this facility were nurses registered with the Nursing and Midwifery Council (NMC) in the field of adult care and RNs registered in the care of children. The education, training and expertise acquired for each specialism is different.

The Children's Nurses worked a 12-hour shift exclusively on the Day Care Unit. I asked what happened if children were too unwell to be discharged at the end of the shift when the Children's Nurses went home. I noticed Tim gazing at his shoes in a rather reticent manner before responding, rather vaguely, that this rarely happened. I was puzzled by his hesitancy and later in the day I asked Helen the same question. She assured me that this very rarely happened, and the children would be transferred to the children's in-patient surgical ward overnight. This would impact on the beds available for children requiring longer hospital stays and have significant consequences to the in-patient waiting list targets. I queried if the agency's Children's Nurses could cover the day unit's night shift. Helen replied that this extra expenditure would impact on the already overspent budget and would irritate Tim.

I asked Helen how well she worked with Tim. She appeared flustered by the question, uttering that she avoided Tim when she could. Helen went on to say that they did not have a lot in common, she found him ambitious and not really interested in the care of children. I commented that the Clinical Director, in charge of the directorate, seemed very engaged with his clinical workload, leaving potential opportunities for inventiveness in the way they managed the directorate. Helen replied that every day was a staffing challenge, she constantly worried about Tim undermining her and did not see any opportunities for creativity. As Helen left for her next meeting, she claimed that she had a long-standing working relationship with the Clinical Director, but saw little of him in recent times as he appeared more involved with Tim.

As I reflected on the morning and the high numbers of children receiving day care, it seemed unusual that some children would not recover well enough to go home on the same day. I spent time talking to staff, listening to conversations, observing behaviours, and whilst recognising that my presence would impact on their usual patterns of work and conversations, I hoped to gain some understanding of how the unit functioned.

I remained curious about the Day Care ward. I noticed how closely the Children's Nurses worked with their Adult Nurse colleagues and how Tim seemed to be their key contact for the Children's Directorate rather than Helen. Tim also had a good relationship with the surgeons and appeared to work well with all the nursing staff on the Day Care Unit.

After a few days, I decided to meet the night staff, as the routines and ways of working are often different at night-time. On entering the Day Care

Unit, I was disappointed to find three children requiring overnight care. They were too unwell to be discharged, needed overnight observation and were being cared for by Adult Nurses not registered in the care of children. They said this was a regular occurrence and explained that Tim had an agreement with the surgeons that the Adult Nurses would care for the children as they 'only needed babysitting'. When I asked what happened if children became acutely ill, it appeared that Tim had arranged for the surgeons to be informed but not the Children's Directorate staff.

I decided to call Tim at 11pm at night. As an RN (child branch), I also work under the NMC Code of Conduct and needed to ensure that the children were cared for by appropriately trained staff overnight now that I was aware of the anomaly I had stumbled upon. There was capacity for a nurse to move from the children's ward to the Day Care Unit that night. Tim reluctantly agreed and we met the following day along with Jane the Director of Nursing and Helen the Directorate Nurse Manager.

It was an uncomfortable meeting and I made it clear that I did not want to reproach anyone but wanted to understand the thinking behind the arrangements and where the level of accountability lay for the well-being of the children. Both Jane and Helen said they were unaware that children were staying overnight or of any staffing agreements. Tim said angrily that he was accountable, but the staffing shortages meant there were never enough beds open to achieve the number of operations required. He had an agreement with the surgeons and Adult Nurses, which enabled him to achieve the waiting list targets, and was struggling to see how his solution had significantly compromised professional and clinical standards.

We began a series of conversations that turned out to be confrontational and hostile as we explored Tim and Helen's working relationship. I was clear that I was not a counsellor or psychotherapist, but wanted to work with them on their relationship and how they avoided confronting their frustrations and anxieties whilst under pressure from so many competing demands.

As I reflected on the situation, it became clear that the conflict within the managers' day-to-day relationship had led to the emergence of a potential patient safety issues. As a consultant, I wondered what was preventing them from dealing with their difficulties and why there was such a stand-off in relations.

As I pondered on this question further, I recalled the initial conversation with Jane. She had contacted me about the CEO's concerns about the

Children's Directorate's poor management of performance targets and the clash between the two managers. After speaking with Tim and Helen, both had a view as to why the other was behaving in a certain way or would behave in a given set of circumstances. It seemed that in the interweaving of their intentions on how best to do 'good', they created a situation that put children at risk.

Although the focus of attention for the situation centred on Tim and Helen, other staff were likely to have known about the arrangements. The day-care-registered Adult Nurses would have known that they were not qualified to care for children. The Director of Nursing (an RN), and the Clinical Director, must have known that every child requiring Day Care treatment would not be fit for discharge on the day of operation. The lack of inquiry or intervention of these two senior managers particularly enabled them to withdraw themselves and by remaining distant, the spotlight centred on the two more junior managers.

In many hospitals, the blueprint for managing the care of patients requiring minor surgery is to admit patients into a specialised Day Care facility. This was the scheme organised within this hospital and it was decided to accommodate the care of children requiring minor surgery within this format. Rather than create a bespoke system of working pertinent to the local situation, it seemed logical to use a blueprint, a tried-and-tested plan, which enabled staff to 'focus on the tangible products of conversation, the organisational designs, performance profiles, business models, strategic frameworks, action plans, lists and categories with which we seek to grasp the reified complexities of organisational life' (Shaw 2002, p. 10).

Tim was well versed in 'tangible products of conversation' (ibid.) given his rationalist approach to the waiting list situation. He implemented what he considered to be a tried-and-tested national blueprint to reduce waiting times. To Helen, the waiting list targets represented everything she despised in instrumentalising an approach to the care of children. However, by disengaging from anything to do with performance targets, she had unwittingly contributed to an unsafe situation.

The creation of systems and formulation of plans to organise healthcare in the public sector is a very complex activity. Characterising healthcare as a system has been the dominant way of thinking for many decades and will be considered in the next section.

A Systems Approach to Management

Systems thinking has had a profound impact on the way that organisations are understood. This way of understanding the National Health Service (NHS) has prevailed for decades and has impacted the thinking, structures and processes across the Health Service. Taylor (1911] 1967) wrote extensively about scientific management in the early 20th century and is cited as the 'founder of scientific management' (Jackson 2000, p. 27; Pugh and Hickson 1989, p. 90). Taylor's 'scientific management' was based in engineering. It involved the systematic observation and measurement of fundamental tasks along with their underpinning management systems, but was criticised as 'reducing workers to the level of efficiently functioning machines' (Pugh and Hickson 1989, p. 93).

Systems thinking was further developed by Ashby (1956) and Wiener (1948) into cybernetics. In cybernetic systems, goals are set as pre-reflected targets that are regarded as optimum for the functioning of the system: a thermostat on a radiator is a cybernetic device. The characteristics of this approach when taken up in organisations include setting targets and other performance measures which are perceived as a 'given' and not questioned by practitioners. These objectives are reviewed and scrutinised by groups, such as senior managers, Trust Board members or even external agencies, who apply these rules or controls to the domain of work understood as a system, and draw conclusions as to what needs to be accomplished next. Current outcomes are compared with anticipated targets, and managers/ directors use the information consistently to correct towards the original target.

Stacey and Griffin (2006) contend that there is an implicit assumption that public sector organisations, 'even those as large as the NHS, are actually cybernetic systems and can be operated as such' (Stacey and Griffin 2006, p. 30). In the NHS, goals are set by government, which then measures the hospitals' performance against these goals. It is the function of the regulator (or hospital organisations) to monitor and control the environment to reduce instability and ensure that action is taken to reduce any variance in performance from the set targets.

In my work to support Helen and Tim to make sense of how their daily interactions had led to the problems, it became clear how Tim used the tried-and-tested blueprint for adult patients to reduce the waiting list for children. Helen, as discussed earlier, was indifferent to the notion of performance planning. This brought significant challenge within the management team and their performance reflected on the overall success of the hospital.

In Health Services, recently there has been a movement away from a strictly cybernetic approach towards an interpretive systems approach, which is frequently referred to as 'soft systems thinking' (Jackson 2000, p. 211), based on the work of Checkland (1978). The principles of soft systems thinking include a focus on people or agency rather than the organisation understood as a system. It involves reviewing process and skills and concentrates on perceptions, values, beliefs and interests. People are seen as having free will rather than being a mechanistic component within the system. Across the NHS, there has been a change over time as clinicians organise their work in a more patient-focused way, challenging a more 'automated' approach.

March (2007) argues that people find it natural to interpret their choices on a presumption of human purpose and have invented terminologies associated with values, needs, objectives, goals, aspiration and drives. Targets and performance management are understood to be a cybernetic approach to managing the NHS. In this context, the human agency and purpose, as proposed by March, is illustrated clearly in the NHS Oversight framework (2019) where the focus is on a new framework where local performance will be set against a core set of national requirements at system and/or organisational level (ibid., para 33). These will include the quality of care, population health, financial performance and sustainability and delivery of national standards (ibid., para 8).

So, the reliance on thinking about the organisation as a system remains, but the boundaries now include the broader social and political dimensions to achieve performance targets. The 2019 NHS Plan suggests a 'reorientation away from principally relying on arms-length regulation and performance management to supporting service improvement and transformation across systems and within providers' (NHS Plan 2019, para 7.7). Nevertheless, the mainstream thinking in healthcare still focuses on the expectation that national standards be implemented, measured, monitored and corrective action taken to rectify discrepancies.

Williams asserts that 'leaders are the local advocates of macro policies as they are the energisers of processes of control designed to ensure that others enact behaviours that are consistent and compliant with respect to the wider policy orientation of their service' (Williams 2005, p. 146). Note the focus on the terms 'control', 'enacting behaviours', 'consistent' and 'compliant' in this sentence. There is clearly no suggestion of opportunities for creative thinking in their role as local advocates of macro policies. As Briggs (2022) in this volume points out, 'deviation from documented "best practice" is viewed harshly; practitioners learn early that being right (as opposed, for example, to be wise or creative) is crucial to their success' (Briggs 2022, p.22 in this volume)

The CEO and Tim were both anxious about the threat of admonishment from the wider NHS and regulators. NHS managers are constrained by the threat of sanctions, which is legitimised through the institutionalisation of the authority of government and through the monitoring of performance by agencies such as the Care Quality Commission (CQC). They also feared that poor leagues table results would give rise to 'naming and shaming' on an organisational and personal level. A problem with performance metrics and league tables is that by their very nature, only 25 per cent can be at the top of the league and 25 per cent at the bottom. As Elkington (2022) argues in this volume, it is unlikely that there will be complaints about this approach from those at the top of the league whilst those in the bottom quartile will not complain because it would be seen as defensive.

In the initial meeting with the Director of Nursing, she asked me to help understand why targets were being missed, why the relationship between the two managers was dire and why the team did not follow through on improving performance planning. Rather than suggest that a better plan or 'blueprint' was required, or more harshly, the recruitment of more able staff to implement the blueprint, I am suggesting instead that it was the different values and expectations of how best to implement the national plan to reduce waiting lists, which was the problem. When considering other competing values such as patient safety and efficiency and staying in budget, then delays in treating children requiring surgery could risk compromising some or all of these values to a greater or lesser degree, depending on the treatment each individual child required. People are not rule-following entities or mechanical components within an organisation understood as a system; they are individuals who have the free will to make autonomous choices often related to their personal beliefs and values.

The avoidance by those involved in dealing with the conflict within their relationships and lack of sharing their expertise to provide solutions essentially led to a way of working that was unsafe. Much more challenging, but possibly more productive, would have been to call attention to the differing values and patterning of their power relationship. Tim believed that rational management, the implementation of a blueprint, would improve efficiency and effectiveness and be a 'good thing' for patients (and for which there are some benefits), and Helen experienced this approach as dehumanising. Had she questioned the night care arrangements, different agreements might have emerged, but this was an unlikely conclusion, given the poor relationship between the two managers. As I reflect on my assumptions about what resulted in unsafe clinical practice, whilst useful, it played scant account to the power dynamics that were a major issue in the drive to 'improve performance'.

I will now compare alternative perspectives on power. Every day, power is understood predominantly in the sense of directing others to do things, and in another, the emphasis may be as much on the productive effects of power, although it does not lose the first emphasis.

Power as a Possession

In the earlier narrative, Helen described her relationship with Tim as 'leaving her powerless', suggesting that Tim was more powerful, even though their roles were of equal status in the organisation. Tim had responsibility for implementing the performance management targets on which the success or failure of the directorate relied, and Helen rationalised that his role was seen by 'the organisation' as having more significance and influence than hers. In her mind, his views would dominate and he was more powerful. Helen was describing an unhelpful pattern of relating, which illuminates the type of friction and rivalries that occur not only in healthcare settings, but within many relationships in the workplace when performance metrics are used in instrumental ways. They come to represent a particular set of valuations of the good.

To understand power further, Clegg (1989) argues that there is no single all-embracing definition of power but describes a number of 'family relationships between some closely related but nevertheless differentiated concepts' (ibid., p. xv). Equally, Wittgenstein (1967) posits that in different contexts, the meaning of power changes so that there is no single definition of power that covers all usages. Each usage takes place within local, tacit or explicit theoretical systems that we construct or take for granted (Haugaard 2002).

American writers such as Hunter (1953) and Mills (1956) concentrated on the methods by which political groups were constructed, contending that social order required unambiguous planning and organisation. This school of thought was known as the 'elitists' (Haugaard 2002), in which the power of the ruling elite was implicit by virtue of their evident status in society. Dahl (1957), attempted to study a more situational and relational concept of power, describing it as something held by people (rather than, for example, an organisation). He proposed a behavioural science approach and recommended a methodology whereby power could be measured by studying its exercise. Dahl studied the rate of individual success in decision-making situations, describing the notion of power as intentional and active. Within Dahl's framework, A has power over B to the extent to which A can get B to do something that B would not otherwise do. Therefore, the power of A could be measured through the reactions of B. An individual could exercise power to prevent another from doing something that they would have preferred to have done. Dahl (1957) concluded that there was no ruling elite, but rather a myriad of different people and interest groups involved in a multitude of issues. Although this model was felt to be limited and assumes that the effects of power are visible to be measured, it challenged the previously less rigorous research approaches proposed by the elitist proponents.

Lukes (2005) argues that the insidious exercise of power prevents people from having grievances, by shaping perceptions and preferences in such a way that people accept the existing order of things. This elucidates the relationship between Tim and Helen. Helen accepted that there were financial constraints on the nursing budget and Tim expected Helen to work within the constraints and not question their application. As Helen disliked conflict, it possibly suited her not to contest the decision even though this resulted in her working clinical shifts, reducing time for her managerial role and negatively influencing her credibility as a manager. This could describe Helen's perception of Tim 'having power' over her, which she felt impacted on her successful performance as a manager.

Assad (1987) stresses the relationship between discipline and organisational virtue or achievement. The mechanism for this achievement, argues Clegg (1989), has come to be termed 'disciplinary practice'. For example, a system's approach to measuring performance data, supervision, policy-making and appraisal could be seen as a way of controlling the behaviour of the individual. It could be argued that this power dynamic was the approach adopted by the CEO when describing the poor performance of the Children's Directorate

A prominent health policy academic, Chris Ham (2005), refers to power and regulation as a collective phenomenon within the NHS. He argues that the health service is subjected to an amalgamation of rheostats (or controls) – some hierarchical and some regulatory – that combined will confine the power of local healthcare organisations. Ham describes the friction between desires to devolve power to local organisations alongside the execution of politically set national targets. He expresses concern that the inconsistent message from government constrains managers and clinicians from delivering quality healthcare. Staff invested time and resources negotiating their degree of authority at a local service delivery level, to then meet national targets and reassure local and national regulators.

In these perspectives, power is understood as a possession implicit by virtue of the status in society or within an organisation of those thought to hold it and that it can be used as a tool to silence or control those who don't hold it. In general, in the NHS, it is difficult to talk about power because the everyday understanding is that managers 'have it' and those they manage don't.

Power as Consensual

A different way of perceiving power is that power is not something owned; rather, it is a functional quality of all relationships. Instead of focusing on one person's power 'over' another, Arendt (1970) maintains that 'power is never the property of an individual; it belongs to a group and remains in existence only as long as the group keeps together' (ibid., p. 44). She argued that power in government survives only as long as people support it. Arendt draws a distinction between the exercise of power through politics and violence, maintaining that politics and violence are opposites; where violence prevails then politics disappears.

Three major scholars argue that power can facilitate as well as constrain: Parsons (1967), Foucault (1979) and Arendt (1970). Parsons defines power as a:

> ... generalised capacity to secure the performance of binding obligations by units in a system of collective organization when the obligations are legitimized with reference to their bearing on collective goals and where in case of recalcitrance there is a presumption of enforcement by negative situational sanctions – whatever the actual agency of that enforcement.
> (Parsons 1967, p. 306)

Parsons's (1967) structural account of social order links power with authority and the pursuit of collective goals. Although power carries the threat of sanction, this is legitimised through the institutionalisation of authority.

Authors who take a functionalist view, such as Parsons, construct empirical models of how society works in which power is consensual and decisions are made in the best interest of community. This way of thinking brings validity to the notion of performance management goals in the NHS, where there are many examples of standards being set that result in positive outcomes, for example, with access to treatment for serious diseases such as cancer or access to mental health services. An unintended consequence might be the threat of sanction being so great that managers fear for their jobs at times, and there are examples of where statistics have been falsified in order to meet the target (Windmill et al. 2007). As indicated earlier, for Parsons, there is a duality between individual freedoms and the demands of the system.

Power as Co-Created

Elias (1978) perceives no such duality. Like others, he argues that power is not a 'thing' or an object that is owned (Clegg 1989; Foucault 1979), but is part of an ongoing relationship. Elias understands power as a feature of all human relating, by which people are interdependent. They have a mutual reliance, based on who needs whom the most. These constant shifts in interdependence both enable and constrain all activities within relationships.

Elias further argues that human organisations are not edifices, nor are they the objects of individual or group design. It is through the concurrent conflicting, competitive and co-operative relationships in organisations that everything happens. This insight helps me make better sense of the narrative in which Helen commented that Tim's approach to managing the directorate left her feeling powerless. Nevertheless, I now see that there was some level of passive resistance in her comment that she was not Tim's 'bean counter'. Tim's power advantage was not absolute: his authority depended on Helen accepting that she was less effective or persuasive and that she was more dependent. Although she felt she had been treated unfairly, she had also co-created the power dynamic by her actions. In summary, I am arguing that the notion of power is premised on relationships in which people are interdependent and where the level of dependency changes according to the degree of need of each other. Elias describes relationships as a 'fluctuating, tensile equilibrium, a balance of power moving to and fro in relationships' (Elias 1970, p. 131).

As I tried to make sense of the intertwining of the different relationships that maintained the way of working for children requiring overnight care, it became clearer that it was the interdependency between those involved that maintained what staff experienced as feelings of a 'balance of power', that is, powerful or disempowered, depending on who needed whom more at that particular moment. Tim could not have implemented his plan in isolation; it was dependent on the co-operation of others. Helen found the waiting list directives tedious and did not want to participate or be drawn into finding alternative solutions. When the targets were missed, she could blame Tim, and when her colleagues complained about working with targets, she could maintain her identity as the person 'looking after' the children. If she did suspect that children were staying overnight, neither Jane nor she could admit to this as it was an established way of working and questions would be asked about why they had let it happen for so long. Jane's role therefore complexified this issue beyond that of Helen and Tim's relationship being 'the problem'. Similarly, the Clinical Director and CEO appeared disinterested in the detail of operational management and as the adult day care nurses did not raise concerns, even though they must have been aware that they were in breach of their Nursing and Midwifery Code of Conduct, so the plan for attaining the targets remained. I also disrupted the previous power figurations by my presence, as they knew I would be reporting my findings. I also needed them to co-operate with my investigation as my reputation was at stake.

This way of understanding power as highly social identifies how the effect of power moves or changes based on need or dependency and how shifts in power relationships affect the patterning of who is included and excluded from the group. Thus, the role of power as an enabling/constraining aspect of any relationship is important in understanding that power is co-created by individuals and groups rather than as a function that is possessed and regulated by an individual. Elias offers a more fluid understanding of the notion of power in which the dynamic is, paradoxically, constraining and enabling, inclusive and exclusive, conflictual and harmonious at the same time.

Inclusion and Exclusion as Dynamics of Power

The emotions associated within power relations are experienced through feelings of inclusion and exclusion within social groups; 'power is thus felt as the dynamic of inclusion and exclusion' (Stacey et al. 2000, p. 353).

Perhaps Helen's contempt for a target-driven environment appeared to be fostered by feelings of alienation as performance management is engaged with market-oriented terminology such as 'tariffs', 'access targets' and 'commissioning'. The lexicon embodies specific meanings and has a currency that is shared by healthcare managers, but this was a vocabulary Helen chose not to embrace. She felt that Tim's relationship with the Clinical Director left her feeling excluded. Equally, Tim appeared to show little interest in the clinical care of the children and families, possibly feeling equally discounted by his nursing colleagues. So, perhaps it is towards people's relationships at work that we should turn our attention.

Stacey (2007) asserts that 'if there is a good enough holding environment so that people can contain rather than submit to or avoid the anxiety, then insight and creativity may be generated' (p. 113). Walker (2005) argues that 'demands and pressures can be more easily managed, and quality services developed if the experience of anxiety in the present moment is attended to' (ibid., p. 3). While acknowledging the interdependence of doctors, nurses and managers as their power relationships ebb and flow, it is important to recognise that they are continually renegotiating their enabling and constraining relationships. They are included at certain times and excluded at others, depending on the changing dynamics of the groups. The risk of potential exclusion can provoke feelings of anxiety.

I noticed that the Children's Nurses, who worked ostensibly in day care, saw themselves as an inclusive part of the Day Care team, with little or no connection to the Children's Directorate. There was perhaps a history of an insider/outsider dynamic between the Day Care team and the Children's Directorate, which suited the latter and enabled Tim to form an 'in' group of their own. This constraining and enabling dynamic of the relationships raised several issues for the Director of Nursing to investigate, including why the Adult and Children's Nurses had not raised concerns about the overnight practice and why the Children's Nurses had not sought clinical supervision from their Children's Unit colleagues.

Perhaps the adult day care nurses felt recognised and appreciated by Tim and shared the 'values' that they were benefiting the children, believing that they were the 'good' ones, which was reinforced by the recognition from senior management. If they had felt bullied by Tim, given what was at stake, it would be more likely that someone would have blown the whistle. They might have thought that it was the children's ward and ineffective management who were the ones putting barriers in the way of their innovative approach to clear the waiting list for children.

Clearly there needed to be a process to enable children to be admitted for their operations. I have not described this scenario to allocate blame to the actions of particular staff members. Rather, I have attempted to show how, within this situation, the patterning of their relationship to avoid conflict and the lack of reflection on the day-to-day challenges of their working relationship resulted in unintended consequences for sick children, which could have been catastrophic. This apparent clash of values provoked conflict in which both managers felt compelled to fight for what they believed to be right. As I described earlier, the cult value of 'good care', for example, was operationalised in the form of waiting list targets, which got taken up by staff in different ways. Tim implemented a blueprint to manage the waiting list in a way that conflicted with other values at play, such as Helen's vocational ideals to have children 'properly looked after'.

In my experience, taking time to make meaning of the experience of working with the uncertainties, instability and unpredictability of daily life is not an approach favoured by most organisations. I believe that having conversations acknowledging the vagaries of organisational life with its differences, conflicts, differing ambitions and values can bring a different sense-making to our working lives. Whilst this may be anxiety provoking and might not necessarily resolve differences, being able to talk about these diversities brings more opportunity for creativity and innovation to emerge rather than the repetitive, stuck conversations Tim and Helen endured.

In summary, it is important to recognise how the diverse understanding of power described above led to different ways of identifying and interpreting the phenomenon. If we conceptualise power as a dynamic quality of relating rather than being the possession of individuals, then power is not a function of a role or managerial status, but rather a way of relating co-created in the mutually dependent relationships between staff. There was a central NHS policy directive to 'cut the waiting lists', which needed to be operationalised. Tim saw value in cutting waiting lists in terms of patient care and his own career. His solution was to use a tried-and-tested Adult Day Care facility blueprint, with hazardous consequences. Helen did not see her role within a waiting list initiative, as it did not sit well with the values that brought her into nursing. The enabling and constraining power relationships between the two managers, the RNs, the Clinical Director, the Director of Nursing and possibly a host of other clinicians and managers, all enabled this practice to continue.

I am not arguing against the sharing of good ideas, initiatives and blueprints. I am arguing that to completely take over a way of working in one context and expect it to be adopted in the same way in another is unlikely to be successful because of the differing power relationships, and values, that constrain and enable relationships within the workplace.

I mentioned to Tim and Helen at the beginning of our work that there appeared to be opportunities for creative ways of problem-solving, especially as the Clinical Director seemed to have a 'light touch' management style. As I worked with Tim and Helen, I noticed the stuck pattern of relating which were producing more of the same types of problems. I was keen to explore how the two managers might begin to talk about their differences, build on their individual expertise and work towards a more creative relationship.

Novelty and Innovation

Stacey argues that it is only through the negotiation of conflicting constraints that novelty arises (Stacey et al. 2000). He points out that this might result in the emergence of constructive or destructive patterns of behaviour, but nevertheless has the potential for people to notice what is emerging and perhaps pay attention to it in a specific and local situation. Rather than focusing on the need to achieve the waiting list targets, an alternative was for both managers to begin a conversation about how their ways of behaving, the inherent patterning of their interactions, had contributed to the success or failure of their work.

There are a myriad of frameworks and models that analyse the notion of innovation and the emergence of novelty in the literature. Bessant and Tidd (2007) characterise innovation within three core themes: generating new ideas, selecting the good initiatives and implementing them. They acknowledge that this is fraught with uncertainty, relying on trial and error to find out whether an idea is good. They maintain that even if project managing the resources and budget to produce a new product or service is successful, there is no guarantee that people will adopt it. They argue that 'innovation is a not a simple flash of inspiration but an extended and organised process of turning bright ideas into successful realities' (ibid., p. 298). Innovation, they maintain, is an output of a new product or service and the process of making it happen.

Traditionally, research has regarded innovation in terms of phases of invention, implementation and dissemination. These phase models, despite often being described as messy and iterative, may, however, be inadequate for investigating and supporting innovation as an integrated part of the ongoing problem-solving within the workplace (Seo et al. 2004; Smith and Tushman 2005).

Organisational change models have the potential to provide defences against anxiety by covering over uncertainty through the organisation of rational tasks and focus on what the future will look like and the journey to get there. Tim and the Chief Executive's approach was to implement a 'top-down' approach to the waiting list problem, as they were constrained by the need to reduce the waiting lists within a timescale to comply with the national policies. For them, combining the Day Care facility for adults and children appeared to be a simple solution with few complications or contradictions.

Smith and Tushman (2005) suggest that understanding how organisations effectively manage contradictions is an important question in the management of innovation. They conclude that balancing contradictions in decision-making is rooted in cognitive frames and processes, which means that the senior management team is encouraged to embrace rather than avoid contradictions. Based on the assumption that the existing ways of working and the new innovation must both succeed, managers confront the differences and similarities between the new and the old and manage the contraindications through cognitive frames.

This runs counter to Schumpeter's (1934) idea of the 'winds of creative destruction', where new innovation destroys old ways of working. Similarly, Ham (2014) argues that 'many innovations depend on existing services being decommissioned in order to fund new services to take their place' (ibid., p. 36) rather than providing the same services in new settings. Equally, Anandaciva and Ward (2019) recognise that to keep within financial boundaries, new ways of delivering care needs to be developed rather than finding more efficient ways of delivering existing models of care.

Creativity and Innovation as Complex Responsive Processes of Relating

Describing creativity and innovation as an emergent characteristic of complex responsive processes of human relating brings a significantly different way of thinking about the matter (Fonseca 2002). I will describe how a complex responsive process perspective may add to an understanding of how the dynamics of social processes promote novelty and innovation. From this view, organisations are seen as patterns of relationships between people. Self-organisation means that 'agents interact locally with each other according to their own local principle of interaction' (Stacey 2007, p. 321), an insight Stacy offers by drawing on the work of pragmatist GH Mead.

For GH Mead (1938), novelty emerges in the interaction between people rather than through following rules that can be decided in advance. Mead (1934) argues that mind, self and society evolve together and at the same time. Fundamental to being human is our ability to reflect on ourselves as objects to ourselves, a paradoxical property of human biology which he thinks of as an 'I' responding to a 'me'. That is to say, as we become socialised, so an individual is able increasingly to take the attitude of the group towards themselves through private silent conversation. The 'I', our spontaneous response to our social context, is mediated by our general sense of what others think of us. There is no split between the 'I' and the 'me'; they are two inseparable aspects of the same social act, but the 'I's' response to the generalised sense of the other is potentially novel and can surprise us.

This silent conversation with ourselves we call thinking is the private version of the vocal, public conversations between people: they are two sides of the same coin. This suggests that the individual and the social are inseparable phenomena, not two discrete ones. This more paradoxical perspective holds that meaning does not occur in the mind of an individual who then takes action; it continually emerges between people and within social relationships. It is in these interactions that patterns of conversations arise which, paradoxically, reveal both continuity and transformation, as there is the potential for new ideas to emerge.

In Mead's (1934) way of thinking, there is no one person or group controlling or driving forward the development of novelty, but the potential for novelty arises in our everyday interactions. No external designer can possibly control or steer the way that novelty arises in the everyday exchange between people. Rather, it is by observing the detailed interactions that people may increase their awareness of how change is already emerging in their organisations. This is not a completely random process, as individuals perpetually and unpredictably constrain and enable each other within the social norms of the local structures. Within these relationships, people attempt to influence, lobby, coax and persuade.

Fonseca (2002) notices that as new themes emerge from conversations, people may start to amplify a change. As the new ideas are shared with others, the meaning is further altered and refined through conversation. I am not arguing that implementing change need not be organised, nor am I arguing against reviewing systems and processes in a systematic way. But I am drawing attention to the patterning of conversation in which meaning is continually negotiated rather than simply conforming to a preconceived prescriptive blueprint or framework.

When I worked with these two managers I reiterated the opportunities I saw for them to work together to bring to fruition their ideas to meet the performance challenges better suited to the unique situations of their directorate. Eventually, the conversations in the Directorate did start to change and new thinking began to emerge as how best to manage the care for children. Tensions remained, doors were slammed and frustrations expressed as new approaches to day care emerged, which were eventually presented to the Executive Board of the hospital.

The importance of effective communication is a significant factor cited in many of the traditional change models and organisational change frameworks. However, this tends to be understood in terms of a 'sender-receiver' model of communication in which clear messages are formulated and delivered for cascading throughout the organisation as part of the implementation process.

From a complex responsive process perspective, communication is also seen as central to how innovation emerges in organisations, but it is understood very differently. The perspective offers an explanation for how global thematic patterns of conversation emerge from local human interaction which are both formed by and forming each other at the same time (e.g. what it means to 'keep children safe').

Rather than identifying change as a project, innovation is seen as an ongoing aspect of daily life. Of course, it is impossible to know what may have happened if the two managers' relationship had been different had they been able to discuss, rather than avoid, the issues they were concerned about or if a more suitable solution might have been found. I am not arguing that focusing on relationships is a panacea because the outcome of our interactions is never fully predictable. We cannot know the result of our actions until we see the response from others. But by engaging with difference such as appreciating the range of values in play and taking the risk of drawing attention to stuck patterns of conversation might bring the possibility of change. Whether the change is for the better or worse is subject to how it affects existing power relationships, depending on whether those involved feel they have gained or lost as a consequence of the innovation.

The perspective of complex responsive processes thinking draws attention to the importance of fluid conversation; Stacey (2007) and Fonseca (2002) stress the importance of trust within relationships. To recognise this is to privilege the importance of difficult conversations to explore the factors that might develop or destroy that trust. As I described at the beginning of the narrative, a lack of trust and significant anxiety underpinned the managers' relationships. The consequences of my discovery of unsafe care and the requirement to give an account of this to myself, Jane and others focused attention on their troubled relationship. It forced us to realise that they and their respective team members all had to make an effort to listen, lobby, coax and persuade each other to enable a different way of working to begin to emerge.

Tim and Helen were individuals, not a blueprint of a cloned senior nurse and healthcare manager. They brought their experience, strengths and creativities as well as their anxieties and fears to the day-to-day experiences of their working relationships. They were familiar with the stability and security of habitual ways of behaving, and when I, the outsider, introduced a different discourse, it provoked feelings of anxiety and threat. However, as the patterning of conversations change, so did the configuration of feelings of inclusion and exclusion, which had the capacity to change the power relationship. According to Stacey (2007), 'organisations display the internal capacity to change spontaneously only when they are characterised by diversity' (ibid., p. 446).

In summary, if, as I am contending, novelty and innovation are emergent phenomena and occur in the known and unknown qualities of the social patterning of interaction between people, then it is difficult for those new ways of working to emerge from a predetermined blueprint. What was seen as a new and dynamic approach to clear the waiting list in one place may not necessarily be successfully adopted in another. The unique working relationships, the conflicts and power struggles all contribute to ways of working from which innovation may or may not appear.

Conclusion

Using my experience of working with complex relationships, I am attempting to make sense of how two managers and their colleagues had co-created a situation, which had the potential to put the lives of vulnerable children at risk. This was not their intention, but arose out of their lack of ability to pay attention to their relationship and to think reflexively about what they were doing together.

As public sector organisations are required constantly to adapt to economic and political change, structural reforms, which aim at retaining central control, are inevitable. However, it is important to recognise that people are not part of a system; they have choices in how they interpret what is asked of them in the context of their mutually dependent relationships, which are diverse and unique in each situation.

I have argued that power is not a function of a role or managerial status, but rather a way of relating, co-created within the mutually dependent alliances between staff. Therefore, the local implementation of any central policy directive is reliant on these relationships. Referring to a blueprint is insufficient for knowing how to go on together. Developing a coherent plan outlining the processes to be followed is clearly of value, but the implementation of that plan will rely on the power dynamics, the conflictual relationships and making the time to reflect and make sense of unique day-to-day situations.

In my experience, taking a more reflexive approach to understanding the way that we perceive the structure and processes of organisational life, and the power dynamics of day-to-day relationships, provides a sense of freedom. To others, the notion of reflexivity generates feelings of anxiety and a loss of control, and they can dismiss the idea as idealistic, time-wasting and exasperating.

Whatever the reaction, I think it is important to reiterate that thinking about organisations from a complex responsive process perspective is not an organisational change management tool. Rather, it offers an opportunity to examine and begin to make sense of who, what and how we are shaping the notion of 'this is the way we do things around here', in order to operationalise central policy directives and consider the moral and ethical implications of what we are doing together.

If the aim of healthcare reforms is to make organisations more responsive to patient need and cost-effective for the public purse, creativity and innovation need to be at the heart of working life. Again, this is contingent on the ability to build trusting day-to-day relationships where conversations, acknowledging the vagaries and struggles of organisational life, have the potential to increase the opportunity for ingenuity and originality to emerge.

References

Anandaciva, S. and Ward, D. (2019) How Is the NHS Performing? July 2019 quarterly monitoring report. https://www.kingsfund.org.uk/publications/how-nhs-performing-july-2019 (Accessed 15 July 2020).

Arendt, H. (1970) *On Violence*, London: Penguin.

Ashby, W.R. (1956) *Introduction to Cybernetics*, New York: John Wiley.

Assad, T. (1987) 'On Ritual and Discipline in Medieval Christian Monasteries', *Economy and Society* 16(20): 159–203.

Bessant, J. and Tidd, J. (2007) *Innovation and Entrepreneurship*, Chichester: John Wiley and Son Ltd.

Checkland, P.B. (1978) 'The Origins and Nature of "hard" Systems Thinking', *Journal of Applied Systems Analysis* 5: 99.

Clegg, S.R. (1989) *Frameworks of Power*, London: Sage.

Dahl, R.A. (1957) 'The Concept of Power' in Scott, J. (1994) (ed.) *Power: Critical Concepts*, London: Routledge, 201–215.

Elias, N. [1970] (1978) *What Is Sociology?* London: Hutchinson and Co.

Fonseca, J. (2002) *Complexity and Innovation in Organisations*, London: Routledge

Foucault, M. (1979) *Discipline and Punishment: The Birth of the Prison*, Harmondsworth: Penguin.

Ham, C. (2005) 'From Targets to Standards: But Not Just Yet', *British Medical Journal* http://www.bmj.com/cgi/content/full/330/7483/106 (Accessed 15 July 2020).

Ham, C. (2014) *Reforming the NHS from within*. https://www.kingsfund.org.uk/publications/reforming-nhs-within (Accessed 25 August 2020).

Haugaard, M. (2002) (ed.) *Power A Reader*, Manchester: Manchester University Press.

Hunter, F. (1953) *Community Power Structure: A Study of Decision Makers*, Chapel Hill: North Carolina Press.

Jackson, M.C. (2000) *Systems Approaches to Management*, New York: Kluwer Academic/Plenum Publishers.

Lukes, S. (2005) *Power: A Radical View*, (2nd ed.), Basingstoke: Palgrave Macmillan.

March, J.G. ([1976] 2007) 'The Technology of Foolishness' in Pugh, D.S. (ed.) *Organisation Theory*, (5th ed.), London: Penguin, 329–352.

Mead, G.H. (1934) *Mind, Self and Society*, London: University of Chicago Press.

Mead, G.H. (1938) *The Philosophy of the Act*, Chicago, IL: Chicago University Press.

Mills, C.W. (1956) *The Power Elite*, Oxford: Oxford University Press.

NHS Oversight Framework 2019/20 (August 2019) Available at https://www.england.nhs.uk/wp-content/uploads/2019/10/nhs-oversight-framework-rev-oct19.pdf

NHS Plan (2019) Available at https://www.longtermplan.nhs.uk/wp-content/uploads/2019/08/nhs-long-term-plan-version-1.2.pdf

Parsons, T. (1967) *Sociological Theory and Modern Society*, New York: Free Press.

Pugh, D.S. and Hickson, D.J. (1989) *Writers on Organisations*, (4th ed.), Suffolk: Penguin Business.

Schumpeter, J. (1934) *The Theory of Economic Development*, Cambridge. MA: Harvard University Press.

Seo, M-G., Putnam, L.L. and Bartunek, J.M. (2004) in Poole, M.C. Van de Ven (eds.) *Handbook of Organisational Change and Innovation*, Oxford: Oxford University Press.

Shaw, P. (2002) *Changing Conversations in Organisations*, London. Routledge.

Smith, W.K. and Tushman, M.L. (2005) 'Managing Strategic Contradictions: A Top Management Model for Managing Innovation Streams', *Organizational Science* 16(5): 522–536.

Stacey, R.D. (2003) *Strategic Management in Organisations*, (4th ed.), Essex: Prentice Hall.

Stacey, R.D. (2007) *Strategic Management and Organisational Dynamics*, (5th ed.), Essex: Prentice Hall.

Stacey, R.D. and Griffin, D. (2006) (eds.) *Complexity and the Experience of Managing in Public Sector Organisations*, Oxford: Routledge.

Stacey, R.D., Griffin, D. and Shaw, P. (2000) *Complexity and Management*, London: Routledge.

Taylor, F. ([1911] 1967) *Scientific Management*, New York: Harper Brothers.

Walker, D. (2005) *The Experience of Anxiety When Leading a Changing National Health Service Trust*, unpublished DMan Thesis, University of Hertfordshire.

Wiener, N. (1948) *Cybernetics: Or Control and Communication in the Animal and the Machine*, Cambridge, MA: MIT Press.

Williams, R. (2005) *Leadership Power and Ethics in the Educational Sector*, unpublished DMan Thesis, University of Hertfordshire.

Windmill, A., Harvey, S., Liddell, A. and McMahon, L. (2007) *The Future of Health Care Reforms in England*, London: Kings Fund. http://www.google.co.uk/search?hl=en&q=Kings+Fund++windmill&btnG=Search&meta

Wittgenstein, L. (1967) *Philosophical Investigations*, Oxford: Oxford University Press.

8

REWORKING MEANING THROUGH PROCESS CONSULTANCY INTERVENTIONS

Åsa Lundquist Coey

Introduction

The Scandinavian welfare models have in common ideals around equal distribution in access for all regarding health, education and social services, adapting central policies to local needs and a right for citizens to participate in democratic decision-making.

The public sector in Sweden looks a little different compared to the neighbouring countries of Denmark and Norway as a result of historic differences, but also recent policies. Sweden has opened up for strong profit-orientated growth in private services in the last 30 years, whilst Denmark has the largest share of non-profit sectors and Norway a mix between the two, depending on the area of service. Different regulations are used in each country in different service areas, but Sweden is the most marketised.

Later influences since the 1980s have been directives from the EU and national regulations of public procurement. However, the most influential international feature regarding the work being done in organisations has been the implementation of new public management (NPM) tools. Having swept internationally through advanced welfare states, it promotes global competitiveness rather than focusing on the state as a social provider for people. This has meant an increase in market economy thinking, with calls for privatisations and 'freedom of choice' for everything from hospital care to what schools to send your children to.

The previous management discourse I and my clients in the public service sector in Sweden worked in had been criticised for having become too bureaucratic and high-handed in the last decade. It was accused of becoming micromanagerial, thus creating more problems than solving them. Rather than micromanagement, NPM advocated abstract goals, reviews and evaluations which meant more administration and manualisation of the public sector. The NPM's argument has been that by promoting the profit motive, fewer resources would be wasted. Problems could thus be solved with the help of measurements, calculations and quantifying outcomes. Quality conferences further promote the documentation of control, effectiveness measurements, quality indexes, ranking lists and quality scores as well as heart rate monitors and pedometers in order to make sure that everybody keeps healthy and fit. Organisational Behaviour Management (OBM),[1] for instance, seen as a branch of scientific management,[2] has been in use in the public sector in Sweden during the last decade. It tries to influence, or 'nudge', the actions of an individual employee before the action occurs, antecedently. Nudges (Thaler and Sunnstein, 2008) are defined as triggers, presenting something in the environment that will increase the likelihood that a certain behaviour will occur. The consequence is defined as change in the environment, which increases the likelihood of it continuing to be exhibited in the future.

Increasing beliefs in rationality and all things measurable reduces human action to figures and diagrams. Complex questions where practical judgement is needed have been given less and less space in managerial thinking. Rather than being sensitive to differences in situation and context, the hunt for global and scalable solutions goes on.

While there has been an increased focus on the tools and techniques of management aimed at controlling the behaviour of individuals, measuring and ranking, there has also been a growing critique of this approach. The government has tried to ensure that monetary resources for schools or elderly care homes do not disappear in profits and that an acceptable level of quality of service is maintained. New reforms were thus introduced in Sweden between 2016 and 2019 that advocated a new way to govern through introducing the concept of trust. This was seen as a 'tool' for the furthering of a citizen-orientated and efficient organisation. Public authorities emphasised the challenges ahead and favoured the influence the reform could have on governance structures as a counter to the emphasis on measurement. Five public authorities have so far implemented the reform with varied results.

My working field of consultancy is located in this discourse of managerialism in Sweden. The role of a consultant is often traditionally seen as objectively analysing data, presenting them, standing back and letting the organisation deal with the outcome themselves or designing strategies and objectives for securing pre-reflected outcomes. It builds on assumptions of management and consultancy as a linear and instrumental social engineering science and consultants as able to design and predict outcomes, even in unexpected and uncertain domains. However, in the practice of leading management teams in development processes, disturbances and conflict inevitably emerge unexpectedly when differences in opinions occur, despite the focus on metrics and tools and techniques.

In my practice in the early days, I tended to avoid situations that were hard to quantify or measure and which were not particularly easy or straightforward. But the strains and stresses my clients, public service managers and employees were dealing with, when they were judged as not being effective or competitive enough in comparison with the private sector, have gradually made me come to question some basic assumptions of my profession. I have come to challenge one assumption of process consulting in particular, namely that conversational activities and communicative processes – which are considered the core of process consultancy – can be designed, directed and controlled. If they could be, we could indeed avoid disturbing and uncomfortable situations and conflicts. But over the years, I have increasingly noticed how I have occasionally felt helpless in dealing with unforeseen situations that have felt like (unnecessary) deviations from achieving my and my clients' designed and desired outcomes of interventions. It has been like walking around with a small irritating pebble in my shoe.

I have tried to provide alternative ways of viewing situations in order to diffuse tensions when disturbances have occurred, sometimes feeling unable to help and uncertain how to proceed when witnessing people leave the process in various stages of anxiety. I have gradually come to understand process consulting – which is what I do – as deeply social, situational and contextual. Alternative ways of thinking about what we are doing together in organisations had however largely been left unexplored until I joined the Doctor of Management and Complexity programme at Hertfordshire University in 2012. This meant taking my every day experience more seriously.

Even though the broader management context has been one of design and delivery of intended outcomes in the abstract, the different management teams I've worked with and I have frequently found ourselves involved in addressing pressing human issues. We have been caught up in having conversations around the pressures this dominant way of viewing delivery of pre-reflected outcomes at work has on employees, who have had to adopt different coping mechanisms.

There are still few ways of dealing with high levels of anxiety and worry, which are then often expressed as disturbances and outright conflicts between all of us. Sensing that we, process consultants, managers and employees, are unlikely to be able to produce the desired results commonly gives rise to feelings of anxiety and shame. The numbers of stress-induced conditions at work are still rising in Sweden. What is left unsaid is that expectations of predictable outcomes are unrealistic, an idealisation. The actual *process* in process consultancy, as I am taking it up, is important. These are conversational processes built on encouraging openness and curiosity with the help of a coaching and enquiring approach. The broader process approach in public service is still one of predictability, based in a positive and constructive context which means that a premium is placed on agreement, harmony and consensus.

This was evident in a workshop in the Star organisation, where emotions regarding a proposed surveillance routine made the managers oppose and resist the changes. However, being together in conversational processes of relating which involved conflict offered potential for changing our sense of self, who we thought we were, in which new understandings did emerge.

The Workshop

The Star organisation is a state-owned organisation running large infrastructural projects all over Sweden. Mary, the human resources (HR) director, asked me to conduct a number of process consultancy sessions with her HR department and a few other managers in a development team. The purpose was to create more effective ways of working to meet the future expectations that were about to descend upon them, in particular increased competition from the growing private sector in Sweden. She wanted me to 'stir things up' in the sessions, as she found the newly founded team to be too complacent and therefore ineffective. She wanted me to conduct feedback exercises in order for us to get things moving. She felt that people were being too quiet and seemed frankly disinterested. She assumed that this was one of the reasons people were not performing well in the meetings.

I had sensed some urgency in her plea, but I felt that bringing feedback exercises might be a too instrumental an approach and suggested encouraging more conversation around the different issues they were supposed to look into. After a lengthy conversation, to my relief she agreed to just having conversations as she had previous experience of me encouraging this as a way forward.

Going Live – Making Conversation

The participants, the HR department and eight other managers, some of whom I had met before, were gathered in front of a room when I arrived, waiting for it to be unlocked. We had some casual conversation, when they asked what I was doing there. I explained my role was facilitating conversations on issues that they might want to explore in order to make sense of their mission, what they were to do in this newly founded team. I detected both tension and relief at this, and somebody jokingly said, "Well, I hope you are not going to destroy the harmony we have built in the group." I joined in the laughter at this, reflecting about their worry and worrying myself at the same time. Did I have a reputation for doing that? It was puzzling how contradictory this message was to Mary's, who had asked me to 'stir things up'.

We were going to meet another four times and I explained my function in the group and it being a process, after which I invited them into a first conversation: what they were going to do in this particular team and why. This did not create much liveliness and only short, odd comments. I therefore suggested they first speak in pairs before bringing issues up in the larger group, thinking they would have to communicate then. This made the energy go up a bit, and eventually discussions came about a little bit more. But it was still curiously hard to get the conversation going, and I reflected on this being similar to other encounters I had had in this organisation, both with individual managers and with the management team. People did not easily come forward or open up. There seemed to be a pattern of holding back, and I experienced it yet again in this workshop. They all knew each other quite well, so what was going on? I felt irritation welling up and decided to leave the simple structure I had anticipated using as it started to feel pointless and instead told them about my feelings of it being hard going. "What is going on? What are you thinking about?" I asked. Out of the corner of my eye, I could see Mary fidgeting on her seat. This was obviously not what she had expected me to do. A few of the participants looked uncomfortable.

A manager I had met earlier said, "You are right, I am just so mad at the moment at these new log-ins we have to do in the computer systems". He glanced in Mary's direction; she looked very distressed. He continued, "Are we really going to be carrying out this kind of dirty business? The Government controlling how we are controlling each other? That is creepy". We were all a bit taken aback, but the strong wording had a releasing effect on conversation. A few minutes later, everybody was engaged in a heated discussion regarding this new directive. Mary was defending the initiative, clearly under attack from several directions. I was trying to get her out of the line of fire and started insisting on background information; this new directive had been given by the Government due to perceived security breaches, presumably from the Star organisation, in the form of unauthorised peeking into and even leaking of classified material connected to a large project. The directive meant managers had to carry out spot checks on employees, randomly checking who had been looking at specific files and whether they were authorised to do so or not. These checks had to be carried out at least twice every month and demanded more personnel resources than they currently had. Accusations left hanging in the air concerned that the HR department and Mary had been far too complacent in this matter and agreeing to it without demanding explanations as to how it could be certain that the supposed security breach came from the Star organisation in the first place.

The whole idea seemed preposterous. Surveillance activities were not exactly the routine thing recommended in Sweden in the public service with its commitment to fairness. It was also contrary to the 'freedom of choice' thinking a market economy advocated. Why would the employees in Star consider this 'proposition' a choice?

Mary now defended the idea whilst the other HR employees looked on. She explained that it was not necessary to make such a fuss about it; this was mostly a simple administrative task. This made the managers more irritated. "We don't have to do it then, it being such a simple administrative task?" No, it had to be done, Mary claimed. At this the manager that had first spoken said, "I am not going to do this. I think it is a shame you [he nodded in the direction of Mary's co-workers] are trying to coerce us into doing something like this". This was a very powerful display of resistance. Mary pleaded, "But, you need to …", "I don't need to do anything", he replied angrily:

> and I am not going to either. I have neither the time nor the resources. And, for that matter, I think this is disgraceful in a modern organisation. It is a kind of activity I don't want to be involved in!

The other managers looked like they were going to applaud. This was a rebellious act, and Mary needed their co-operation if this was going to work. She had little control of the situation. I felt bad having started it, but at the same time I felt there had been little choice; we could not continue being overly polite, nobody talking about what was clearly on everybody's mind. But taking a hidden transcript[3] into the open was risky, would we be able to get out of the situation in a sensible way? Preferably with less anxiety. The tension was high. Everybody looked at Mary now except for her co-workers, who seemed to be studying their shoes. This was hardly Mary's doing. I intervened by telling everybody to slow down and attempt to disentangle the situation. Everyone settled. The discussion started over again, with heated arguments that eventually became more intimate. I semi-forced them to hear each other out and pose more questions around the issue rather than presenting right/wrong views or try to solve, fix, the situation. More and more people came forward eventually, including Mary, who confessed to feeling very anxious about it initially, saying that she had not supported the idea either really but felt pressured to carry it out.

During a break, I heard the Communication Manager (CM) whisper to Mary, "I thought we had an agreement", her tone was dissatisfied. Mary giggled nervously and replied, "I thought she was going to do feedback exercises". I wondered what she had promised that I would deliver. We had not agreed to my doing feedback exercises. I manoeuvred myself closer to the CM, whom I knew a little, and asked her about work in general. She told me about the different communication concepts and platforms they were currently developing. "We should be working more with the concept of feedback, but in a nice way", she said, "We don't want to upset people". I asked her what she thought of this way of working, what we were doing right now, isn't this a kind of feedback, to all of us? "Well, it's not very harmonious, is it?" she replied, "It must be possible to talk to each other without arguing. It is not exactly nice to have these kinds of surprising discussions popping up at all times". The look on her face was genuinely worried. "Is this common here?" I asked. She hesitantly answered:

> Well, HR, for instance, isn't an easy place to be in when decisions often are being overruled. They are supposed to know best what is right to do with or for people. To overrule them affects my function as well in a negative way.

"Why are they not being taken seriously?" I asked, meaning the decisions. "I don't think they like her", she answered, referring to Mary.

The talking became livelier, but paradoxically also more nuanced. We finished on a hopeful note, agreeing on the helpfulness of not jumping too soon to conclusions or accusing each other. They testified to gaining different thinking in the process of conversation, which was helpful regarding the surveillance. "We may not even have to do it", somebody jokingly said, "just pretend to", which suggested a political awareness.

Sociologist Norbert Elias points to the interdependency of people and power as a relational phenomenon, a structural characteristic of all human relationships (Elias, 1970, p. 74). Depending on the different structural dependencies we were all caught up in, we act out our various intentions in these webs of relationships, which may result in unintended outcomes. For example, one of the managers said, "I am not so angry any more" when leaving the room.

Situations like these are more or less everyday work in organisations. Process consultancy always deals with conflictual, disturbing and uncomfortable situations which are located in a wider discourse of predictability and control that dominates management today. There would be no need for bringing a consultant in if things were running smoothly without interruptions, tensions or conflicts. Important issues are always at stake when bringing in my colleagues or me; they are political, emotional, factual.

Meeting after the Workshop

The meeting with Mary and the HR department that followed was full of emotions, relief that the workshop ended well and also various degrees of general worrying. "Well, this workshop was a bit of a surprise!" Mary said. Conversational patterns often reproduced themselves in Star, the same tropes being recycled. The sustainability manager had told me once that she wanted 'no surprises' regarding the content of an employee day I was going to be in charge of. Mary had used exactly the same sentence in regard to the management programme I had been responsible for carrying out with the board prior to the workshop. She had wanted an extensive report on the progress of the management programme when it had just begun, making sure there would not be any 'surprises' at the end. The CM had worded it as 'surprising discussions popping up all of the time'. The workshop had now come out as yet another 'surprise', something they could neither predict nor control.

I knew Mary had a personal history of being away for various periods of time due to stress-related issues. I often sensed a great deal of anxiety surrounding her. When walking me out, she said, "I may not be cut out for this job. There are too many pressures in it. I shouldn't be a manager. I am not good enough".

Mary often suggested that to adapt was imperative, to do more lobbying for the HR function and thus reform their identity to fit in with the organisational games being played out, even to the point of reproducing the same dominant language, as in 'no surprises'.

One of the core assumptions within dominant management thinking is that it is fierce competition in our field of work: we have to be quick in creating a brand as the most attractive employer of the future, otherwise nobody wants to work here. This can get played out in situations where process consultancy is brought to bear. We are always trying to foresee and forecast where opportunities or new fields for our services or products could emerge next. This creates a need for tools, methods and measurements that may help us in predicting the future. The ideology behind this implies that what we are doing at present is not good enough and needs constant improving with the aid of war-like strategies. This technocratic worldview suggests that people also need to be improved. This leads to a constant struggle to get rid of our perceived weaknesses. It also creates an ongoing sense of urgency, as displayed when Mary wanted me to 'stir things up' in the workshop. The ideology implies that we need to be striving for something better than what we are in at present. We should attempt to improve ourselves to enhance effectiveness, be 'right up there', 'leaning in' and preferably ahead of the competition. Effectiveness is a word frequently used within conventional management and is often described as the capability to produce a desired result or an intended or expected outcome. It relates to getting the right things done and 'can and must be learned', according to Peter Drucker (2006), an influential management thinker and writer.

This attitude seems to lead to prescriptions and feverish attempts at implementation of things we have already been trying, more of the same, and this has, in most cases, not prevented or predicted disturbances or undesired or, indeed, desired outcomes so far. We are still in the dark (and always will be) as to what exactly produces certain outcomes of the interventions that leading, managing and process consultancy inevitably are about.

Moving to a Social Understanding of the Star Organisation

Alternatively, the Star organisation can be viewed as a social arena being formed by all the members, managers, employees, clients, advocates, stakeholders. It is influenced by and, in turn, is influencing in ongoing processes in volatile and versatile ways, forming and being formed at the same time. The culture in Star was one of anxiety, and was felt by me too. I had rarely encountered processes with such high levels of tension, whether working through or with the HR department and Mary or the managers in the workshop or in the earlier process consultancy interventions I had been involved in there. The highest level of anxiety had been displayed in the top management team about a year earlier. Individually, they had all approved of a development process, but when we were underway, the process frequently froze, making it heavy going and very confusing. I felt little response to my gestures to the point of losing confidence and starting to question my competence in running the process. I had felt relief when the process finally ended as opposed to feeling sad as I often did in other organisations when it was time to part from the group.

They had all spoken openly to me in private but clammed up when in the team. I had eventually come to understand more of the relationships of power in the group that had been played out in unhelpful ways with an excessive competition amongst them.

Process Consultancy Evolving

Traditional definitions of process consultancy (Schein, 1987; Block, 2000) are as a philosophy of helping and a methodology of intervening. The consultant is seen to be a highly qualified professional with insights into and understandings of psychosocial dynamics. Initially, having an observing role, she/he later designs interventions and participates in the process through giving feedback, paraphrasing and asking questions. Schein wrote about it as being an art of knowing what to look for, how to look and interpret it and act upon it. His idea was to help in instituting patterns that the client wished for. His take on process consultancy came from a systemic perspective, a participant-observer view and did not take change variables into account. On the one hand, he understood process consultancy activities as "a patterning that cannot be understood as intended by any single person or group." On the other hand, he suggests that people can introduce new patterns that they 'do intend' (Shaw, 2002, p. 9). This contradiction that we may be able to introduce new calculated patterns intentionally into processes has been and still is heavily influential in mainstream management. This leads to us, consultants and managers, being expected to fill the looming gaps of structural voids in the organisation, to fill them with concepts, matrices, frameworks, policies, exercises and structured agendas. This approach only takes a single narrative into account (the most powerful) rather than the multitude of stories that makes up the organisation. I now believe that taking multiple narratives more seriously and encouraging conversations around specific issues may be helpful in creating movement.

During my first years as a consultant, I basically agreed with the first definition of process consulting (above) and believed it possible to implement this or that intervention into the organisation. I believed people to be competent and willing to take the new concept up as intended. Gradually taking my experience seriously after many years of practice has changed me. The character of work has changed also. The way I take up process consultancy today is with an increased awareness of the importance of context and sociality. This means taking account of relationships, how figurations of dependency and power are being formed and played out in the organisation. Process consultancy as a mutual, co-created activity attempts to deal with disturbing, uncomfortable and conflictual situations in specific contexts focusing more on relationships rather than individuals. Problematic situations can be more fully explored through talking about them, exploring multiple interpretations, context and the relationships, all the particularities that participants bring into it.

When Mary was in the line of fire from several directions in the workshop, I attempted to talk about it. I wanted to untangle it from too polarised views for us to be able to collaborate more around it, talk about it first in a factual way and then address ideologies and intentions, the cause of different interpretations. Encountering and acknowledging differences and talking about them may be one way of moving forward together; however, the outcome of such an activity will still be as unpredictable as doing nothing (which also is an activity).

Surprises – The Rhetoric in Star

I am used to dealing with tension in groups, but there had been an unusual high degree of it in the Star organisation, even with occasional eruptions as illustrated in the workshop.

This wish for harmony and pleasantness in Star may have stemmed from events that had produced disturbing and uncomfortable emotions earlier, for instance, when in the case of Edward, a manager, there had been a "lack of communication with staff". Edward never wanted to be a manager but the personnel came with the job. He largely ignored the responsibility of leading and co-ordinating their efforts and complaints mounted, which eventually saw him transferred to another department and eventually to leave the organisation. This made new emergent situations with disturbing elements reproduce old emotions and create avoidance behaviours when everybody protected themselves from the anxiety this could create.

The Edward story had occurred a few years earlier. At the time, I was asked to provide a proposal for the top management team. The HR team in charge of the tender liked the ideas in it and wanted to go ahead. They told me the proposal had to pass through Edward first, though. He was one of the senior project leaders in the management team and had insisted on this. Otherwise he might be working against it, the HR team explained. With his perceived history of obstructing, it was felt that it would be advisable to try to win him over. In this short introduction, they had clarified the rules of the game we were going to have to play if we wanted to secure the carrying out of the leadership programme. Edward's position was important, overseeing large infrastructural projects of which he was in charge more or less single-handedly. HR had recently helped manoeuvre him into this position in the hope that he could do the least damage there, as his handling of staff in the earlier position had been disastrous. After much negotiating, he had been transferred to another department as senior project leader; in reality, a more senior position, although he did not have people directly reporting to him.

In the meeting that followed, where the proposition I had made was going to be discussed, those present included me, two HR representatives, one leadership strategist, the director of communication and the senior project leader, Edward.

After initial greetings, Edward gave a lengthy account of what a leadership program should contain and what issues to address. None of this was in my proposal. I started to wonder whether he had read it. A coaching approach was nothing the organisation needed, he declared, as he already had a coach once and knew 'all about that'. I kept quiet mostly while the rest of the team were struggling to get into the conversation when he ridiculed what they said or brushed it aside, claiming it was 'irrelevant'. The room grew increasingly quiet as nobody challenged the assumptions being laid before us.

Edward was a large and loud male, the rest of us were all female. It felt to me as though he seemed to be using every trick in the book to intimidate us through displaying different domination techniques, sometimes called 'master suppression techniques'. This is coined by the Norwegian psychologists and philosophers, Ingjald Nissen and Berit Ås. Defined as strategies of social manipulation, the idea is to indirectly suppress or humiliate opponents:

> In some situations, men may express their resentment that women are there at all, stating that they are "taking a place away from a man". It is

not only inequalities of power that leads to domination techniques, but a conscious or often unconscious sense of entitlement to privilege.

(The Centre for Gender Equality, Norway, 2001)

This overpowering behaviour may have been an act of resistance directed towards the representatives in the room. The HR department had been the prime executioners in stripping him of being manager of personnel earlier. At the time, he had appeared to be satisfied with the solution, but there may have been ambiguity involved if he didn't feel competent in dealing with personnel issues. The whole setup now with HR, the strategist, the CM and me may have been anxiety provoking and identity threatening. There were five of us, he was alone, and the people in HR had been instrumental in removing him from his last position due to his lack of ability to deal with people. The person responsible for communication in the organisation was present and the proposal was mainly geared towards leadership communication improvements. He may have felt compelled to clarify his position in this new game being laid before him, technically more powerful now in his new position. If he identified himself as someone unable to communicate well, he was not likely to sanction a programme aimed at improving communication that might have posed a threat to his current identity. If he was inclined to such open demonstrations of power or felt that he had a conscious or unconscious sense of entitlement to privilege, the organisation had enabled it by promoting him.

Edward may exemplify a phenomenon in the public sector, where people are moved around, given promotions and demotions, as it is not easy to get rid of them due to work environment laws, instead of dealing with difficult behaviours or uncomfortable situations. Edward had difficulties communicating with his staff and was, in a sense, rewarded for having these by being promoted into a higher-status position with a grander salary. These activities were likely interpreted by the rest of the organisation in many unintended ways. The easiest way out of the hot situation had been to free him from staff responsibility and give him some interesting business projects instead, naively thinking that he could do less harm as there would not be the same degree of communication and relating to people in this position. The effect had been a decline in business projects instead.

I sensed anxiety and insecurity in the small planning team and in Edward. The power play that had been on show in the meeting may have been a need for recognition in the new role he had not himself consciously chosen to play but been forced to accept. He may not have intended to silence us, but this became the effect.

A couple of years later, I eventually did leadership training with the management team, with Edward by now gone and replaced with a 'people person', as HR termed it.

This earlier event, removing direct reports from Edward and his subsequent departure was rationalised by HR as a practical solution for avoiding the conflict. This avoided their dealing with Edward's anger and staff disappointments and the emotions surrounding the events. I felt these were lingering in the background, occasionally seeping through, as in the meeting following the workshop. There was no forum in which to reflect together on these repetitive patterns, no place or time to talk about their feelings regarding them. They somehow had to work these out for themselves before they eventually could come to rest. Many emotional issues that arose in the workshop felt resolved, but were soon revived in new or stressful situations or provoked when perceived threats or new uncomfortable situations were felt by the team. The rationale was that these bygone events were not of importance anymore, but I sensed that emotions were still looming in the background, informing the patterns of communication today, provoking tension and nervousness as they had stirred issues of recognition, identity and power expressed in the language used as 'no surprises please'. Mary had now lost interest in the incident as she now seemed to want everybody to brush aside these 'unnecessary' emotions and free us all up for other activities, regroup, create and adapt into other figurations of relationships.

The CM's preference for working with feedback exercises in a 'nice' way suggested her desire to maintain the status quo, 'do not upset us or stir things up', as my way of being open regarding what I felt was going on had not exactly created harmony, she said. She had been genuinely worried and I experienced the tension too. As the CM, she was expected to communicate in an upbeat and positive way to keep morale high in the organisation, and it would be hard to maintain staff morale if people were arguing or got upset.

Mary's and the CM's messages seemed ambiguous and contradictory. Mary wanted me to stir things up, but the CM wanted me to maintain harmony. Mary wanted feedback exercises, and in my experience of doing feedback exercises in general, people do get a bit upset. We are protective of our sense of self, our identity, and giving honest feedback may not always be done in a way that feels comfortable. It would possibly have stirred and provoked various degrees of defence mechanisms. Things can be well intentioned but still have harmful effects. Apart from this approach being instrumental, this may not have gone down well with the CM, although the turn the events had taken without feedback exercises had not gone down too well either. This, however, does not preclude that things can be nicely meant and nicely felt, as meaning emerges in the social act of our gesturing and responding (Mead, 1934, p. 80). In a conflict, we struggle to negotiate meaning in the situation. As there had been anxiety and attempts to avoid the disturbing situation regarding the surveillance that was clearly on everybody's minds, it might have produced defensiveness that erupted when there was a forum for them to do so. It seemed to me that they were all able to live with the outcome of the workshop, although there had been 'surprises'.

Thinking and talking together had moved us all into more pragmatic views. Rather than coming out of the workshop with a number of bullet points on what actions to take, we had gained a better understanding of what was going on for us.

Changing Identities

We are radically social selves because we are born into a network of relations, and all the contingencies, ideologies, intentions and power struggles will influence the self we become. It involves our capacities and talents and political struggles. Our identities are forged in such struggles, and are not prior to it.

The sense of self or identity is not a riddle locked inside our bodies. It is nothing that can be found inside of us, but arises from social activity with other people. We become who we are through being in social settings making conversations, being influenced and influencing. We all became different through changing in multiple ways in the workshop. Identities are made and can be seen as pluralistic, unstable and subject to radical change over a lifetime, but paradoxically there are also ensembles of habits and hence a deep and stable/unstable sense of self. We carry internal voices, an invisible audience past and present which we perform for, voices in the organisation. The power relations we were caught up in meant limited choices in taking up the proceedings of surveilling staff or not. The specific situation that caused unrest in the workshop, the manager voicing his refusal in doing as the Government and HR had intended, thus arose in the workshop. The meaning emerged in the negotiating in the social acts of gesturing and responding. Mary had declared that there was no choice in taking up the requirements demanded. This may have been felt as coercive and caused even more resistance. Unsure about how to go on, as her gestures had not been taken up in the way she had intended, she had backed off the official stance, hoping we would come around, otherwise her position would have felt untenable. Coming back to ourselves and complying with what is expected of us may be an act of choosing to trust the leadership in the organisation or of coercing ourselves into submission and rationalising: "It is probably being done for the best".

When people are socialised into accepting and believing a view of themselves and their interests, their face may grow to fit the mask. Philosopher Foucault describes modern forms of social control in his work *Discipline and Punish* (1977). Retribution was enacted on the criminal's body earlier in history, and physical punishments are still in use in many parts of the world. However, Foucault argues that today's societies have mostly abandoned public spectacles for disciplining citizens, but depend instead on surveillance. Individuals are carefully disciplined within a social order, according to a whole range of techniques. A telling example of how disciplinary power functions can be found in Foucault's description of the Panopticon. A Panopticon is a physical central observation tower placed within a circle of prison cells. It allows for continuous observation of inmates, as each cell is housing a prisoner. But the prisoners cannot see into the tower. It relies on the power of implied surveillance. This instils states of docility in the prisoners, who cannot tell whether they are being surveilled or not. There is no need for direct violence or force anymore; the surveilled subjects discipline themselves.

Performance metrics in the shape of documentation of control, effectiveness measurements, quality indexes, scores and ranking lists are common techniques in NPM and examples of the techniques of disciplinary power Foucault describes. These techniques may conflict with values of openness and trust and severely constrain for the individual feeling spied upon when being subjected to spot checks. What will they do if there is a conflict aversion and somebody breaks the rules? What if they break the rules themselves? The rhetoric will be that this is being done for the 'good' of the organisation, such as promoting pedometers for organisational good health, through ensuring compliance with efficient/effective practice.

In a sense, we disciplined each other in the organisation as it was being played out in the workshop. Disciplinary power and its techniques are not only negative though. Modern organisations and societies rely on them to sustain sufficient productive order for carrying out complex tasks. My critique points more to the fact that we were covering it over in Star organisation. We pretended that this was being done in order to improve organisational outcomes. This happened in a contradictory and confusing experience of organisational talk in Star: "We are being surveilled to ensure we in turn surveill employees, find the wrongdoers and secure a better fit into the fabric of the organisation, but it is really mostly an administrative task". These techniques, taken to extremes, mean we risk losing awareness of the ethical dimension of work, what the morally responsible thing to do is. The managers in Star resisted this in the hidden transcript until there was an opportunity to bring it into the open. Their reluctance to speak, bringing the hidden into the open, is always risky due to relations of power.

Idealisations and Reality in Process Consultancy

The group was to constitute a development group, and although I initially tried to focus on their interpretations of this, what exactly they were going to be doing and why, my gestures were not taken up with any particular interest. As consultants "themselves are participants in the ongoing pattering of relations that they seek to change" (Mowles, 2011, p. 8), I was curious to know how the purpose of the group was interpreted by them.

As there had been little or no response and due to my own irritation and impatience when that emotion emerged, I asked what was on everybody's mind. I made the choice to take my experience of discomfort seriously rather than follow the scheme I had planned initially. This could be seen as development (which was the purpose of the team), as it helped us encounter our differences. It was due to the disengagement I experienced in response to my first questions that other questions emerged. They may have come across as uncomfortable or challenging but did have a tongue-loosening effect.

Had there been a certain level of conversation, disagreement or agreement, the need would not have arisen. Twelve people in a room, hardly talking, create bodily sensations of something being at stake.

In the interplay of different intentions change happens, unexpected and undesired or desired population-wide patterns can emerge which no one single person, however powerful, can control (Elias, 1994/2000, p. 366; Stacey, 2011, p. 484). The experience of being together can only manifest in local interactions. A leader, manager or consultant is a powerful player and formulates visions and goals (that are equally influenced by local interactions), but there is no knowing how these will be taken up. The responses to powerful gestures can never be predicted. People could be seen to conform, but this may be an empty pose to minimise discomfort or exposure.

Not being able to deliver something more tangible than just 'making conversation', like bullet points or a strategy or policy for development, often makes those responsible for the workshop (in this particular case, Mary and I) unsure of how to describe what we are actually doing. We are drawing attention to this, which may not be particularly welcome or common in mainstream management settings. Mary and I were attempting to stay in relation and explore the tense, ambiguous and contradictory situation, as could be advocated from a complexity view. We had hopes that this would provide us and everybody else involved with information and clues as to what was being avoided and why, thus illuminating new or different meanings and understandings that we may have wanted to take up.

The workshop did eventually shed light on these issues. We did not make the rebellious manager into a patient, somebody to cure, who was being disruptive and in the wrong. We did not make his relationship with Mary the main issue and coached or coerced him into a suitable way of behaving. The route we finally took was an attempt to make the issue our common responsibility, and through drawing attention to information and questions attempt to address the emotional attachments within the situation, still remaining involved but making an effort to self-distance.

The process was helpful in illuminating and increasing an awareness of a change, not of content (refutation of old errors) or of theories (modifying models) but through rethinking, finding out what ideologies was governing our views with the help of participative enquiry:

> Consequent organizational effectiveness, a moderate amount of substantive conflict is necessary, but affective conflict should be minimized, and

organizational participants should learn to use the five styles of handling conflict to deal with different conflict situations. In other words, if the variables, other than conflict, that affect organizational learning and effectiveness are controlled, effectiveness can be maximized if effective conflict management strategies are implemented. This indicates that the management of organizational conflict requires proper understanding of the effect of conflict on organizational effectiveness.

(Rahim, 2001, p. 65)

The quote is a typical example of literature dealing with conflict in general. Teaching "the five styles ..." may help distance ourselves from the situation, and perhaps the group would have felt more comfortable than with the conversations I insisted upon. If we had gone down that route, we would, however, first have had to control the other 'variables' as well as had a proper understanding of the effects. This technocratic worldview dominates mainstream conflict management and builds on a science of certainty rather than complexity.

Conclusions

The difference between solutions, resolutions and dissolutions can be viewed as the first two aiming for something better, a future desired state, solving or resolving something, whilst dissolution is a felt effect, not aiming at anything apart from helping us to think. I have come to think of the actual process in process consultancy as a solution in a sense disguised as a dissolution. When addressed differently or explored in wider and deeper contexts, the process of conversation dissolves many issues at stake. Conversations have the potential to help us change our minds, increasing awareness of disputed issues and their interrelatedness and providing a sense of solution when we actively participate in conversational processes of human organising. This sense of resolution, rethinking and feeling differently around an issue (it being pushed, contested, challenged, supported) when socially involved, is what I like to refer to as a felt dissolution, the problem is no more. As employees and managers in the public sector increasingly find themselves in need of internal as well as external co-operation, having to compete with a growing number of private actors in Sweden, the conversational processes is in general seen as constructive and helpful.

Conflict is a universal feature of human society, deeply and socially embedded in our societies. What we do on a daily basis seems to be inherently conflictual and takes its origins in culture, ideological and political differences, psychological development and economic differentiation. Disturbing, conflictual and uncomfortable states are normal when what we value is at stake and people with different ideologies and intentions are trying to create results together. Further, they seem to be necessities for movement, creativity, innovations and norms and ethics to emerge in the forming of new and different ways of engaging. Too restricted social control (being cult-like) may trigger anxiety and resistance and cause surprising, unpredictable and disruptive situations that paradoxically require new instruments of social control, causing further anxiety and resistance requiring new instruments of social control and so on.

Prescriptions stemming from idealised management thinking may actually cause the same conflicts and disturbances that we are trying to avoid. Prescriptions simplify the lives of human beings in organisations through not taking issues of our social location or power relations sufficiently into account. Attempts to implement certain steps or procedures into organisations, as advocated in these idealisations, may cause even more resistance and more social conflicts owing to us feeling coerced and unfree.

In the process of making conversations, we are trying to make sense of how we can contain anxieties which arise from these different opinions in the organisational melting pot and in a good-enough way to allow us to go on together anyway, although we may not fully agree with the perceived outcome. We do not always make sense of situations either and have to leave them with a feeling of unfinishedness, incompleteness and confusion. We settle for relative disharmony, with harmonious disharmony.

A dilemma for the manager or consultant lies in encouraging a level of maintaining what is paradoxical and contradictory in our thinking whilst avoid collapsing into finding solutions to problems too soon. Keep the transitional space. A sense of movement may occur only if there is an identity movement, and as we are guarded when it comes to our sense of self, this may not occur without a certain amount of discomfort.

One task of process consultancy, apart from being in the process and thus making a difference, may be captured in the words of Deetz as an analogy:

> The point of research ... is not to get it right but to challenge the guiding assumptions, fixed meanings and relations, and reopen the formative capacity of human beings in relation to others and the world.
> (Deetz, 2001, p. 37)

'Reopen the formative capacity' is what I find myself doing as I have been invited into the organisation for a reason. As a process, it is geared towards a common investigative exploration of the bothersome and the stressful in trying to achieve results together. Without providing ready-made answers, giving wanted or unwanted advice or recommendations to soon, but rather accepting there being no solutions means inconclusive confusion may lead to other and further inquiry.

Engaging in thinking at the same time as we are thinking about how we are thinking, reflection and reflexivity in action[4] are activities which differentiate man from animal. It is how our identities are felt and can be reformed. We are enabled but also constrained in and by our interactions. Hence, social interaction evolves from thinking of what we are doing, and we evolve from our social interaction.

This chapter is a shortened and a more comprehensible recap of an actual situation that I have been writing about in my PhD thesis in 2016; link: http://hdl.handle.net/2299/17120

Notes

1. A sub-discipline of applied behaviour analysis (ABA); its emergence stems from the foundations of behaviour analysis developed by B.F. Skinner (1938).
2. Originally inspired by Frederic Taylor (1911/1967).
3. A 'hidden transcript' represents a critique of power spoken behind the back of the dominant that every subordinate group creates out of its ordeal (Scott, 1990, p. 18).
4. Stacey (2012, p. 108).

References

Block, P. (2000) *Flawless Consulting*. New York: University Associates, Inc.

Deetz, S. (2001) Conceptual foundation. In F.M. Jablin & L.L. Putnam (eds.), *The New Handbook of Organisational Communication: Advances in Theory, Research and Methods* (pp. 1–46). London: Sage.

Elias, N. (1970) *What Is Sociology*. New York: Columbia University Press.

Elias, N. (2000) *The Civilizing Process*. Malden, MA: Blackwell Publishing.

Foucault, M. (1977) *Discipline and Punish: The Birth of the Prison*. Translated by Alan Sheridan. New York: Pantheon Books.

Mead, G.H. (1934) *Mind, Self & Society*. London: University of Chicago Press.

Mowles, C. (2011) *Rethinking Management*. London: Gower.

Rahim, M.A. (2001) *Managing Conflicts in Organisations*. Westport, CT: Quorum Books, Greenwood Publishing Group.

Schein, E.H. (1987) 'Process consultation, vol. 2. Lessons for managers and consultants'. Reading, MA: Addison-Wesley.

Scott, J.C. (1990) *Domination and the Arts of Resistance*. London: Yale University Press.

Shaw, P. (2002) *Changing Conversations in Organizations*. London: Routledge.

Skinner, B.F. (1938) *Behavior of Organisms*. New York: Appleton-Century-Crofts.

Stacey, R.D. (2011) *Strategic Management and Organisational Dynamics*, 6th edition. London: Pearson Education Ltd.

Stacey, R.D. (2012) *Tools and Techniques of Leadership and Management – Meeting the Challenge of Complexity*. London: Routledge.

Taylor, F. ([1911] 1967) *Scientific Management*. New York: Harper Brothers.

Thaler, R.H. and Sunstein, C.R. (2008). *Nudge: Improving Decisions about Health, Wealth, and Happiness*. New Haven, CT: Yale University Press.

The Centre for Gender Equality, Norway (2001)'Domination techniques: What they are and how to combat them' (pdf), p. 12. Retrieved 2010-01-29.

9

COMPLEXITY AND THE PUBLIC SECTOR

Key Themes

Chris Mowles and Karen Norman

On Method

The chapters in this volume are granular accounts of what it is like to manage in the public sector across three countries in the Global North where profound changes are taking place in the function and valuation of public services. They are specific examples of particular management dilemmas experienced in health care, in the civil service, in a university and in a state-controlled organisation undertaking infrastructure projects. Each of the authors has given an account of how they have navigated strong expectations which form the background to their work. In all cases, there are taken-for-granted ways of dealing with the work dilemmas, drawn from a discourse we have described as managerialism, which assume that whole organisation approaches based on best practice, blueprints or idealisations are the best way to approach the work. In order to manage at the grand scale, it is inevitable that managers would reach for such abstractions. It is hard to imagine managing in any other way, particularly if equity and universality of service provision is one of the guiding principles. As citizens, ex-managers in the public sector and having offered consultancy to public organisations ourselves, we are in favour of high-quality public services which are well managed and evaluated against standards. However, this does not preclude an inquiry into what the accepted ways of working promote and what they obscure, what they enable and what they constrain.

The authors in this volume research in a tradition that assumes that what makes management complex is that social life is predictably unpredictable; it repeats in complex fractal patterns which are recognisable, but never in exactly the same way. Consistent with this perspective, they take the position that employees are not parts of systems, or human resources, but creative, interdependent, highly social individuals with imagination and agency who are sometimes unpredictable, sometimes even to themselves. The patterns they form by co-operating and competing together to undertake work may be helpful or may impede it, and it is on this point of inquiry that the chapters turn. Authors explore the extent to which managerial schemes and blueprints bring about the transformation in quality and attitudes that the discourse claims. Detailed inquiry is needed in whichever sector one is working; a research perspective which more fully takes not just the abstract, but the particular and contextual difficulties of managing. One which pays attention to what human beings actually say and do in order to get the work done. Similar insights are explored in the companion volumes to this one (*Complexity and Leadership*, Chauhan and Crewe, 2022; *The Complexity of Consultancy*, Solsø and Sarra, 2022).

To continue to draw attention to method, each of the chapters turns on every day concrete examples of dilemmas in the workplace in public sector organisations. They bring to life the embodied sense of what it means to co-operate or compete together, which no appeal to best practice in the abstract can sufficiently render. In each case, the author stands back and reflects upon the matters in hand, and by doing so become reflexive. Reflexivity is extensively covered in the literature (Cunliffe, 2003; Alvesson et al., 2008; Antonacopoulou, 2010) and is particularly useful for a method which pays attention to the interdependences between colleagues trying to get things done together. It is invaluable for noticing the changes in relationships between the authors and their colleagues as they emerge in the negotiation of interdependence. Each of the authors demonstrates what Antonacopoulou (2010) highlights for us, that reflexivity enables a critical ability to question the taken-for-granted ways of going on together, particularly if they are proving unhelpful. Critical, reflexive engagement with the everyday politics of working in the public sector cannot necessarily achieve the grand claims of managerialism for 'transformation', but as each of the authors demonstrates, it can create degrees of freedom to work differently, to pay attention to different things, to recognise each other and perhaps to make the workplace more humane. In order to do so, it requires the authors dwell longer in the mess and uncertainty of not knowing what to do and to hold on to their anxiety for a little bit longer to allow for the potential for different outcomes to emerge in the hurly-burly of everyday organisational life. They demonstrate greater fluency with the public and the private, the formal and the informal, the inherent uncertainty of being human and trying to act in concert with others.

To manage in or offer consultancy to the public sector demands the kind of critical attention that the authors in this volume portray so vividly. As scholar-practitioners, they demonstrate the importance of paying attention to experience, then reflecting and theorising from it in order to find more helpful ways of working. This involves focusing less on tools and techniques and grand schemes for organisational transformation and more on the qualities of human relating to think about trust, freedom, prejudice, politics, values and ethics. One of the perennial problematics of public services is that in their aspiration for universalism, they can lose sight of the unique and the individual: this is equally true for citizens and for employees in the sector. The aspiration for equity can sometimes compromise recognising plurality and difference. Management in the public sector demands both a commitment to general standards combined with an attention to the particular and contextual of every individual's needs and the values that the relationships imply.

The Particular Complexities of the Public Sector

We make an additional claim in the introduction to this volume that managing in the public sector is more complex than managing in the private sector. This is because public provision has meaning for us as citizens and as members of communities. This is not to say that the meanings are always generative, because the extent and quality of public services arise as the direct result of political contestation over valuations of the good mediated through the state. Though public services have an ethic of universality, this does not guarantee that they are or are experienced that way: some groups will always fare better than others in their access to and enjoyment of what the state has to offer. The recent pandemic offers very clear examples of this, and gives further evidence that in times of crisis, already marginalised or vulnerable groups are likely to fare worse (Bambra et al., 2020). The 'meaning' of public services in these instances is that some lives matter more than others. But the way we fund and offer services, and whether we choose to fund them at all, speaks to what we choose to value and the degree to which we consider ourselves interdependent. They are what GH Mead (1938) terms a social object, a pattern of relating that produces education, care or regulation which also shapes our we-identities as citizens of a particular country as well as buildings, equipment and procedures. Managers in the public services are also citizens and will have their own sense of themselves and their membership of particular groups in relation to what they do, which will be called out in them as they undertake their tasks every day. This may provoke a good degree of ambivalence and private conflicts about whose interests they serve and how.

Emergent Themes in the Chapters

Feeling Bodies Co-Operating and Competing

One of the first casualties of working methods which lay claim to rationality and to be based in scientific values of evidence can be feelings and emotions, which may be portrayed as irrational: as an example, in Chapter 3, Elkington's manager argues that managing with metrics is much better than using 'gut feeling'. The authors in this volume find that rather than getting in the way of the work, experiencing often strong emotions allows them to find themselves in relation to others and to work out a way of going on together. They are 'data', alongside other data, which help them to manage more skilfully. Emotions can be surprising in managerial environments which are surprise-averse. But in each of these chapters, paying attention to emotions proves more valuable than simply trusting in a tool or technique.

In Chapter 2, Briggs gives a number of examples where the appeal to evidence and best practice is silencing and the professionals involved in thinking about their co-operation don't allow themselves to scratch beneath the surface. In Chapter 3, Elkington notes that trust in the neutrality of performance metrics calls out the very opposite of what it aims at achieving: rather than creating an environment where colleagues calmly discuss neutral numbers, they find themselves caught up in rivalry, triumphalism, schadenfreude and acts of subversion. Meanwhile, Yung (Chapter 4) is paralysed by a meeting which quickly polarises around two competing communities of practice and is unable to locate herself in the struggle as long as she tries to stay 'neutral'. Being able to admit that she has prejudices, understood as prejudgements and identifications with a group, allows her to find herself again to take a stronger position in the dilemma she has to resolve.

In Chapter 5, Filbee experiences bodily the ebb and flow of emotions involved in the negotiation of trust in her workplace where trust in numbers is privileged. She realises that trust is a dynamic phenomenon and cannot be taken for granted: paying attention to how one is feeling in the moment offers clues to what might be going on for others in the group. Filosof (Chapter 6) experiences the parallel process of heightened virtuous feelings while resisting the proceduralisation of virtue in her university, where her managers try to reduce her broad understanding of social responsibility to a series of measures. Marriott (Chapter 7) finds herself caught up in mediating between colleagues who are at loggerheads, but who are unable to express to each other what matters to them and what they feel about it, which leads to a crisis in care for vulnerable children. In Chapter 8, Lundquist Coey surprises her client in a working environment which depreciates surprises by inviting participants in a workshop to talk about what they are feeling, to stick with the difficulties rather than avoiding them.

Ideology, Power and Politics

Managerialism as ideology is shy of the discussion of power and politics because of its claim to value neutrality. The assumption is that it's not that the tools and techniques of management cause a particular pattern of domination; it is simply that they are the best instruments to bring about the most effective outcomes. With this assumption power is covered over. There are scholars (Davies, 2014) who argue that a reliance on control through performance metrics allows for managers to create a particular kind of uncertainty which tilts power in their favour. However, the authors show that an inability to negotiate, contest and put forward plural valuations of the good in public can leave the work impoverished. This is particularly important in the public sector where there are profound discussions about public values from incommensurable positions: from a liberal perspective, some basic state provision is a prerequisite for citizens to participate freedom in the polity; from a neoliberal position, the highest degree of freedom is to be found in market mechanisms and broad public provision creates a kind of dependency. In each of the chapters where broader currents of contestation are bubbling beneath the surface, politics is practised as subversion or breaks out into public view. Paying attention to power and politics, encouraging people to recognise each other in their differences is no guarantee of 'effective' work, but it might allow things to become unstuck when they are blocked.

Briggs (Chapter 2) points to the ways in which appeals to the idealisations of best practice can cover over the discussion of power relations and render it superfluous to the holy grail of best practice. To pretend that power is not a quality of working together allows a lot to be ignored. In Chapter 3, Elkington describes feeling stuck in the middle managing by performance metrics and being managed by metrics in her turn, can lead to feelings of powerlessness. Yung (Chapter 4) finds herself having to tackle the unspoken but obvious traditional medical hierarchies in order make any progress in combining two teams into one, which involves locating herself in the hierarchy and assessing her power position. Meanwhile, Filbee (Chapter 5) points to the ways in which fealty to numbers is an indicator of loyalty to a group: to challenge the numbers is taken as a power play and risks exclusion. Filosof (Chapter 6) explores and experiments with the degree to which she needs to play the game in order to stay true to herself and to what she is obliged to do, which requires her to be fluent in her assessment of power. Marriott (Chapter 7) notes the way in which certain narratives about organisational values play out in the rivalry and struggles between colleagues and tries to keep in view the foundational value of quality of care. Finally, Lundquist Coey gets her hands dirty and does not shy away from dealing with the strong feelings and conflict which emerges in response to a new work initiative. The failure to do so would have threatened a blockage in the group's ability to go on together and requires her to draw attention to power inequalities.

Practical Judgement

We observed previously that managerialism is strong on abstractions and weak on particularity. Grand schemes for organisational transformation are assumed to be applicable in all contexts, all things being equal. But as MacIntyre has observed (1985: 91), the difficulty of generalising in the social sciences is that we can never be confident in which circumstances things are equal, in a world where social regularities never repeat themselves in exactly the same way. One of the key skills required for managing day-to-day in any organisation, *phronesis*, or practical judgement, is exercised locally, contextually and taking history into account. As Eikeland (2008) argues, *phronesis* is the paradoxical ability to make general knowledge, *episteme*, useful in a particular context at a particular time, with particular others. And that particularisation always involves questions of the good, what is of most value to us in this moment as a community trying to get things done (Shotter and Tsoukas, 2014a, 2014b). We have already noted the broader socio-economic trends affecting the public sector which pose a profound challenge to idea of the public good, which is translated instead into profit and loss, efficiency and effectiveness or market competitiveness. In each of the chapters, the authors contend with exercising their practical judgement trying to keep questions of ethics in view, considering what is best for the particular groups they find themselves working with, in the context of their traditions.

For Briggs, abstract conceptions of interprofessional collaborative practice (ICP) are insufficient help to know how to go on in this particular team at this specific time. She recommends that teams pay attention to their power dynamics by being able to talk about every day practice. Elkington acknowledges how tightly performance regimes can hedge managers round, but this doesn't do away with their agency entirely: there is still room for exercising practical judgement in the way she manages others to avoid the tyranny of metrics. Yung notes how the idea of the neutral facilitator was no help to her in navigating the conflict in which she found herself: it required her to interpret her own tradition in that particular group of conflicting professionals. Filbee describes herself constantly making judgements about when to push forward and when to retreat in navigating her membership of groups in the civil service. Meanwhile, Filosof makes continuous judgements about how to navigate the set of expectations placed on her and, in turn, placed on her boss. She has to anticipate the anticipations of others in a complex web of power relationships. Marriott notes how the quality of relations between colleagues enables or constrains the ability to make good judgements about the work and thus act in the best interest of vulnerable others. And Lundquist Coey has to make judgements contrary to contractual expectations about how to run her workshop in the face of colleagues who wanted her to keep things calm.

Conclusion

To manage within the discourse of managerialism often means rushing towards an idealised future, embarrassed by the past, unable to dwell in the paradox of continuity and change. The authors in this volume, informed by the perspective of complex responsive processes of relating which Mowles outlines in the preface, assume that continuity and change are co-present in everything that we do: it would be impossible to change everything all of the time. To take a non-linear position on change means assuming that large-scale programmes of transformation might achieve very little, while at the same time small variations of behaviour might escalate over time to population-wide transformation. The non-linearity of change is popularly referred to as the butterfly effect. However, as German sociologist Hartmut Rosa points out (2015), continuous change is both one of the assumptions and outcomes of modernity, which leads to what he describes as frenetic standstill. We never stand still long enough to take stock and think about what we are doing and find our feet before embarking upon the next series of changes. But this doesn't necessarily lead to the greater quality and efficiency that managerialism promises. We offer no idealisation that somehow the pace of change can be halted; rather, we encourage enhancing teams' ability to strip the engine down while they are still driving. All of the chapters in this volume turn to a greater or lesser extent on reflection and reflexivity, which we understand in Elias's terms (1956) as becoming more detached about our daily involvement in the work.

We accept that there are aspects of public services which demand reform and improvement, just as there are aspects which are worth preserving because of what they tell us about who we are and what we choose to value as societies. Constant change, dressed up as transformation, can never be an obvious good in and of itself without our inquiring into change on behalf of what and for whose benefit. To engage critically with change programmes is to drop the assumption that employees are naturally change-averse, questions the idea that the proposals for change are obviously for the good and problematises the suggestion that employees are obliged to 'align' themselves and their values in harmony with what is being proposed. Organisations in whichever sector have to cohere enough to function well, but this should not involve abstaining from contestation, critical inquiry and thinking about what's going on. As Arendt (1971) reminds us, thinking is what might save us when the chips are down. And in terms of our public provision and how it is funded and managed, there is a lot at stake to think about.

The authors in this volume describe in detail what it means to bring into focus feeling human bodies caught up in political games with each other, exercising practical judgement as they contest different valuations of the good. We make no claim that the episodes described in this volume and the authors' responses to them are generalisable, in the sense that is directly applicable for managers in and consultants to the public sector everywhere. But in putting together this volume, we aspire to provoking resonance in other public sector managers and consultants, the experience of recognition. We imagine that many of the difficulties described here, the pervasiveness of metrics, the aspiration to a 'no-surprise' working environment, the appeal to evidence and best practice, the grand schemes of organisational transformation, the avoidance of conflict and expression of feelings will be familiar to an interested reader. We hope that the reader will find them plausible, interesting and relevant to their work.

References

Alvesson, M., Hardy, C. and Harley, W. (2008) Reflecting on reflexivity: reflexive textual practices in organization and management theory, *Journal of Management Studies*, 45: 3.

Antonacopoulou, E. (2010) Making the business school more 'critical': reflexive critique based on phronesis as a foundation for impact, *British Journal of Management*, 21: S6–S25.

AredNT, H. (1971) Thinking and moral considerations, *Social Research*, autumn, 38(3): 417–446.

Bambra, C., Riordan, J.F. and Matthews, F. (2020) The COVID-19 pandemic and health inequalities, *Journal of Epidemiology and Community Health*, 74(11): 964–968.

Chauhan, K. and Crewe. E (eds) (2022) *Complexity and Leadership*. London: Routedge.

Cunliffe, A. (2003) Reflexive inquiry in organizational research: questions and possibilities, *Human Relations*, 56(8): 983–1003.

Davies, W. (2014). *The Limits of Neoliberalism*. London: SAGE.

Eikeland, O. (2008) *The Ways of Aristotle: Aristotelian Phronesis, Aristotelian Philosophy of Dialogue and Action Research*. Bern: Peter Lang.

Elias, N. (1956) Problems of involvement and detachment, *The British Journal of Sociology*, 7: 226–252.

MacIntyre, A. (1985) *After Virtue: A Study in Moral Theory*. London: Duckworth.

Mead, G.H. (1938) *The Philosophy of the Act*. Chicago, IL: University of Chicago.

Rosa, H. (2015) *Social Acceleration: A New Theory of Modernity*, New York: Columbia University Press.

Shotter, J. and Tsoukas, H. (2014a) In search of phronesis: leadership and the art of judgement, *Management Learning and Education*, 13(2): 224–243.

Shotter, J. and Tsoukas, H. (2014b) Performing phronesis: on the way to engaged judgment, *Management Learning*, 45(4): 377–396.

Solsoe Iversen, K. and Sarra, N. (eds) (2022) *The Complexity of Consultancy*. London: Routledge.

INDEX

Note: Italic page numbers refer to figures and page numbers followed by "n" refer to end notes.

agency 150, 192; influence of 23; metrics and 52, 60, 64–67; performance regimes and 197; power and 155; soft systems and 150
Alvesson, M. 192
Anandaciva, S. 161
Antonacopoulou, E. 192
Arendt, Hannah 9, 154, 155
Ås, Berit 180
Ashby, W.R. 149
Assad, T. 154

Bambra, C. 194
Barad, K. 20, 25, 29, 31, 37, 44
Barberis, P. 1
Beauchamp, T.L. 27
Beer, D. 56, 63
Benner, P. 28, 31, 32, 37
Berg, D.N. 102
Bergum, V. 28, 34, 37

Bessant, J. 160
Blair, Tony 3
Bleakley, A. 32
Block, P. 178
Bond, C. 120, 121
Bourdieu, P. 19
Bowen, H. R. 117, 141n1
Bret, J.M. 84
Briggs, M. 30, 151
Brown, A.D. 104
Brown, E. 118
Brown, W. 9
bureaucracy 10, 107, 118, 127
Burkitt, I. 62, 63, 65, 102

Canadian Interprofessional Health Collaborative (CIHC) 20, *21*
Chauhan, K. 192
Checkland, P.B. 150
Chia, R. 24
Childress, J.F. 27

CIHC *see* Canadian Interprofessional Health Collaborative (CIHC)
Clegg, S.R. 152, 154, 155
Clinton, Bill 3
Cloke, J. 118
CMS *see* Critical Management Studies (CMS)
Cochrane, Archie 106
Collini, S. 57
community of practice, *vs.* practice of community 31
competition 3, 34, 38, 54, 63, 138, 172, 176, 177, 178, 194–195
complexity(ies): anxiety and 105; in microinteractions 42; organisational behaviour and 81; practice and 38–39; of public sector 148–149, 191–192, 193–194; in public service management 7–10; relations and 19; research and 43; uncertainty and 96
complex responsive processes 10, 24, 29, 81, 86, 89, 96, 101, 103, 135–136, 161–164
consent 52, 154–155
conversation, controlling, to manage difference 83–84
co-operation 5, 32, 75, 80, 126, 127, 138, 156, 174, 187, 194–195
Corporate Social Responsibility (CSR): Critical Management Studies and 122; limitations of discourse on 119–123; managerialism and 121; metrics and 123–131; metrification and 134–138; origins of 117; public sector and 117–118; universities and 118
COVID-19 pandemic 73–76, 92–93
creativity 93, 106, 111, 146, 157, 159, 161–164
Crewe, E. 192
Critical Management Studies (CMS) 122

Crouch, C. 9
CSR *see* Corporate Social Responsibility (CSR)
cult values 73–76
Cunliffe, A. 192

Dahl, R.A. 153
Dargies, C. 2
datafication 56–58, 70n7
Davies, W. 9, 63, 195
Dawson, S. 2
Deetz, S. 122, 189
Deleuze, G. 28, 30
Denmark 168
Dewey, J. 20, 36, 104, 105, 108
Diaz-Carrion, R. 134
Diefenbach, T. 118
difference: conflict and 86–87; controlling conversation and 83–84; innovation and 106; prejudice and 86–87
Dimmock, C. 60
Discipline and Punish (Foucault) 184
Domination and the Arts of Resistance: Hidden Transcripts (Scott) 61
Dossetor, J. 28, 34, 37
Douglas, M. 8
Drucker, Peter 1, 51, 177

EBP *see* evidence-based practice (EBP)
education *see* higher education
Elias, Norbert 7, 15, 59, 61, 82, 104, 134, 135, 136, 155, 156, 186
Elkington, J. 123, 151
embodiment 24, 31–32, 33, 35, 43, 157, 192
Emergence of Leadership, The (Griffin) 86
Emirbayer, M. 136
emotions, metrics and 62–70
Espeland, W. 62

INDEX 203

ethics: close up 37; normative 34, 36; pragmatism and 36–37; principle-based 28; relational 34–36; representation of, practice and 26–27; of responsibility 34–36
evidence-based metrics 106–111
evidence-based practice (EBP) 20, 22–26, 25; *see also* practice
exclusion 5, 28, 58, 59, 60, 61, 65, 66, 88, 91, 101, 102, 105, 106, 157–159, 196

Fenwick, T. 25
Filbee, S. 112
financialisation 6
Floyd, A. 60
Fonseca, J. 161
Foucault, M. 28, 30, 155, 184
Fukuyama, F. 101

Gabbay, J. 19, 23, 28, 30, 32
Gadamer, H.G. 9, 85, 87
Gaebler, T. 3
Geertz, C. 40
Gherardi, S. 19, 30, 31, 43
Gindis, D. 118
Goldeberg, S.B. 84
Gonaim, F. 60
Goodwin, N. 80
Graeber, D. 8
Graham, G. 60
Griffin, D. 43, 86, 87, 104, 149

Ham, Chris 154, 161
Hardin, R. 101
harmony 12, 15, 72, 86, 91, 171, 172, 179, 182, 188, 199
Haugaard, M. 153
Hawthorne Effect 121–122, 141n2
healthcare: evidence-based practice in 23–24; focus on practice in, implications of 40–45; team rounds in 42

Heidegger, M. 20, 24, 29, 41
Heugens, P. M. A. R. 118
Hickson, D. J. 149
higher education: metrics in 52–54
Hoggett, P. 8
Hood, Christopher 2
Horsley, T. 28
Hoser, Larue Tone 101
Huisman, J. 53
Hunter, F. 153
Huy, Q. 60

IC *see* integrated care (IC)
ICP *see* interprofessional collaborative practice (ICP)
idealisation 5, 7, 11, 16, 45, 64, 75, 80, 81, 82, 105, 171, 185–187
imagination 5, 7, 15, 32, 35, 38, 192
improvisation 25, 28–39, 35, 42, 90
inclusion 59, 61, 66, 101, 102, 134, 157–159, 164
indeterminacy, precision and 40
innovation: complexity and 111; creativity and, as complex responsive processes 161–164; difference and 106; diversity and 159; emergence of 163; novelty and 159–161; public sector and 5
integrated care (IC) 76–79, 80–83
interdependence 7, 32, 34, 39, 59, 101, 103, 119, 120, 133, 134, 135, 155, 156, 157, 192, 194
interest: practice as phenomenon of 24–25
interprofessional collaborative practice (ICP) 20–22, 21, 27, 197

Jackall, Robert 108
Jackson, M. C. 86, 149, 150
James, W. 20
Janus, Irving 106
Jutterstrom, M. 123

Klikauer, T. 1, 2, 3
Kuhn, T. 122

Landsberger, H. A. 141n2
Langly, A. 25
Lawson, Nigel 18n3
leadership: development 33; discourse on 6; as idealised practice 81; practice-based approach to 45; privilege and 85; trust in 184
Learmonth, M. 6
le May, A. 19, 23, 28, 30, 32
Lozeau, D. 7
Lubinow, W.C. 40
Luhmann, Niklaus 101, 102
Lukes, S. 153

MacIntyre, A. 19, 20, 27, 30, 44, 197
Malpas, J. 104
managerialism 92, 95, 130, 170, 191; characteristics of practices in 4–7; Corporate Social Responsibility and 119, 121, 122; defined 1; as dominant ideology 65; marketisation and 3–4; neoliberalism and 4, 9; New Public Management and 2–3, 5, 6, 118; rational 38; success of 2; thinking underpinning 1; transformation and 4–5
March, J.G. 150
marketisation 3–4, 18n2, 52, 53, 54, 65, 168
Marris, P. 8
McNamara, Robert 107
McNamara fallacy 107
Mead, G.H. 20, 24, 34, 59, 75, 113, 161, 162, 194
metrics: agency and 60, 64–67; business school and 54–56; Corporate Social Responsibility and 123–131; datafication and 56–58; double bind of 58–60; emotions and 62–70; engagement and 65–66; evidence-based 106–111; in higher education 52–56; as neutral 59–60; as objective 59–60; power and 56, 60; productivity and 97–100; as shaping the measured 58; shift in favor of 56; as target 57; trust and 108
metrification, as social process 134–138
Micklethwait, J. 118
Mills, C.W. 153
Mintzberg, H. 60
Mische, A. 136
Misztal, Barbara 101, 102
Moral Mazes: The World of Corporate Managers (Jackall) 108
Morrell, K. 6
Mowles, C. 2, 5, 29, 31, 65, 70n8, 82, 86, 103, 104, 106, 113, 185
Muller, J. 55, 57, 120

National Health Service (NHS) 7, 15, 72–93
National Student Survey (NSS) 52, 53, 54
neoliberalism 4, 9, 18n1, 63, 122, 196
neutrality, of metrics 59–60
New Public Management (NPM) 2–3, 5, 6, 118, 123, 168–169, 184
NHS *see* National Health Service (NHS)
Nicolini, D. 19, 25
Niebuhr, H.R. 20, 27, 34
Nissen, Ingjald 180
Norberg, P. 123
normative ethics 34, 36
Northhouse, P.G. 85, 86
Norway 168
novelty 159–161

NPM *see* New Public Management (NPM)
NSS *see* National Student Survey (NSS)
Nyberg, D. 122

objectivity, of metrics 59–60
OBM *see* Organisational Behaviour Management (OBM)
O'Byrne, D. 120, 121
O'Leary J. 52
O'Neill, Onora 9
Organisational Behaviour Management (OBM) 169
Osborne, D. 3

Palazzo, G. 120
pandemic 73–76, 92–93
Parker, L. 118
Parsons, T. 155
PDSA *see* Plan, Do, Study, Act (PDSA)
Peirce, C.S. 20, 36
performativity 24, 31, 35, 44
Peters, T. 51
phronesis 197
Plan, Do, Study, Act (PDSA) 32
Polanyi, M. 44
Pollitt, C. 1, 3, 4, 6–7
Porter, T. 62, 107, 108
positivism 40
power: agency and 155; as co-created 155–157; as consensual 154–155; differentials 14; dynamic relations of 45; exclusion and 102; expression of, in practice environment 34; ideology and 195–196; inclusion and exclusion as dynamics of 157–159; metrics and 56, 60; as possession 152–154; relationship 8

Power, M. 5, 56
practical judgement 9, 109, 110, 169, 197–198
practice: of community 31; complexity and 38–39; as ethical enterprise 31; ethics and 26–27; facets of 25, *25, 35, 41*; in healthcare, focus on 40–45; improvisation and *25*; interprofessional collaborative 20–22, *21*, 27; as moral enterprise 31; as phenomenon of interest 24–25; representation and 26–28; sense-making and *25*; as social enterprise 31
pragmatism 20, 34–37, 104, 138, 161
precision 39–40
prejudice: as aspect of organisation 84–86; conflict and 86–87; defined 92; difference and 86–87; as process 87–90
privatisation 3, 4, 6, 7, 18n3, 169
PROCEED (Projected Completion and Employment from Entrant Data) 53
process consultancy 178–179, 185–187
productivity 97–100, 109
public sector: complexities of 148–149, 193–194; Corporate Social Responsibility and 117–118; interprofessional collaborative practice and 20–22
Pugh, D.S. 149
Putnam, R.D. 101, 102, 110

quantitative fallacy 107
Quest for Certainty (Dewey) 105

Rahim, M.A. 187
rational idealism 40

Reagan, Ronald 8
Redman, S. 45
Reinventing Government: how the entrepreneurial spirit is transforming the public sector (Gaebler) 3
relational ethics 34–36
representation 26–28, 31–32, 38
representationalism 24, 40
Ridgway, V.F. 107
rounds, team 42

Sackett, D.L. 22
Sameshima, P. 25
Sandberg, J. 19, 24, 25, 26, 28, 29, 31, 44
Sarra, N. 192
Schatzki, T.R. 19, 23, 24, 30, 31, 37
Schein, Edgar 83, 84, 178
Scherer, A. G. 120
Schumpeter, J. 161
Scotson, J. 59, 61
Scott, J. 57, 58
Scott, J.C. 6, 20, 109, 118, 137
Seeing Like a State: How Certain Schemes to Improve the Human Condition Have Failed (Scott) 109
sense-making 25, 28–39, 35, 103–104, 105–106
Seo, M-G. 160
Serra, J.P. 36
Shaw, P. 178
Shotter, J. 25, 28, 30, 43, 197
Simonet, D. 118
Smith, K.K. 102
Smith, W.K. 160
social manipulation 180–181
Social Responsibilities of the Businessmen (Bowen) 117
Solsø, K. 192
Stacey, R.D. 5, 22, 29, 31, 37, 43, 58, 66, 75, 81, 82, 86, 103, 115n2, 134, 149, 157, 159, 161, 163, 164, 186

Stevens, M. 62
stimulus overload 83
Sunnstein 169
Sweden 18n2, 168, 169, 170, 171–172
systems approach 149–152
systems thinking 87
Sztompka, P. 101, 102, 110

Taylor, Charles 104
Taylor, F. 51, 149
Taylor, M. 123
Teaching Excellence Framework (TEF) 52–53, 54
team rounds 42
TEF *see* Teaching Excellence Framework (TEF)
Thaler, R.H. 169
Tidd, J. 160
transformation, managerialism and 4–5
transparency 9, 53, 95, 107
trust: defining 100–101; fragility of 102–103; key aspects of 102–103; knowledge and 28; leaders and 84; metrics and 108; relating and 101; relationships 96; risk and 93; scholarly interest in 100–101; sense-making and 105–106
Trust in Numbers: The Pursuit of Objectivity in Science and Public Life (Porter) 107
Truth and Method (Gadamer) 85
Tsoukas, H. 19, 24, 26, 28, 29, 31, 43, 197
Tushman, M.L. 160
Tyranny of Metrics, The (Muller) 55

uncertainty 8, 13, 37, 42, 43, 59, 63, 83, 92, 96, 102, 103, 105, 145, 160, 193

Van Oosterhout, J. 118
Venugopal, R. 18n1

Walker, D. 157
Ward, D. 161
Washington consensus 3
Weber, Max 10, 40
Weick, Karl 103, 104
Wenger, E. 31
Wetherell, M. 63
Wiener, N. 149

Wilkins, S. 53
Williams, R. 150–151
Windmill, A. 155
Wittgenstein, L. 152–153
Wooldridge, A. 118

Yankelovich, Daniel 107–108

Printed in the United States
by Baker & Taylor Publisher Services